The Rambler in North America, Mdcccxxxii-Mdcccxxxiii
by Charles Joseph Latrobe

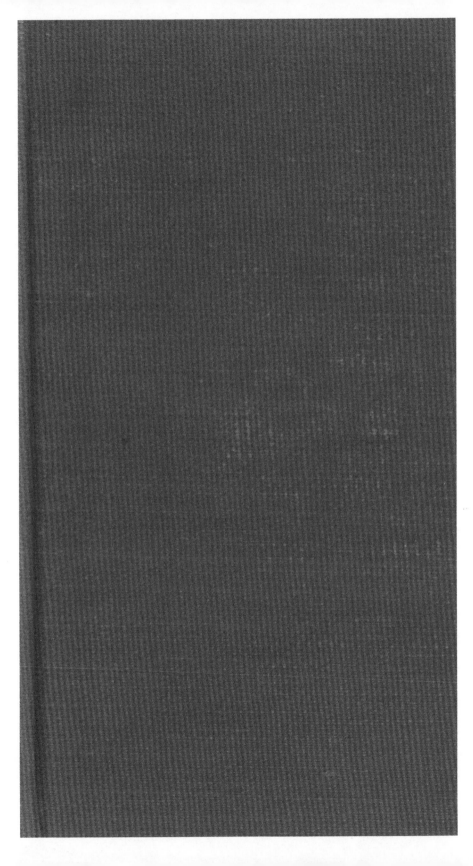

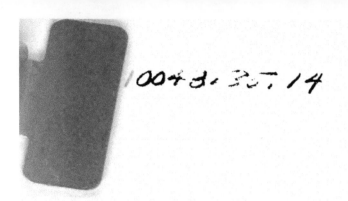

THE RAMBLER

IN

NORTH AMERICA,

MDCCCXXXII——MDCCCXXXIII.

BY CHARLES JOSEPH LATROBE,
AUTHOR OF THE "ALPENSTOCK," ETC.

"Cœlum non animum mutant, qui trans mare currunt."
HOR. EPIST.

IN TWO VOLUMES.

VOL. I.

NEW-YORK:

PUBLISHED BY HARPER & BROTHERS,
NO. 82 CLIFF-STREET,
AND SOLD BY THE PRINCIPAL BOOKSELLERS THROUGHOUT THE
UNITED STATES.

1835.

$2v @ 37\frac{1}{2} = 7$

CONTENTS

OF

THE FIRST VOLUME.

LETTER I.

We have both, by this time, become aware of a
melancholy truth. We have both seen, that, however
a common lot may be awarded to the young members
of a family in early life; to whatever degree a common
education may strengthen the natural affection im-
planted in their bosoms—blend together their youthful
associations, and form their tastes on the same models;
—in fine, however potent the spell which pervades
their spirits, and seems to unite their hearts indis-
solubly together—the approach of manhood rarely fails
to scatter the little band to the four winds; and the
time comes when long periods of separation and absence, though they may not choke a generous interest,
or stifle affection, must impair, if not destroy intimacy. Epistolary correspondence may, it is true, offer
under most circumstances a partial remedy, and to
that we have hitherto had recourse to fill the chasms
produced in our intimacy, from having for many years
pursued diverging paths. May we never quite neglect it!

You may recollect, that when boys at school, I
seemed, as you were my junior, to have a certain
natural right to stretch the sceptre of patronage over
you. When fatigued of looking up to my two elder
brothers as models of scarcely attainable perfection
and wisdom, it was encouraging to turn and cast a
glance of complacency on you, with the reflection,

that in your eyes at least, I must appear a personage of equally superior intelligence. At this later day the doubt may well occur to me, whether the two or three years by which I was your senior, had in fact given me a very decided advantage over you in moral and physical alertness or power. This however I keep in remembrance, that you certainly looked up to me with a far greater degree of respect than I merited, and with a degree of affection, which, whatever may have been the fate of the former sentiment, has in no degree been diminished by added years, different pursuits, and long terms of separation.

But it may be admitted, that even at the present day, when both are well advanced in manhood, there still exists a certain weakness in my manner of looking upon you. When addressing you as at the present time, I persuade myself that in your breast at least there are sentiments which will prove far stronger than the spirit of criticism. Moreover, I am still, without fear of contradiction, a few years older, and if I dare presume to instruct and amuse any one, it may be yourself. In this spirit I take up my pen to reply to your last letter.

You say you continue to be interested in every step I take, and feel curiosity to follow me through the scenes which have been presented to my view on the opposite shores of the Atlantic. I will try to answer your interest, and satisfy your curiosity, and, as far as circumstances allow, to give you a history of what my comrade and myself have seen, achieved, or suffered for some time past. A period of tranquil and sedentary existence has succeeded to a long term of travel and constant activity, and a portion of its hours cannot, perhaps, be employed to better purpose.

I might, it is true, as an alternative, send you a portmanteau, full of papers of all descriptions, printed and manuscript, which, in spite of many efforts to the contrary, has been added to my travelling equipage, and, generously telling you that they contain no secrets, bid you pick and choose, and burn or read, as you may feel inclined. But in so acting, I should do you no justice, and myself perhaps yet less.

I may be mistaken in my estimate of your peculiar taste, and in my judgment as to that part of the heap which would be most in accordance with it. Tastes differ. I received a letter while in America from a common friend of ours, one worthy of both attention and esteem, and one whom I should be proud to oblige. It was in return to one of mine, which I had closed with a well-meant inquiry, whether I could be of any service to him. The following is an extract from the reply: "We have had plenty of descriptions of the American House of Representatives, the President's levee. Tell me how the poor are provided for;—what sort of people are the overseers?—have they vestry meetings for the relief of the poor? How are the work-houses arranged and regulated? What is the bill of fare in such places? What do the inmates cost per head? Are they farmed or not? Is there any remnant of a religious establishment? Railways, are they increasing? Do they pay or not?" and so forth; the whole concluding with this pithy piece of advice, "let your letters, in short, be about men, and not about mountains; and let them inform me of what I have never heard, not what has been presented to the world a hundred times before."

What do you say to this? It was, in my humble opinion, treating a gentleman in search of the picturesque no better than a church-warden. There was the advantage of having a political economist for a correspondent! In you I have, at any rate, the comfort of believing that I may indulge in less prosaic and less matter-of-fact subjects. He might as well have required me to furnish him with a set of essays upon the casuistical divinity of the middle ages; and well it is for you that I know how to interpret your expressions of curiosity, or you might fare as ill as R., who to this day has never received an answer to his queries, though I was far from being indisposed to gratify him, had I been able. Had he asked me to give him intelligence about geological phenomena, the courses of rivers, the Indian tribes—to inform him which was the most approved mode of hunting a bear, or catching a raccoon, I should have known to whom to apply, and how to obtain the necessary knowledge ; but about poor-rates and poor-houses, the rent of pews, and the success of the voluntary system, I never could get any but the most vague and partial intelligence.

I asked one gentleman, for example, how the poor of his town were provided for ? He answered promptly, " Poor, sir !—we have none."   Of course all the succeeding queries which I was fully prepared to put, fell to the ground.

In other places I perhaps fared better, and found that there were absolutely poor people, and did not fail to make notes of all the information I gleaned.   But I soon grew tired of my quest on this and other like points of interest, and the prosaic company into which it introduced me ; and more than all, of the endless shades of distinction in the systems under trial, among a people spread over such a vast extent of country, and under such very different circumstances.   This led me to change my mode of proceeding.   I got possession of all the books and pamphlets, right and left, which appeared to shed light, or to bear upon these and similar subjects of general interest, and these are all at your service, and especially at that of our worthy friend. Therefore, when you see him, pray tell him so, but advise him not to apply to me either by letter or orally for such information.

Our brief period of intercourse in town, during the winter of 1831–2, made you aware of the principal objects of my proposed visit to the United States of America ; and also of the feelings which predominated in the anticipation of it.

Whatever natural regrets were involved in a departure from Europe, there was little but pleasure in anticipation. Without a feeling of satiety, much less of disgust, to spur me forward, I was content to turn my back for a season on the society and scenery of the Old World, and look forward with a sensation of undefined pleasure and curiosity to those western climes, whose characteristics were so different from any I had yet seen. I longed to wander among the details of that sublime scenery which the fancy associates with the New World, as so peculiarly her own : her wide-spread streams, interminable forests, and foaming cataracts ; and to be a guest in the lodges of that race, of whom men speak as doomed speedily to disappear from the face of the earth.

I desired to follow into their places of refuge and retreat, the crowd of human beings which the last two centuries had sent in annual swarms upon the pathway opened across the great western waters by the constancy and patient daring of Columbus ; men of all nations, of all ranks and degrees,—those of unsullied purity of life and character, and others who were steeped to the lips in crime ;—the patriot, the dreamer after Utopian schemes of happiness or liberty ;—men goaded by political and religious persecution ;—the disappointed in heart and purpose ;—hundreds incited by speculation, thousands by poverty ;—the tens of thousands who, having all to hope and nothing to lose, had disappeared from the countries of the East, had gone and seemingly buried themselves under the deep shade of the western forest, or beneath the tall grass of the western prairie.

Preparatory to this visit, my efforts were more negative than positive ; by which expression is meant, that I attempted to keep my imagination and my mind unbiased and uninfluenced by preconceived notions, from whatever source they might be drawn, rather than, by reading the works, or listening to the opinions of preceding travellers, to run the hazard of adding the prejudices of others to my own. As a foreigner, and, above all, an Englishman, about to travel in a country where comparison would force itself on the mind at every turn, it was to be feared that there were obstacles already existing in my own bosom, in the

2*

way of forming a sound, unbiased judgment of men and things. Education, habit, political bias, and tastes, might all be arrayed on the opposite side, even supposing there were an absence of violent and uncontrollable prejudice. For the rest, I flattered myself that I had some advantages to counterbalance the great disadvantage of being born within the sound of Bow Bells. I laid some claim to the character of an old traveller, having seen divers countries besides my own. Difficulties and asperities which might disgust others from their novelty, might not work with equal effect on the temper of one, whose European rambles had made him pretty fully acquainted with both the rough and the smooth passages of a traveller's life. Providential circumstances had, as you are aware, prepared for me a home, and a place in society, as long as I should remain in America. I was, as you may recollect, no very violent politician; and was inclined, whether from natural indolence or dull good-nature, to allow a very considerable diversity of opinion in my neighbour, as long as he took care not to contradict me. I had seen enough of mankind in divers countries, to believe that no system of government is of general application, and that the government must be made to suit the people, and not the people to suit the government. I loved my own country and its institutions better than any other on the face of the earth, and had no fear of giving a preference to any other, however its peculiar advantages might excite my admiration: and I need hardly add, that no change has been wrought in this feeling, in which I hope to live and die. I possessed in my friend and your acquaintance, young Count de Pourtales, a cheerful and accomplished travelling companion, who, I believe, was bent like myself on forming opinions from observation. We wished to identify ourselves as much as possible for the time being, with the feelings of the people we were going to visit; and, as long as we were among them, to try to feel with them as far as it was reasonable to do so. Lastly, I resolved that nothing should tempt me into the manufacture of a book, a resolution which I have magnanimously maintained to this moment.

And now I still ask your patience, not while I make promises as to what I intend to do, but rather while I warn you as to certain things which you must not expect from me. Take my letters for what they are worth. If you find it a trouble to read them, be sure that it has cost me yet more to write them; and, moreover, if you find me at any time particularly dull, as some one has said before me, be sure that I have a design in it.

It is not my intention in a general way to give you descriptions of places and scenes described a thousand times. You will not look to me for elaborate sketches and dissertations on transatlantic politics, for I am quite ready to own my poverty of satisfactory information on that head. Virulence of party, with all its concomitants of misrepresentation, falsification, and personality, is found within the United States in as great a degree as within the bounds of Britain; and leaves little for a stranger like myself to do, after attempting to pry into the state of politics in America, whether by means of the public prints, or of private inquiry, more than to turn away with mingled disgust and despair.

You must not expect pages of statistical information; relations of stage-coach, steamboat, and tap-room colloquies with Captain *This* or Judge *That;* anecdotes abounding in slang, and stories at second-hand; much less, sly peeps into the interior of families who may have exercised the rites of hospitality towards the stranger.

As to the first, you may find them elsewhere; and, moreover, however correct at the time I might have procured them, they would probably be erroneous by the time you might wish to draw deductions from them. The second and third have now neither novelty nor good taste to recommend them; and as to the last, you may miss a great deal of egregious amusement, but I respect myself, even if I did not love my neighbour, too much, ever to repay the confiding hospitality of private families by such cold-blooded displays of disloyalty.

I have been now for ten years more or less a wanderer; and if any man should have learned to revere hospitality, and entertain a horror of the term 'ungrateful guest,' surely I should be that man. There is something in the warm, unchecked, and open-hearted conduct of a family circle, which should ever prevent the stranger from judging what he there witnesses with a cold eye and heart, as though he had nothing in common with it. Modern philosophy, it is true, finds an apology for this, but what is that to you or me?

As to the rest, commonsense and common reflection will show you, the more you see of human society, high or low, at home or abroad, that there exists scarcely any modification of it that has not its "*ridicules.*" Few, if any, are regulated by such unquestionable laws of good sense and propriety in every particular, as not to give legitimate cause for ridicule. Every one affords matter for caricature. None is so perfect that the satirist and the cynic may not see abundant occasion for a sneer; and, moreover, at the present day, a greater degree of neglect and contempt will frequently be awarded to any ignorance of, or deviation from, rules, fancies, and fashions, the adoption of which is but conventional and capricious, than to absolute departures from moral rectitude, and sound principle.

I regret that my prefatory epistle has proved so long, but I now bring it to a decent conclusion.

LETTER II.

You are aware when and how I left London for Paris in March, 1832; having, in consequence of the appearance of the cholera in England, determined to set sail from a French port in preference to an English one. You will doubtless remember also, how, at the very outset, I found myself entrapped with a whole steamboat load of my migratory fellow-countrymen, by our French neighbours at Calais, and that we were cooped up in durance vile, to perform unwilling quarantine in an old dilapidated fort without the town walls, in spite of reiterated protestations and expostulations of ' *Mais, Monsieur, je ne suis pas cholerique ! Mais, Monsieur, ma femme et moi sommes très pressés !*' &c. There is something ludicrous, as well as vexatious, in disappointment, and there were certain among us who did not fail to extract a good deal of amusement from the unquestionably disagreeable position into which we found ourselves suddenly transported, and which we had subsequently to endure for three long days.

I might amuse you with sundry pictures of men and manners as they then moved before me; rejoicing your English heart with sly remarks upon our Gallic neighbours. I might tell you how, on our approach to the wharf, the French craft, great and small, and the rogues in them, got out of our way as if we had been a fire-ship; how busily fumigation was carried on by a bunch of sanatory officers, peering out of a temporary hut, while, baboon-like, they made a cat's-paw of a poor doctor; how we were given over by the medical authority to the civil—by the civil to the military—and finally handed over to no authority at all, but shut up pell-mell in the old dismantled fort, to live or die, as it might happen, under the protection of the yellow flag. I might describe the miserable

state of all within the forlorn enclosure : how rude
barracks of boards formed the sole accommodation,—
and how for these we were indebted to the pestilence-
defying cupidity of the hotel-keepers of the town
alone, the government having provided absolutely
no shelter. These huts were capable of housing but
thirty out of the hundred sufferers of all ranks, shut
up together, and were, of course, filled to suffocation.
It would excite your commiseration to learn, how
'first come' was 'first served,' while the rest had
to lie on the grass of the ramparts, under the lee of
the counterscarp, or wherever they could ; how,
moreover, it rained ; how, where the rats gambolled
in long undisturbed possession five days before, milord
and milady were now glad to lay their dainty heads.
The scramble for beds was only equalled by the
scramble for board. Sorrow, but not surprise, might
be elicited on reading that some of my wise-headed
countrymen insulted the health-inspecting dignitaries
at their noontide visit, threatened an appeal to the
British government for the national outrage perpe-
trated on our sacred persons, and that in consequence
the time of sorrow was lengthened instead of abridged.
You would have been amused to see our motley band
of men and women, of all nations and degrees, English,
French, Belgians, and Americans; and you would
have marvelled to hear how the English maundered,
grumbled, and groaned together; to see the Belgians
play at dominoes and chuck-farthing from morning
to night; to listen to the French singing, smoking,
and jesting, repeating constantly '*à la guerre comme
à la guerre ;*' and, lastly, to watch the American lie
from morning to night on his back in the straw, ab-
stracted and speculative, with the rain dropping into
his ears.

Moreover, I might tell you how my post was upon
the seaward bastion, overlooking the comic scene of
petty misery and amusement on one side, and, on the
other, the troubled straits, and the long white sea-wall
of my own land, and show you how many a warm and

anxious thought winged its way thither—but all this is foreign to my present purpose.

The same observation will apply to any detailed notice of my release—journey to Paris—sojourn there —and final departure with M. de Pourtales from the port of Havre de Grace, in the second week in April, in company with Washington Irving, our future companion in many a day's adventure.

A voyage to America is no longer a circumstance worth signalizing as a marvel. It is, as you know, literally, an every-day occurrence. Hundreds, nay, thousands of white sails now bespangle that wide, blue, and restless ocean, which, a few centuries ago, was, in truth, a solitary sea ; and, though I write to one who was never yet out of the limits of the British Isles, I cannot persuade myself that a sheet full of extracts from "my log" will add much either to his amusement or instruction. The Havre, such was the name of the stout New-York packet-ship in which we sailed, was a fine vessel, in no whit inferior to the others of her class in build, or in the commodious arrangement of her interior. She was commanded by a high-spirited, generous-hearted, gentlemanly seaman. He was one whose character could not fail to impress the mind favourably with regard to the service and land to which he belonged. He was accused, but wrongfully I think, of having a tendency, in sailor's phrase, to " spin a long yarn" now and then, or, in other words, to exaggerate. You may contrive to swallow a tale of considerable size at sea. We were upwards of two hundred on board, and of these one hundred and seventy were steerage passengers.

You will doubtless know that on a prosperous passage,—and such in fact we had, though not a quick or a direct one—adverse winds, and now and then a rough gale, producing a fearful destruction of the ship's crockery,—extraordinary sights and events are hardly to be looked for. A week or two was sufficient to make us " au fait," as to every phase of our position. The ability to read, with any degree of steadiness on ship-board, is not granted to every one, and I must say, that, to me, a voyage is in that respect nearly lost time. The study of character, however, both of rational and irrational beings around you, may afford a never-failing source of amusement, and, in this instance was truly such to us.

None of us have forgotten the first mate, little D., a round, fat, good-humoured man—an off-set of the hardy stock of Nantucket, or Martha's Vinyard, I forget which—a narrator of incredible stories about whales. He was proud of bearing the same patronymic as a ci-devant president of Yale College. He had scraped a good deal of information together, and had a very laudable desire to add to the stock—was much given to walk the deck, smoke, and philosophize; and was altogether an unexceptionable character, though he owned that he had been bred a quaker, but had clipped his broad-brim and painted it white the day he came of age. The young second mate was a special favourite, and was generally called " right and left ;" because if he saw any fight among either sailors or steerage passengers, he dashed into it, and before asking a word of explanation, just knocked down the two men nearest him. Names, descriptive of some peculiarity in form or manner, were soon concocted by our little knot of humorists, for all the more noted characters before the mast.

The position of the poor emigrants—men, women and children, Jews, French and Germans, stowed a-midships—was at the best unpleasant. As long as the weather was fine, matters went on tolerably smoothly, and we had then chirping and singing enough : but a gale set them all at loggerheads, and rumours of fights and feuds not unfrequently came aft. Three Frenchmen, (Jews and sharpers if they were not maligned,) seemed to be just so many stumbling-blocks to the honest Germans ; and even the quality in the great cabin took a spite against them. One of their number from his oracular and star-bleached countenance, was dubbed Sidrophel, and it was whispered that they conjured up bad and adverse winds. The majority of the steerage passengers were Alsatians and Bavarians, and were speeding, with their little all collected around them, to settle in a new land. They were most of them musically inclined, and when the level beams of the sun began to glance over the bows, they usually gathered in a knot round the mainmast, and sang the songs of their native land, which they and theirs had now quitted for ever. Many a pleasant hour did we thus spend, as our vessel was gently heaving beneath us, and pressing toward the setting sun.

Of our more immediate companions, I say nothing: they were in general too well bred to excite much attention. We had a proportion of females and pretty children among their number, and I add my testimony to that of many, as to the pleasant, chastened, and agreeable air which their presence dispenses on shipboard.

But this is not all—do not think I am going to pass by that most fertile field of harmless amusement, the dumb animals on board, among which we numbered a cow, ass, divers pigs; and a numerous, but daily-decreasing horde of ducks, turkies, geese, and poultry—besides a snappish pointer with two whelps, and a setter; not to forget a tom-cat, several canaries, and last but not least in favour, a mocking-bird.

Tom seldom made his appearance till about nightfall, and then he might be seen skulking slily along, close under the shadow of the spars lashed to the bulwarks, always contriving, however, to retreat if detected. His movements were never quite free from suspicion—and he was no great favourite aft, in spite of its being alleged, in excuse of his vespernal excursions to our end of the ship, that the mice frequenting our state-rooms were his lawful perquisite: and it was soon found that Tom had, in fact, other ends in view. It was remarked that he had taken a particular fancy to haunt the purlieus of the large wicker cage in which our little musical favourite, the mocking-bird, was

confined—in preference to all the allurements held out
to his attention by the plumper denizens of the coop :
and he was frequently detected in its immediate vicinity, sitting with an air of great meekness, eyes half
shut, as it were, quite lost to the world in sweet en-
trancement, while the pretty bird poured forth its
melody. But this was all a sham. He had no more
ear for music than the ship's counter, and, in fact, he
was twice discovered in the attempt to make a meal
of our playmate. The second time the whole cabin
was in arms, and Tom received such summary punishment that he never visited the round-house again.
We thus secured the merry little songster's safety.
The latter was somewhat capricious, but very diverting—sang like the canary, quacked like the duck,
chirped and cackled like the poultry, mewed like the
cat, and finally tucked his little wings close to his side,
and looked up to the mainmast-head like the Captain.

I have told you that our voyage was protracted.
After long trying to make our way to the northward,
we stood to the south of the gulf-stream, and soon
exchanged bleak blowing weather and stormy seas, for
gentle breezes, blue skies, and tranquil waters.

I cannot forget how pleasingly the monotony of our
voyage was broken about the middle of May, by our
coming within sight of the Bermudas, that little step-
ping-stone in the vast ocean between the continents,
and how every animate being on board seemed moved
with the aspect and atmosphere of the land.

To cut a long voyage and long letter short, I will
close by noting the 21st of May as the day when the
former ended, by our arriving off Sandy Hook, with
the heights of Neversink to the left, Long Island to
the right, and the deep outer bay of New-York before
us ; and when the sun set over the land, our ship might
be seen with sails furled and anchor a-peak rocking on
the threshold of the New World.

The following morning, we advanced with wind and
tide through the outer bay and the Narrows, till abreast

of the prettiest quarantine ground under the sun, and dropped our anchor off the shore of Staten Island.

In consequence of the casual indisposition of my comrade, it was thought advisable to stay on board the Havre for a few days, instead of accompanying our fellow-passengers to the city : and it is very comprehensible that both curiosity and six weeks imprisonment on board, made me glad to while away a few of the hours of detention in a ramble on the green shores and wooded heights, which were directly in front of our anchorage.

LETTER III.

THE New World! You may imagine, but you cannot feel the degree of curiosity with which I first set foot upon it. It may be readily granted that the emotion of interest with which an American steps upon the shores of Europe, must be of a higher character; yet to me, this change of position from countries where the forms of external nature had in a great measure become familiar, and lost the charm of novelty, to another in which she was to appear clothed in a different garb, and develope other phenomena, was nevertheless an epoch in my existence. It was the renewal of youth and boyhood. Many a sensation, to which I had been a stranger for years, returned to the breast after it might seem to have left me for ever. I felt all that excess of prying curiosity into the productions of nature, which had been a strong principle of my soul twenty years before, when we used to explore the vallies of the Air, Wharf, and Calder in concert, bring home pockets stuffed with plants and stones, and heads filled with supposed discoveries. Such they were indeed to us. These fresh and natural feelings of excitement, which had been of course weakened or lost, when every object had become familiar, and there were no more discoveries to make, now stimulated me as warmly as ever; and while eagerly examining every tree, shrub, bud, and reptile, that came across my path during my first solitary stroll, I could almost smile at my boyish and buoyant feeling.

The spring had been tardy in appearance, and unfriendly in its character; yet as I rose from the margin of the bay, and surmounted the first slope, covered with the straggling village, the lively green of the enclosures, the blossoming peach, and other trees, and the budding forest were all delightful to the eye after the monotony of the ocean. The scenery presented by the outer Bay of New-York is not striking, and however we had been pleased to approach the green shores, and gaze upon the fixed and firm land, we had hardly been able to chime in with the enthusiastic expressions of admiration uttered by our American fellow-passengers, as we sailed up the Bay, at the peculiar beauty of their native country. Yet, when, after an interrupted climb, I gained the hightest point of the wooded range above the Narrows, and looked forth upon the wide extended view then spread before me, I did them justice. The knoll upon which I stood rose above the wooded skirts of the hills, and immediately overlooked the Narrows to the right, with its forts, and the long, green, cultivated shores of Long Island beyond. To the south-west the eye gained a glimpse, over the back of the Island, of the strait separating it from the main shore of New Jersey, the undulating outline of which formed the horizon in that direction. Directly over the village below, rising with its clean white edifices on the margin of the Bay, you saw spread before you, the capacious inner harbour, with the distant city, and the entrance to the Hudson, stretching far inland in the perspective, a broad expanse of water dotted with innumerable sails. The wind was fair for the passage of the Narrows, and many a noble ship was passing the Quarantine ground, and steering under their white cloud of canvass for the distant outlet into the Ocean, which appeared distinctly to the southward, over the long, low point of Sandy Hook. The feature of the landscape, whose mere outlines I have portrayed, were quite devoid of boldness of character, but they were such as to impress me greatly.

And it may here be observed, that when exactly two years after, by a singular coincidence, we again entered the same port on returning from Vera Cruz, having in the interval penetrated into every part of the Union, and latterly gazed upon many a scene of tropical and mountain magnificence in Mexico, I was anew constrained to admit the propriety of the epithet "beautiful," being attached to the Bay of New York. That is its characteristic, whether the observer looks down upon it from the elevated point I had chosen, or from the neighbourhood of the city. And yet it is difficult to define where the main charm lies. The aspect of the latter is far from being picturesque on a near approach. You see a long line of level wharves, and slips crowded by endless tiers of shipping, and tall brick warehouses peering over them; a few uninteresting church-steeples rearing themselves from the central parts of the city, which rises so gradually from the water's edge, that, at a distance, it seems to be built on a dead flat. There is neither beauty nor sublimity in such an object. Then the adjacent shores of Long Island and New Jersey opposite, though well wooded, are not particularly bold; the small low islands scattered over the nearer portions of the Bay, are far from being either well clothed, or dignified by handsome structures; the swelling back of Staten Island, is too distant to form a prominent object in the landscape; still, come from what quarter you may, you are struck with the air of beauty.

Much is doubtless to be attributed to the extreme mellowness and transparency of the atmosphere, which gives colour to every object on land or water. In this, the climate of New York is truly Italian. There is a freshness in the verdure that covers the sloping and gentle shores, a harmony in the outlines,—and above

3*

all, there is a life in the aquatic scenery, which I never witnessed elsewhere in an equal degree. An air of gaiety and festal enjoyment, which contrasts singularly with the unholiday appearance of men and things in the interior of the country, reigns on the waters of the bays and rivers, in the vicinity of the cities, to a surprising degree.

At all times of the tide, at every hour of the day, whatever may be the wind, the Bay and its outlets appear alive with craft and shipping, from the dark mass of the frigate, or line-of-battle ship, which often lie moored abreast of the city, and the colossal steamboats hourly seen careering over its surface, to the light skilfully-managed wherry of the Whitehaller.

But we will not for the present linger in New York, where I only passed a single week subsequent to landing. This city, and its rivals on the waters of the Atlantic, have been frequently described, and they may therefore be passed over with few remarks.

The acquaintance which my comrade and myself had begun with Mr. Irving at Havre, and cemented on ship-board, was resumed ashore, and led to that series of common projects and common wanderings, which kept us bound together as a trio for the greater part of the summer and autumn of this year. To him all was new again, after seventeen years' absence from his native country.

The month of June was employed in visiting Philadelphia, Baltimore, and Washington, previous to the assumption of our more extended projects for the summer.

The arrangements for public convenience in travelling by steam-boat and rail-road, along the whole line of interior communication, from Rhode Island into the very heart of Virginia, demand the admiration of every stranger, and that of an Englishman more than any other, he being of all travellers, the most impatient and unable to endure the loss of precious time with equanimity. Each of the cities named, though resembling each other in many points, has its own distinctive marks. New York is the most bustling; Philadelphia the most symmetrical; Baltimore the most picturesque; and Washington the most bewildering.

At New York you pass hours with delight under the trees on that beautiful breezy promenade, which the good taste of the citizens has preserved at the extreme point of their island. You follow the example of more illustrious travellers in doing justice to the ample tables of your hotel or friends, not forgetting to pass judgment on rock fish, American oysters, and above all, on shad fish, if in season. You enjoy many a stroll along the gay and cheerful pavement of Broadway, the principal street, running for miles through the heart of the city, with its handsome edifices, shops, and public buildings. You admire the commodious disposition of the interior of family mansions, with their folding-doors, clean, cool, indian-matted floors, and the groups of pretty faces by which they are adorned. You marvel at the incessant bustle and proofs of flourishing commerce visible in all the narrower streets devoted to business, diverging right and left toward the North and East rivers; and on the crowded slips and wharves. You step into a steam-boat, and cross over to Brooklyn, or to the Jersey shore, where you may immediately bury yourself in the delicious walks of Hoboken, where the squirrel climbs as free, and apparently as undisturbed among the grape-vines, as in the depths of the forest. You glance up the Hudson, which laves the grassy margin of the promenade, and see him walled in by the perpendicular pallisadoes and green shores of Manhattan Island, covered with sloops and steamers —and own that in your brightest moment of fancy, you never dreamed of the creation of an equally glorious river, or a city whose position is more strongly marked by all those characteristics which are desirable in a great commercial emporium. Returning, you hear the cry of fire, and repair to the scene of disaster, but go home disappointed, because you find that the good people of New York never give a fire a fair chance, but knock down the house to preserve it from the flames.   You walk out on a Sunday evening, and are fairly elbowed into the gutter by the broad-spread bonnets and *gigots de mouton* of the sable beauties, who, with their beaux, have then the possession of the pavement.

At Philadelphia, "the city of Brotherly Love," you are struck with the regularity of the streets,—their numberless handsome mansions,—the lavish use of white and gray marble,—pleasant avenues and squares, —noble public institutions,—markets,—the abundance of water,—and the general attention to dress visible in every one you meet.   As in New York and Baltimore, you are surprised with the great proportion of handsome female faces, and delicately moulded forms which crowd the public walks and saloons, like so many sweet fresh May flowers.   You make the usual visits right or left, dictated by taste or reverence; including the romantic scene at Fairmount, and the spot where the celebrated treaty was concluded between Penn and the Delawares; and you taste that hospitality and frank unostentatious kindness which, with all their faults, proved or imputed, the American ever offers to a stranger who conducts himself courteously.

At Baltimore, "the city of Monuments," snugly sheltered within its deep bay, and rising from an oblong basin of the Patapsco toward the amphitheatre of wooded hills on the west, you marvel to hear how, from a period of time within the memory of some yet living, the small village of a dozen houses has sprung up into a large capital, overspreading an extended area, abounding with noble public and private edifices, and possessing an increasing commerce with every port under the sun.   You admire the neat style of building, —the bustle of the Bay,—the beauty of the shipping, —and the lovely scenery in the environs.   You welcome a southern climate in the perfume of many odorous flowers, and, more than all, the delightful society for which Maryland is pre-eminent—frank, polished and unaffected.

At Washington, "the city of magnificent distances,"

with the haste and eagerness of a new comer you visit the lions ;—ascend to the capitol ;—criticize its architecture, whether properly authorized to do so or not,—listen to the proceedings in either House for an hour or two,—pay your respects to the President,—visit the country-seat and grave of our great and good opponent Washington. You plan, but do not execute, an excursion to the Falls of the Potomac,—get more and more bewildered with the study of the city, which seems to have been contrived with an eye for the especial advantage of the hackney coachmen ;—get squeezed out of all equanimity at a Presidential levee ;—retain your appetite, but lose your patience at a scrambling dinner at Gadsby's Hotel,—and finally retrace your steps to Baltimore as we did, with a resolution not to return to Washington till there should be a less suffocating heat in the places of public resort, less dust in Pennsylvania avenue, more water in the Tiber, and more elbow-room in the hotels.

I have, however, no hesitation in saying, that our first impressions, of America, were every way pleasing, both as to men and things. We saw the country and the society under the best auspices ; and the season at which we made our first journey, was also one which naturally incited us to contented enjoyment.

In returning northward, we made a halt of a fortnight in Baltimore and its neighbourhood. Many of the country-seats which stud the environs upon the upland slope, at various points and distances from the city, are singularly well-situated and tastefully arranged ; and I look back with unalloyed gratification to the hours spent among them, and the hospitality there enjoyed. Rural fetes are ordinarily given in these villas at this beautiful season of the year, when every tree and shrub appears in its freshest green, and every natural object cites to amusement and recreation.

The numberless white four-petalled flowers of the dog-wood, which we had left, in the latitude of New York, in full beauty, had, it is true, become

discoloured, and half hidden by the green foliage
which they precede; but the catalpa was in blossom
in the vicinity of the country-seats; the shrubberies
were in their beauty, and on the margin of the forest,
which generally thickened to the back of these villas,
the evening air was perfumed with the rich odour of
the magnolia, whose snow-white blossom peeped out
from its covert of glossy leaves. A thousand beautiful
trees, either transported from their concealment in
the woods, or tastefully preserved for the purposes of
ornament, surrounded the lawns in front of the open
colonnade.

It was not till my return to Europe, in the height
of summer, after a very short passage, that I was
struck with the totally different character of the verdure, both of the field and forest, on the two Continents. After the bright sward, and the varied summer foliage of the Western woods, with their great
ponderance of light greens, the English landscape
seemed to exhibit nothing but evergreens, such was
the depth of shade observable in the blue verdure
of the rounded and heavy masses of foliage, of our
ordinary forest trees, and on the dark and thick meadow grass of our humid climate.

A few hours before sunset, the different visitors
generally assembled, by far the greater number consisting of the young and unmarried of both sexes,
under the shade of the trees, tables were covered
with the delicacies of the season,—among which the
delicious fruit, from which these Strawberry Parties
took their name, was ordinarily seen in the greatest
profusion, with its appropriate concomitants of cream
and champagne. Many an enchanting spectacle of
natural beauty and human contentment and pleasure,
have I observed spread before me, while sitting in
the portico of one of these rural retreats, as the sun
sunk slowly to its setting. The view from many of
them commanded a wide prospect, to the south-east,
over the forests and fine undulating slopes of the country in the direction of the city, whose domes and

edifices peered over the woods, or were descried bordering the irregular lake-like divisions of the river. More remote, lay the wider bay of the Patapsco, glistening with white sails, merging far in the distance into the broad Chesapeake; the long promontory of North Point, with its light-houses glistening in the sunshine; and, beyond all, the hardly perceptible thread of gold which marked the utmost limit of the horizon, and the eastern shore of Maryland.

If to this noble view you add as a foreground, the sweet intermingling forest, lawn, and shrubbery in the immediate vicinity of the dwelling, with the gay and graceful groups scattered over it; you would own with me, that you had rarely gazed upon scenes so truly beautiful and guilelessly cheerful; so animated, so full of innocent pleasure, and so devoid of false glitter and glare, as those presented by the Maryland Strawberry Parties. Later comes the brief but beautiful twilight, with the wailing cry of the whip-poor-will, the flight of the night-hawk, and above all, myriads of fire-flies filling the air with sparks, dancing in the deep shade, or streaming with their intermittent and gentle light among the groups, as they stroll in the open air, or sit in the porticoes.

The frank manners and uncontrolled intercourse between the young people of both sexes, and the confidence with which they are on all occasions left to their own discretion, form one remarkable feature in American society, and one that must strike every European. Unattended as this open confidence has hitherto been, with perhaps the rarest exceptions, by unpleasant results, it is a proof that thus far the society of the New World has an advantage over that of the Old, where circumstances throw such difficulties in the way of most early marriages; where the poison of libertinism is more generally diffused, and where the whole structure of society warrants the most jealous care in the parent, and the utmost caution and reserve on the part of the daughter.

Though compared with future tours, a short excursion we made from Baltimore during this interval, may sink into insignificance; yet as it was the first which led us away to any distance from the coast, it may not inaptly find a corner before I conclude my third sheet to you. This was a visit to the Point of Rocks on the Potomac, and the village of Harper's Ferry, at the junction of that river with another off-spring of the wooded Alleghany, the Shenandoah, which, in the upper part of its course, waters the lovely valley of Virginia. The celebrated rail-road, planned with an object of forming a junction with the waters of the Chesapeake and the Ohio, had then already been carried as far as the Potomac, upward of seventy miles from the city of Baltimore, and in the first part of its course up the varied and beautiful glen of the Patapsco, presents scenes of great and peculiar beauty.

The spirit with which such gigantic undertakings are conceived, the millions furnished for their pro-secution, and the immense works which they render necessary, carried forward by private companies, often without even the assistance of a loan from the State Governments, are worthy of great admiration. None is more so than that displayed in the prosecution of the rail-road in question, which is conducted by bridges, viaducts of massive granite, deep excavations, em-bankments of great extent and height, for seven miles to the entrance of the more confined valley of the Patapsco, through which it subsequently winds, fol-lowing the curvature of the precipitous and rocky hills on both sides for many miles, till it reaches the divid-ing-ridge between the waters of that river, and the tributaries of the Potomac. Here, forty miles from the city, you ascend the first inclined plane, of which there are two on each side, and over which you are conducted by a stationary engine. Fourteen miles from the western slope of the planes, the rail-road traverses the Monocacy valley, and a few miles farther you see the forested ridges of the Catoctin mountains, and the broad stream of the Potomac opening before you.

At the time when we made this excursion, the traffic and the arrangements on this newly-constructed work were in their infancy, and a few rude barracks put up here and there in close proximity to the forest, were but slender indications of the changes about to be effected along its line; but long before we quitted the country, a large village with hotels and warehouses had sprung up at the Point of Rocks; the traffic upon the rail-road was incessant; locomotive engines took the place of horse-power; and hamlets sprung up along its line. The natural resources of the country began to be available; the inexhaustible stores of the finest granite, iron-ore, and breccia, which lay on its very path were conveyed to the city; roads sprung up to communicate with it, and it was gradually advancing into the recesses of the Alleghany, side by side with a canal commenced at the city of Washington, with the same ulterior object.

At Harper's Ferry, where the two combined streams before mentioned, have apparently burst their way through the Blue Ridge, as the advanced chain of the many parallel and continuous ridges of the Apallachian series is called, the scenery is deservedly termed romantic. The precipitous and wooded acclivities of the mountains overhang the wide beds of two noble streams, both interrupted by a long chain of rapids. The picturesque village is situated at the point of junction at the foot of a steep acclivity. A long wooden bridge, resting on stone piers, traverses the united volume of water immediately below, and a mile lower down, the whole, roaring over the Bull's Ring rapid, rushes impetuously through the Gap. The scene presented from the crest of the mountain above the village, of the course of the rivers both before and after their junction, is one of the most striking in the United States. The channel of the Shenandoah to the right, appears obstructed by low reefs of slate rock, as far as it is visible, and that of the Potomac to the left, furrowed by rapids and broken by wooded islands. The mountains overhanging both vallies, are rocky and well wooded, and present fine picturesque scenery along the course of the two canals, which have been constructed for the distance of a mile up each for the convenience of the manufactories of carbines and muskets, established here by the General Government, allured by the defensible character of the position, the vicinity of coal, and great 'water-power.' The arms furnished by this manufactory, and another in Massachusetts, supply the whole Union. Neatness and economy seem to characterize every department.

Our return to the Point of Rocks on the Potomac, gave us a first introduction to American river-scenery. The mode of conveyance was a boat, about seventy feet in length, manned by a mulatto captain, and six or seven coloured men. Its movements were directed by a large oar at either end. These dusky fellows are bred to their business, and under their guidance the unwieldy machine shot like lightning through the passes of the Bull's Ring rapid, and among the many islands which deck the surface of this " River of the woods," a name which it well deserves. Once at the Point of Rocks, the rail-road carriages conveyed us on our return to the city.

Various shorter excursions and visits occupied the remainder of the month—none more interesting and delightful than that of a few days to the Manor, the seat of Charles Carroll, of Carrollton, the only surviving subscriber of the Declaration of Independence; —a venerable and polished gentleman of the old school, drawing toward the close of a long and active life, and an object of the respect and love of the whole country. We often recalled the events of this visit, with interest, as, before our return from our long excursion westward, he too had passed away from among the living. The simple fact of such individuals as himself, Washington, Hamilton, and others, of their known character and excellence in private life, having eventually taken a share in effecting the separation of the colonies from the mother country, was sufficient to make me feel desirous to look into the causes. There were faults on both sides, doubtless ; but of one thing I have become convinced, that the convulsion which separated us, was quite as painful to the one as to the other, and little desired or anticipated by thousands in America, till necessity and the course of events left no other choice.

Immediately upon my return, and that of my two companions, from our trip southward at the close of June, we made conjointly, an excursion up the Hudson river, and to the Kaatskill mountains, lingering for a few days by the way, in a delightful retreat, in the bosom of the Highlands.

If, after having, with one exception, visited every State and Territory in the Union, I might feel myself authorized to form a judgment, I should venture the opinion, that the United States, taken as a whole, are far from possessing a fair proportion of what we should term picturesque scenery. Italy, Switzerland, Spain, our own group of Islands, and Germany, have, in their character and accessories, those details which render them essentially picturesque; not only because the works of man, by which they are thickly diversified, have made them so, but because the natural disposition of the surface—broken ground, bare rock, wood, water, verdure, mountains and vallies, alternating in quick succession—has stamped that peculiar character upon them. But the abrupt outlines of surface, so usual in the Old World, and the interminable interchange of the various elements of the picturesque, are of much rarer occurrence in the New. I use the epithet in its proper sense. It is in vain to look for its common occurrence in the vast alluvial tracts of forest and prairie in the immense valley of the Mississippi, or in the regions of the same geological formation extending from New Jersey, between the Alleghany and the Atlantic, to the Cape of Florida. You would not expect to find it as an ordinary character of the long parallel, rarely broken, and forested ridges, and the intervening vallies, which, under a variety of names,

divide the waters of the East from those of the West.
It is hardly to be met with in the undulating, richly
cultivated central districts of Pennsylvania, New York,
or Maryland.   Even in the New England States,
though more rocky, and broken, more cut up by internal lakes, and under longer cultivation than the
Southern and Western, I should be sorry to undertake a solitary pedestrian journey, trusting to the
charms and variety of the scenery to while away fatigue
or ennui.   In a continent where the forest still covers
so large a portion of both mountain and plain, where
the undisturbed ribs of rock are hidden within the
mountain sides by the swelling and even outlines of the
mould, protected and increased by the forests of ages,
there must be monotony.

Again, what nature has to a certain degree denied,
man has hitherto done but little to remedy. As to
ancient architecture, it is not necessary to remind you
that there is none ; the styles of building usually
adopted in the United States, however commodious
and pretty, or adapted to the different climates, have
rarely any thing picturesque about them.   The first
operations of the settler in the primeval forest are productive of a deformity which years can scarcely
remove.

Still you must not misunderstand me. Though you
cannot, in speaking of these vast regions, say that the
general character of their scenery is picturesque,—yet
go more into detail, and you will find, though they
may be far apart, scenes of the most exquisite natural
beauty, fully justifying the application of that epithet.
The course of the Hudson abounds with them from its
source till it meets the ocean.   Range all the world
over and you will never see a more lovely valley than
that of the Mohawk throughout its whole extent; or
sweeter scenes than those reflected in the bright waters
of Lake George and its neighbours.   Such are many
of the slopes and vales in the broken country on both
sides of the Alleghany ;—the frequent Gaps burst
through the several chains, through which the redun-

dant streams roll down over the rapids toward the lower country;—many of the scenes on the upper coasts of New England, and none more so than the rarely visited and rarely-mentioned Portland. The upper Mississippi, from the falls of St. Anthony, where the mighty river pours down from an elevated region of marsh and lakes, to its junction with the Missouri, abounds in picturesque scenery. Many parts of Michigan lay a claim to be included, and other isolated instances might be cited as my memory retraces the steps of the last two or three years.

But do not suppose that for the rest there is no charm;—that there is nothing in the Western world to make up for the deficiency of this pleasing attribute. There is a character to which it may proudly lay claim in the face of the East, and that is, sublimity. I know what you would say—I never forget the Alps and their majesty, but they stand almost alone.

Get to the summit of the Alleghany, and look out upon the dark mantle of primeval forest clothing the swelling ridges which roll toward the deep blue horizon, rising and falling like the tempest-stirred ocean; —bury yourself in their recesses among the giant trees;—look forth on her vast estuaries, her ocean-lakes, and bays indenting the shores for hundreds of miles, sparkling in the sunbeams, or reflecting the deep blue of heaven through her own transparent atmosphere;—stand upon her boundless prairies stretching to the westward, a thousand miles of unbroken grassy meadow, bespangled with flowers of every hue, where no hand ever reaps, no finger ever culls, and but few feet ever tread;—sail over her inland seas in calm or storm, and know yourself, though surrounded by the watery horizon for hours, in the centre of a continent! Then mark her numberless rivers, whether thousands of miles from their bourne in the Ocean, spreading under your eye a broad moving mirror of shining water in the vast solitude of the silent forests; boiling down a rapid for miles as white as snow; contracted among their poplar islands to a

4*

torrent—or yet nearer their estuary, amidst the cultivated fields of the lower and more thickly inhabited
lands, when the accumulated waters of a thousand
streams press on in one wide reach after the other, and
expand into broad tide-stirred bays ere they finally
merge in the great deep.

Well may America be proud of such scenes.   All
bear the impress of sublimity.   The feelings which
they convey to the human mind may be less pleasing
and less definite, but they are more durable.

One scene yet remains, which, though you have
gazed upon the Alps in all their splendid alternations
of high sublimity, and acknowledged the presence of
the same feeling while floating on the bosom of the
Ocean in calm or tempest,—still stands forward among
these, the world's wonders, and vies with them, in
claiming its degree of this attribute,—and that is
Niagara; the huge step between the waters of an upper
and a lower world, whence the thunder of water has
echoed through the forests, and the vapour of the great
cataract has ascended for ages, like smoke from an
altar to the great Creator of All.

LETTER IV.

ABOUT the second week in July, after being witnesses of the panic caused in New-York by the out-
break of the cholera, we prepared to follow Mr. Irving
to Boston, where he purposed to give us rendezvous
previous to our visit to the White Mountains, the
hightest group in the Union.   Accordingly, one rainy
morning we put ourselves on board a noble steam-boat;
and proceeding through the East River, we glided
past the redoubted Hell-Gate, Pot, Frying-Pan, Hog's
Back, Hen and Chickens, and other dangers of olden

times, and entered upon the broad surface of Long Island Sound.

Instead, however, of pursuing the ordinary course to Newport and Providence, we were set ashore at the little port of Newhaven in Connecticut, and subsequently pursued our journey through the centre of that State to Hartford and Northampton. In landing among these, the early settlements of the New World, after glancing at the States more to the southward, you are struck with the air of comparative antiquity in many objects. The houses, the enclosures, and the trees planted among them, have a much more English appearance. The towns and villages are more thickly strewed over the face of the country, and their outskirts much less ragged and less incumbered with rubbish and building materials. The population seems to be at home on the soil, and children to have succeeded to the inheritance of their fathers for many generations, old houses of imported brick, aged Lombardy poplars, grass-grown and discoloured pavements and thresholds, and orchards full of gray distorted apple-trees, mark the vicinity of many of the earliest settlements. Here or there stands an ancient tree—the sole survivor of the original forest, and a boundary-mark of the first colonists. The cemeteries are more spacious and more decently maintained than you will observe elsewhere, and within their precincts you see many a time-stained tombstone, of the exact pattern and fashion in ornament and inscription, of those picturesque memorials of the dead which crowd the hallowed church-yards of the mother-country. The signs of long and steady cultivation may be remarked on the face of the landscape, and all these things combined, throw a degree of interest over the country apart from the charms of natural scenery, which contrasts agreeably with that air of rawness and newness which is imprinted upon the works of man in other portions of the continent, and which is so opposed to anything like poetry and sentiment.

The valley of the Connecticut river struck us as one of the most lovely we had ever beheld. Many are the beauties with which nature has decked the verdant, fertile, and park-like shores of that pastoral stream in its lower course, as it winds among flourishing towns, and bears upon its broad bosom the fruits of the industry and commercial activity of a busy population. The numerous villages have a delightful appearance in the distance with their clean-built, white houses; their gardens, and broad streets. The weeping elm is the glory of New England, and trees of great beauty and size not unfrequently line both sides of the streets, and cluster about the older mansions.

Above Hartford the banks of the river rise to a greater elevation, and the whole style of scenery about Springfield and Northampton is lovely in the extreme. Indeed this river is said to abound in romantic views throughout its long and varied course. In the course of our tour, we again came upon its banks, at the little town of Lancaster in New Hampshire, two hundred miles above Northampton, and still found it a broad deep stream flowing in an exquisite vale, in a country where cultivation was gradually wresting the soil from the dark primeval forests, and surrounded by nearer or distant chains of mountains.

From Northampton we crossed the state by the direct road to Boston. Stage-coachmen are here, as elsewhere, a peculiar race; they drive well and fearlessly, but not in jockey style, and in a manner quite devoid of grace. They display no coquetry in dress, and are evidently fatalists, taking always the chances of an overturn against the chances of escape. You see them dash over a steep hill in rapid career, sometimes driving six in hand, and hardly holding in the horses during the descent, seemingly trusting to their stars, the beds of rough stone, deep sand, or the frequent gutters constructed across the roads in the hilly districts to prevent their being washed away, to bring them gradually and safely to the bottom.

While travelling commodiously to and fro in the New England states, the mind is frequently inclined to occupy itself with the singular and striking circumstances of its first settlement. Two centuries and a half have rolled by since the May-Flower and her burden of pilgrims approached the shores of this part of America, then totally unknown and unexplored : and no country on earth can boast a more remarkable and a more chequered history since that period. Whatever may be your modification of religious opinion, you cannot but admire the strength of mind, simplicity of faith and purpose, and almost super-human perseverance and hardihood of character of the early colonists. They were placed truly in fearful circumstances, and it is both instructive and consoling to see how the back became suited to the burden. However rudely transplanted from the bosom of civil-ized society, they 'steeled their souls,' and were gifted with a power of endurance which might be deemed beyond nature by those who have not seen how much strength both of mind and body, man has been endowed with, and is capable of exerting under the excitement of peculiar circumstances, beyond that modicum of either, which he may be called to exert in the common walks of life.

Their minds were not only unappalled by the ex-change they had made, between ' a paradise of plea-sure and plenty, and a wilderness of wants,'—the change of clime and scene, unheard-of hardships and privations, cold, hunger, and disease ;—but evidently gaining strength from the very destitution of their position, their being beyond all certain human aid and help—in the fervour of religious dependence on God they struggled on under all these accumulated causes of trial, and those of a yet more fearful char-acter which awaited them in the roused and impla-cable hostility of the tribes whom they supplanted from without, or the fire of fanaticism and schism within their settlements, and finally triumphed.

You inquire into the origin of most of the pleasant towns and villages of Massachusetts, Connecticut, and Rhode Island, and find few whose early foundations were not laid upon ground bedewed by the sweat and blood of the little band of brothers, which first raised the axe in that part of the forest. The majority of the settlements had their commencement in a few individuals either taking possession of a tract of land ceded to them by the Indian sachems, or purchasing the same of the companies holding a large district under the royal grants and charters. They formed themselves into communities, having their own civil and religious laws and their municipal regulations, and in general submitted to such an unusual scrutiny into individual conduct and private life, as to be a marvel in the present time. They bound themselves soberly together into a body politic, the separate settlements by degrees united, and submitted to a common government. The watchfulness of their magistrates over the public morals was pushed to a most ridiculous extent. But you have only to peruse any of their codes, the Blue Laws of Connecticut for instance, or read any of the chronicles of the time, to satisfy yourself as to that.

In those early times, and under those peculiar circumstances, all men expressed themselves with vehemence and acted with violence. Scarcely had the first colonists landed, before religious feuds broke out and farther separations occurred. Men who had quitted their native country, hand in hand, for the same holy cause, found in the solitude of their new position fresh subjects of difference, which admitted of no adjustment and no mutual forbearance and forgiveness; but proudly drew away from each other deeper into the woods, unappalled by danger and utter loneliness. The severity of manners and morals practised among them was accompanied by distrust, intractability, and rancour. The emigration of the Quakers and Baptists, lent fuel to the flame, and persecution was added to other troubles. From being the oppressed, they became the oppressors.

Fanaticism brought in the end its own punishment, and a terrible one it was. The belief in witchcraft arose and spread like a contagion in some of the settlements, and it was not till after a number of lives

had been sacrificed to it, that the inhabitants awoke as from a dream, and lamented their falling off from reason and true Christianity.

If the history of this people in their relation to one another is worthy of study and full of interest, that of their struggles with the Indian inhabitants of the forest, is not the less so. It is to be lamented that here, as every where else, the superior power and intelligence of the whites only led to the speedier and more certain destruction of the latter; and much of the misery on both sides is to be traced in its first source to the conduct of the former. It is humiliating to mark how extremes meet, and how the fate of the Indian, under the lash of the unsparing zeal and cupidity of the most bigotted Roman Catholic in the central divisions of this Continent, where tens of thousands were sacrificed under the plea of doing God service, was that also the Northern Indian, under the relentless barbarity of the most fanatical among Protestants, who, deeming themselves a peculiar people, turned a war of defence, to which their conduct had mainly given rise, into a war of extermination, and believed they were thus fulfilling the will of God.

However stern the necessity appeared to be, which bade the Puritans seek elsewhere for a land where they might worship God without molestation, according to their own consciences, abundant testimonials are extant of the ardent love and affection with which these early emigrants looked back to the land of their fathers. 'We in this country,' says one of them,[*] 'have left our near relations, brothers, sisters, fathers' houses, nearest and dearest friends; but if we can get nearer to God here,—He will be instead of all, more than all to us. We may take that out of God that we forsook in father, mother, brother and sister, and friend, that hath been near and dear to us as our own soul. Even among the most wicked sinners there may

---

[*] Mr. Whitney, a pastor of Lynn, Massachusetts, from 1636 to 1690.

be found some righteous,—some corn among the chaff,
—some jewels among the sand,—some pearls among a
multitude of shells.   Who hath made England to differ
from other nations, that more jewels are to be found
there than elsewhere? or, what hath that island that it
hath not received?   'The East and the West Indies
yield their gold, and pearl, and sweet spices—but I
know where the spicy Christians be.   England hath
yielded these, yet not England, but the grace of God
that hath ever been with them.   We see what hope
we may have concerning *New* England, though we do
not deserve to be named the same day with our dear
mother.'

And that this love was real and unfeigned, was
proved for years, by their cherished relations with
home, as they taught their children to call their mother-
country;—by their willingness of dependence;—their
very prejudices;—the blood which they freely shed in
the quarrels of their king, and by a multitude of
other testimonials now thrown aside and forgotten. For
a while this affection grew with their growth, and increased with their strength. It need not have been
estranged, and perhaps never would have been, had
England understood her true interests, and always
acted with justice. But she was only a stepmother
at best. Perhaps temporary oppression from the
measures of government on one hand, and a sense of
growing strength and importance on the other, would
hardly have effected it, despite the democratic feeling
which existed in the country from its earliest settlements. There are other things which are even more
potent than oppression in producing the separation of
colonies from the parent states:—offended pride:
pique; the soreness produced by unmerited ridicule;
the disgust consequent upon being undervalued—and
other passions of that class whose workings are more
hidden, but infinitely more sure and certain in their
effects.

In referring to the early history of this country and
the circumstances of its colonization, there is one

fact which it is perhaps well to bear in mind, at a time when the spirit of change seems to pervade the very air we breathe; and the example of America is frequently quoted, to prove that the advocates for the overthrow of our Constitution, and covertly of our monarchical form of government, are not the rogues or dupes which most honest men would suppose. We are told to look to her, to see how a country may throw aside monarchy, become a democratic republic, —flourish and increase, and give abundant promise of future greatness and power. This is true, the United States do flourish, and they do increase, and they promise great things,—may they fulfil them! But this is to be gathered from their history, that when the American colonies threw off their allegiance to the monarch of Great Britain and his government, they never threw aside the British constitution, which did not intimately concern them.

Many suppose that it was not till the Revolution that the Americans began to govern themselves, when, in fact, they had all along been brought up to self-government. The constitution generally agreed to by the different bands of colonists was a pure democracy; many of them, even down to the time of the Revolution, possessed and exhibited all the essential attributes of free states. The puritans were especially republicans in creed and discipline; and in all their arrangements this principle was predominant. And this the Government at home knew and acknowledged for many years, and had it been always remembered, the bond between us might long before this have changed its character, but it never would have been rudely broken. The royal prerogative of control was wisely and sparingly exercised in the internal affairs of the colonies, even in their earliest and feeblest state; and it was not till it began to be inauspiciously and oppressively put forward, that there was any avowed disposition on their part to resist.

If by these disjointed and hasty remarks, I shall suc-

ceed in directing your attention to an interesting subject, I shall gain my end.

At Boston, we found our companion awaiting our
arrival at the Tremont Hotel, and on chatting over our
projects, we resolved to proceed without delay on our
tour to the northward, the rather, as all minds were
more or less unhinged by the absorbing subject of conversation and dread, the cholera. We had therefore
only time to glance at the Lions. It is a subject of
regret, that neither on the present nor a subsequent
visit, had we a fitting opportunity of becoming more
intimately acquainted with the details and the society
of this large and handsome capital. It is by far the
most English looking city of the Union, and has a
character for possessing much good, well-educated and
accomplished society, male and female. My great
quarrel (for one may contrive to pick a quarrel every
where) is that the good Bostonians pertinaciously per-
sist in crowing over the battle of Bunker's Hill, as
though they had gained any thing on that occasion
worth being thankful for. You recollect, doubtless,
that we were taught to crow over it also as school-boys,
as a victory of King George's. But many of the old,
and apparently settled layers of the brain get strangely
turned upside down by travelling.

Much of the country to the north of Boston, with
the exception of the fertile lands in immediate contiguity to the rivers, might be described in few words,
as a labyrinth of forests, lakes, granite rocks, and
boulder-stones, dispersed over an undulating surface;
with cultivated tracts and flourishing villages and
towns, wherever the courses of the clear streams are interrupted by rocks, and thus rendered serviceable for
the purposes of manufacture, or where the soil is particularly rich. The first day's journey northward
brought us over the Merrimac, to the town of Concord,
in New Hampshire. The beauty of the ponds or lakes,
with which the country is frequently broken, lying
deeply sunk in the forests, diversified by islands and
promontories, and frequently extending twelve or fifteen

miles in length, was the principal feature which caught
our attention.

The second day we reached the shores of Winnipis-
siogee Lake, the largest in New Hampshire, and
between twenty and thirty miles long. On our route
we visited a Shaker settlement; clean, orderly and odd,
but otherwise in no way distinguished from others of
their community dispersed over the Union, and frequently described. To what singular and childish
vagaries will men resort, when through perverse pride
they sacrifice their simple belief in revelation at the
shrine of human reason! How many in our day are
content to grope along by the light of their own sorry
taper, rather than walk in the glorious light which
God has freely offered us!

The lake with the long name, as written above, we
found less beautiful than many of its inferiors in extent; but the scenery from thence to the base of the
White Mountains at Conway, and still farther in their
recesses toward the Notch, is truly romantic. This
detached group occupies the centre of the State of
New Hampshire. The country at the base is, for the
most part, covered with endless pine forests, full of
ponds and tangled streams, through which the smaller
rivers, proceeding from the slopes, filter slowly toward
the more open country. There seems to be going forward, in many parts of these uncultivated districts, a
continual struggle between the two great elements,
earth and water. Large tracts are overflowed at one
season, and the land and its produce drowned beneath
the dark lake; while on the bosom of many of the latter, banks of sand are gradually thrown up by the
action of the waves; shallows are formed, which teem
with aquatic plants, water-snakes, terrapins, and bull-
frogs; piles of floating and rotting timber are stranded
upon them; a vegetable mould is formed, and in the
course of years an island rises, covered with the ordinary forest trees of the climate. The latter, from the
predominance of the fir tribe among them, are of a much
gloomier character than those farther to the south;

but they abound with many shapely and beautiful trees, none more so than the tall sugar-maple; and many sweet flowers peep out from the marshes, or from the thickets of fern and dwarf oak. How wonderful and how imperfectly understood are many of the ordinary operations of nature! No sooner does the axe of the woodman, or the accidental burning of the forests, destroy one class of trees and brushwood—a class that may have apparently covered the soil for centuries—than another race perfectly distinct, rises, as though by magic, from the disturbed and discoloured soil, and covers it with beauty. The proofs of the almost universal principle of spontaneous vegetation throughout both the forest and prairie lands of the New Continent, are so well known and acknowledged, as to need no additional confirmation at the present day. We have met with continual evidences of its truth in every part of the east and west. It would seem that the seeds of one class of plants and forest trees must be deposited by some catastrophe beyond the action of light, heat and atmospheric air; where they lie, supplanted by another growth, and are forgotten, preserving, however, the vital principle for centuries in a dormant or torpid state, till accident or tillage brings them to a position favourable to their reproduction to light and life.

One of the most remarkable instances of this extraordinary phenomenon, of frequent but well attested occurrence, is that the marl dug from pits thirty feet deep in some parts of the Union, on being spread over the soil, becomes instantly covered with white clover; and in New Jersey, this is the case with the mud dragged up from the bottom of the Delaware, and used for the purposes of manure.

From Conway, we followed the valley of the river Saco, as I have already implied, to the Notch or gap in the mountains near which it rises; a remarkable and romantic pass, frequented in summer by numbers of tourists like ourselves; and in the winter, when all the mountains and the countries at their base are often covered for weeks with deep snow, by innumerable sledges laden with cheese and corn, transported through this pass from the fertile vallies of Vermont and the upper country, to the coast.

The ascent of the highest summit of the cluster—Mount Washington, (6234 feet) was attempted by our party, under disadvantageous circumstances: upon gaining the summit, after some hour's toil and much expectation, we were enveloped in heavy mist, which set our patience at defiance, and sent us cold and wet on our downward route. A solitary scramble to the summit of the third in rank, situated in the same chain, which I had contrived to accomplish the preceding day, under better auspices, allows me to give you some faint picture of the scenery of the White Hills.

As a mountain view, it was truly magnificent, though by far the most gloomy I had ever beheld. The entire group, save five or six of the most elevated mountains, which rear their scalps of micacious rock over a belt of dwarf fir, appears invariably clothed to the very summits with the dense northern forest, and excepting here and there in the deepest vallies, or at such a distance that the gazer could but just detect the difference amidst the blue tints of the horizon, where the swelling-surface sank imperceptibly down toward the lower country, the eye was scarcely relieved by the sight of cultivation. No rock could be descried except that which heaped up the highest summits; no bright green pastures were seen on the steep slopes; no white cottages shone like stars from afar; but here and there the precipitous declivities were deeply seamed by tremendous earth-slides, appearing like gashes in the dark face of the mountains. A number of misty lakes gleamed in the distance to the southward, and occasionally you saw the white smoke rising from some upland valley where a hardy son of the soil had pitched his habitation, and begun his struggle with the wilderness and its inhabitants.

From my description you will gather that the upper districts of this mountain region are still in the state of

5*

nature, as wild as when the red warriors, two centuries ago, gathered themselves together in their recesses and leagued for the destruction of the intruders on their coasts; and, with the exception of the Indian tribes, the district is still tenanted by almost the same inhabitants. Here the bear, the catamount, the Siberian lynx, the wolf, and the lordly stag, still find harbour.

By ascending the valley of the Saco, and descending that of the Ammonoosuc, we cut completely across the chain. Pourtales and myself continued our route as far north as Lancaster; and then having parted for awhile from our companion, who was obliged to return for a few days to New York, with an intention of joining company again in ten days' time at Saratoga Springs, we bent our steps to Montpelier, in Vermont, and took our course southward through the whole range of the Green Hills, the back-bone of that State, to Bennington.

The interval spent in thus rambling through the fertile valleys of that chain of beautifully wooded hills, has left a very pleasant class of recollections, but in general of so uniform and ordinary a character, that I do not think you would thank me for delaying my narrative here.

We ascended Killington Peak, a prominent summit of the chain, rising four thousand feet above Lake Champlain, which we descried glistening like a sheet of silver in the distant horizon; and we remained one day in the village of Royalton, upon which I will venture a few remarks; partly because we were stationary and more at liberty to look at the scene around us, and partly because of all the pretty New England villages, and there are thousands, there is none more lovely than that just named, on the banks of White River.

Too frequently you have to remark, in travelling in the United States, how utterly prosaic all the works of man appear; and it is well if there are exceptions now and then, and if you meet with secluded spots where the charms of nature are not blurred by the inharmonious works of human design.

The village in question lay niched in the very heart of the wooded hills on the banks of a crystal stream, flowing over a white pebbly bed, with an occasional mass of slate rock peering above the surface. The hills of medium height, rose steeply on either hand, displaying forested summits and sloping green sides denuded of timber, except occasional groups or single trees, and here and there broken by an isolated mass of rock. A conical hill with a solitary tree on its summit overtopped the lower end of the village. The latter was composed, as usual, principally of one street, with houses irregularly posted, and trees and gardens between. A few of the modern houses had a degree of taste to recommend them, and an old fashioned cluster of low cottages with open galleries toward the street, and steps down to the level of the road, directly fronted the inn.

The church, barn-like as usual, and built with a scantiness of roof which added to its deformity, stood on the verge of a kind of green, not far from the inn, which was one of the best and most prominent edifices of the place. It had the ordinary appendage of a huge staring sign, and lofty sign-post in the middle of the street. The unoccupied spaces and corners in the immediate vicinity of the houses, which at an earlier day, had doubtless been heaped with rubbish, now bore a rank growth of tall plants, among which the mulberry-coloured blossoms and broad white leaves of the milk-weed were conspicuous. There were charming walks along the river bank under the shade of the forest, which hung over the water, from the northern slopes.

The interior of the inn was more calculated for individual comfort than those ordinarily met with out of the principal cities in the United States. I was delighted to observe a large family Bible with the ordinary list of family births, marriages, and deaths, on the side-table of our sitting-room. It was easy to see

that we were in the " land of sober habits," and many
things brought England to mind.

It was here our lot to spend a quiet Sunday. During
the earlier hours of the day, a few loungers were seen
under the arcade of our inn, else the village appeared
deserted. Suddenly divers gigs, light carts, sulkies,
and horsemen, came from all sides, and congregated
under a line of sheds constructed at the back of the
church. The congregation assembled. A plain and
unaffected sermon was delivered by a baptist minister,
prefaced and followed by the congregational singing,
led by the feeble notes of a single flute. The service
ended, the quiet street of the village appeared, for an
instant, full of busy feet; doors were opened and shut,
the gigs and sulkies were filled, and straightway
whirled away; but a few minutes sufficed to restore it
to its solitude, and for the remainder of the day, hardly
a sound was heard. The good people of Royalton
seemed to be quietly digesting the spiritual food thus
afforded them, and their Sunday was literally a day of
rest.

The manners and habits of this great eastern division of the American people are strikingly distinct
from those of their fellow citizens to the southward.
The character of the inhabitants of New England for
diligence, shrewdness, and all those matter-of-fact
talents which tell in a country like this, where every
man is struggling to get and maintain an independence, is probably familiar to you. They are speculative, at the same time that their caution, clearsighted-
ness, and indomitable perseverance, generally ensure
success. In politics, their practical conduct is strikingly
opposed to the theoretical vagaries of the south. They
have often, and not without reason, been compared to
the northern inhabitants of our own island : but, I
think, the New Englanders have all the steadiness and
prudence of the Scotch, with a yet greater degree of
ingenuity. Like the Scotch, they foster education ;
like the Scotch, they are inclined to the more severe
forms of religious discipline and worship ; like the

Scotch, they are fearfully long-winded ; like them they are gadders abroad, loving to turn their faces southward and westward, pushing their fortunes wherever fortunes are to be pushed, and often in places and by shifts where no one ever dreamed that fortunes were to be gained. They may be found supplanting the less energetic possessor of land and property in every state of the Union. They have a finger upon the rim of every man's dish, and a toe at every man's heel. They are the pedlers and schoolmasters of the whole country ; and, though careless of good living abroad, when at home and at ease, they are fond of " creature comforts." No where is the stomach of the traveller or visitor put in such constant peril as among the cake-inventive housewives and daughters of New England. Such is the universal attention paid to this particular branch of epicurism in these States, that I greatly suspect that some of the Pilgrim Fathers must have come over to the country with the cookery book under one arm and the Bible under the other ; though I find in more than one code of ancient laws made in early times, orders issued that no person should make " cakes or buns, except for solemn festal occasions, such as burials and marriages." There are but few boys among them ; many of their children seem to start up at once to puny men. I should not think they were a fun-loving nation, or had great reverence for holidays ; —jokes are an abomination to many among them.

Though, in common with all Americans, they are proud and boastful of their claims to unlimited freedom, they are fond of imposing grievous burdens upon the inferior orders of animals within their power ; and you see horses and cows, pigs and geese, labouring under the most singular yokes it is possible to conceive.

The faults allied to this kind of character are easily recognizable. Where education and religion have had their proper influence, and high-mindedness, and innate sense of honour exist, all this shrewdness and strength of character will add to the respectability of the possessor, and to the good of the social circle. But where they are allied with meanness and littleness of soul, they must bear the stamp of sordid and low cunning in petty transactions, and of uncompromising, ungenerous aggrandisement and selfishness in larger operations. Hence the diverse terms in which you hear the socalled Yankee or Easternman named, and the praise and obloquy with which the character I have attempted so roughly to sketch is alternately drawn. I was never, to my knowledge, taken in by any of my particular or casual acquaintance in any of the Eastern states, and I am far from believing, though I may have laughed at the thousand-and-one-tales related of the extravagant ingenuity and cunning of the Yankee pedlers tramping through every nook of the Union ; but I can easily conceive that there is many an arrant rogue among them, and many an arrant goose among their customers.

I have in pure idleness given you as harmless a sketch of the character of one great division of these doughty republicans as was ever penned, and surely so far I should escape having my name held up to national scorn and obloquy, by my Transatlantic acquaintances, should it ever get to their ears. But I must not make too sure ; for a man sometimes gets spiteful in spite of himself, and I may possibly by and by, in the progress of my relation, arrive at a place where I was both cross and crossed, had the tooth-ache, was disappointed or contradicted, met with dull weather or a cold breakfast, and then you may find that I occasionally see through a bilious medium, and can find fault, like other English travellers, with all and every thing about me.

From Royalton, we crossed the chain to Rutland. We were told we should find in the latter a far more elegant town, which we found to mean, more pretending, more scattered, more staring, and more bustling.

We did not forget our promise to ' byde tryste' at Saratoga on the first days of August, and turning to the westward from Bennington, we crossed the Hudson at Lansingburg, and were there at the time appointed.

I shall not however detain you here at present, but

with permission, will leave any allusion to the gay
motley crowd at that fashionable resort till another opportunity, and will carry you forward with me to Niagara, which we visited in the month of August.

LETTER V.

In attempting in this, or any future letter, to give
you an idea of ' men and manners' in the United States
—which, by the by, would seem to be a most portentous and dangerous subject for any person, male or
female, to meddle with,—I would always have you
bear in mind, that traits which might be introduced as
characteristic of one state of society, or of one class of
individuals, will hardly admit of general application to
the people as a nation.   The only distinctive and really
characteristic marks exhibited by the mass of the population are, perhaps, a hearty detestation of monarchical forms of government on the one hand and a boundless admiration of the republican form under which they
live on the other.

As to the rest, where is their nationality?   The fact
is, that, in their present condition, the people of these
countries cannot be considered to have a national character.   It is even to be doubted whether they will ever
amalgamate sufficiently, under the great difference of
temperament, style of life and habits consequent upon
such diverse climates alone, to admit of one picture,
however broadly sketched, being in every particular
characteristic of the whole.   How can the same description of men and manners be applicable to a mixed
population, spread over such a vast extent of country,
under such very different circumstances, of such different blood and origin?   Turn to whichever part of the
Union you may, manners perfectly distinct from each
other, traceable to the stock from which the individual

sprang, in person, dwellings, prejudices, prepossessions and modes of expression are distinguishable.

Here you will find the children of the Pilgrim Fathers, and the early colonists from the pure English stock; whose descendants have also spread over the fresh virgin soil of Ohio, and the other states in the same parallel, and planted themselves in every part of the Union where shrewdness and industry could win their way. You may trace the French Refugee in West Chester; the Dutch in New York; the German in the valley of the Mohawk; the Swede in New Jersey and Delaware; the Quaker and the German in Pennsylvania, together with distinct colonies of Irish; —the descendant of the Cavalier in Virginia, Maryland, and the States to the south, and the Italian and Spaniard in Florida. On the other hand, between the Creole in Louisiana, and the French Canadian on the Upper Lakes and rivers—you detect many races of men, with peculiar habits and manners, distinct from each other, like all those enumerated, in many particulars, though for the time bound together by a common government, and the ties of common interest.

When, in addition to this evident reason why a given description of 'men and manners' which may be a true picture when applied to one corner of the country, must be inapplicable to another, the unsettled state of a large proportion of the population, the advantages enjoyed by one portion for the attainment of a high degree of civilization, and the disadvantages under which another may labour, are all admitted, who would expect that any description of character or manners were to be considered national? Yet, neither foreigners, nor, it might be surmised, the Americans themselves, appear aware of this. Less surprise may be felt, however, at the temper of mind with which a prejudiced or superficial foreigner sets down any particular trait, (especially if a discreditable one) as characteristic of the whole people from Maine to Florida,—than at the utter perversity and sensitiveness of mind, of by far the greater majority of Americans of whatever class, in

taking to heart and bitterly resenting any chance remarks upon the 'men and manners' of a given district,
when perhaps not exactly of a laudatory description,—
thus making the quarrel of one division of the community the quarrel of all. In this respect there is
doubtless a characteristic nationality of feeling. To
see a gentleman of Boston or Baltimore, resenting by
word and deed, the sketch published to the world of
the society of a district of the West, borders on the
ludicrous, the more so, as, if untravelled, they are frequently as ignorant of the real state of things there, as a
stay-at-home Englishman might be supposed to be. It
impresses one with the idea, that the inhabitants of the
United States, little mercy as they show each other in
their stormy political contests, little measure as they
hold in their terms of satire and obloquy, defamation
and abuse of parties and individuals in their public
prints, are sensitive as a people, beyond example, to
criticism from without, and more particularly so when
the observation comes from an inhabitant of Britain.
This weakness almost amounts to a national disease.
A little thought may, perhaps, suggest some reason
for it.

The English have not, as a nation, whatever may be
supposed by those who gather their estimate of national
feeling from the Reviews, much sympathy with this
kind of sensitiveness. We have arrived at that happy
pitch of national self-esteem, and our national pride is
so little disturbed by unwelcome surmises or suspicions
that in this or that particular we are really emulated or
surpassed by our neighbours, that we calmly set down
any one who comes among us, and tells us that in certain
matters John Bull is surpassed by other nations, or an
object of ridicule to them, as an ignorant or spiteful
twaddler at once, and do not suffer the national temper
to be ruffled. Having now, for so many years, been accustomed to have justice done us by our neighbours on
all main points, however unwillingly, we can even afford
to be satirized, or, as we would say, caricatured, in
some minor particulars, and can magnanimously laugh

at the same. But not so with America. She feels,
and with reason, that justice has not always been done
her in essentials, and by Britain in particular. She
knows that there has been a spirit abroad having a
tendency to keep the truth and her real praise away
from the eye of the world, shrouded behind a vein of
course ribaldry, and detail of vulgarities, which, if not
positively untrue, were at least so invidiously chosen,
and so confirmatory of prejudice, and so far caricature,
when applied to the people as a mass, as almost to
bear the stigma of untruth. She has felt that the progress made in a very limited period of time, and amidst
many disadvantages, in reclaiming an immense continent from the wilderness, in covering it with innumerable flourishing settlements; her success in the mechanic
arts; her noble institutions in aid of charitable purposes; the public spirit of her citizens; their gigantic
undertakings to facilitate interior communication; their
growing commerce in every quarter of the globe; the
indomitable perseverance of her sons; the general attention to education, and the reverence for religion,
wherever the population has become permanently
fixed; and the generally mild and successful operation
of their government; have been overlooked, or only
casually mentioned, while the failings, rawness of
character, and ill-harmonized state of society in many
parts; the acts of lawless individuals, and the slang
and language of the vulgar, have been held promi-
nently forward to excite scorn, provoke satire, and
strengthen prejudice. In short, she has felt that her
true claims upon respect and admiration have been
either unknown or undervalued in Europe, and that
especially that nation with whom she had the greatest
national affinity, was inclined to be the most perse-
veringly unjust.

Hence partly arises, it may be surmised, the querulous state of sensitiveness, to which allusion has been
made, and also that disposition to swagger and exaggerate, which has been laid to the charge of many
Americans, not without reason.

As long as the national temper maintains this morbid tone, I have become more and more convinced that it will allow the justice of no criticism; and that no individual, however honest and striving against prejudice, however conciliatory, however sincerely regarding the people and their institutions with respect, however convinced that he who foments the ill-will and prejudice that may exist between the two countries, ill serves his own, the cause of humanity in the world, or the nobler ends of travel and observation—I say, no one will write a book, depicting the state of things in the United States, as they are, with all their unavoidable crudities and anomalies, and give the public mind in that country satisfaction. Moreover it is to be doubted whether any great good is ever to be effected by foreign criticism, especially in a case like that before you, where the criticized puts himself without the circle in which European rules and deductions, whether political or otherwise, would be deemed decisive. America must correct her failings, by the free course of her own native good sense, and I believe will do it where correction is needful. One thing is certain, she professes to have no more patience with our opinions, or respect for our gratuitous advice, than a painter would have for that of a circle of critics, who surround his easel, to pass judgment upon his projected chef d'œuvre, of which nothing but the preparatory shades appear on the canvass.

As to myself, I was neither tempted while in the country to brood over the disagreeable, nor to look on the dark side, neither can I do so now. I was treated every where with courtesy and good humour, and what less can I return?

Causes for dissatisfaction and disgust will always be discovered by the seeker, whoever and wherever he may be. There is no wit in describing as peculiar to America, that which is common to all the world. As to coarseness and vulgarity of mind and manners, it is not, that abundance is not to be found in our own country, but that it is, from circumstances easily understood, more obtruded for the present into prominent positions in America: at the same time it must be allowed that in most situations, you may escape from its contemplation if you will. Does it not appear to you that there is something essentially vulgar in that mind, which in spite of its alleged disgust, can continually occupy itself with coarseness in others, and load itself and the memory with its details?

LETTER VI.

You may recollect my juvenile weakness, that of being a notorious cascade-hunter. There was something in the motion of a waterfall which always made my brain spin with pleasure. Impelled by this passion, as a boy, I ransacked the moorland and mountain districts of the north of England, in quest of the beautiful but diminutive specimens of this variety of natural scenery with which they abound; and at a later period, there was not an accessible waterfall within my range of travel from the Rhine Fall to Tivoli, that I did not contrive to approach, gaze upon, and listen to with infinite pleasure. So you may well ask what impression was made upon me by Niagara.

I am glad that the position and the general features of this celebrated scene are too well known to need description, and that you will require none from me.

At the commencement of the present century, Niagara, difficult of access, and rarely visited, was still the cataract of the wilderness. The red Indian still lingered in its vicinity, and adored the Great Spirit and 'Master of Life' as he listened to the 'Thunder of the waters.'* The human habitations within sound of its fall were rare and far apart. Its few visitors came,

---

* Such is the signification of the Indian word Niagara.

gazed, and departed in silence and awe, having for their guide the child of the forest or the hardy backwoodsman. No staring, painted hotel rose over the woods and obtruded its pale face over the edge of the boiling river. The journey to it from the east was one of adventure and peril. The scarcely attainable shore of Goat Island, lying between the two great divisions of the cataract, had only been trodden by a few hardy adventurers, depending upon stout hearts and steady hands for escape from the imminent perils of the passage.—How is it now? The forest has everywhere yielded to the axe. Hotels with their snug shrubberies, out-houses, gardens, and paltry establishment stare you in the face: museums, mills, staircases, tolls, and grog-shops, all the petty trickery of Matlock-Baths or Ambleside, greet the eye of the traveller. Bridges are thrown from island to island; and Goat Island is reached without adventure. A scheming company on the Canadian side, have planned a ' City of the Falls,' to be filled with snug cottages, symmetrically placed, to let for the season; and in fine, you write to your friend in Quebec, and give him rendezvous at Niagara for a certain hour, and start yourself from Richmond, in Virginia, for the point proposed, with a moral certainty of meeting at the very day and hour specified, by taking advantage of the improvements of the age, and the well-arranged modes of conveyance by steamers, rail-roads, canals, and coaches.

In short, Niagara is now as hacknied as Stockgill-Force or Rydal-water, and, all things considered, the observation which an unimaginative ' Eastern man' is said to have made, addressing a young lady tourist, who was gazing breathlessly for the first time at the scene, was not so far out of keeping with it: ' Isn't it nice, Miss? Yes, all is nice, very nice, that that active little biped man has done or is doing.'

But do not imagine that we grew peevish at the sight of the blots upon the landscape, to which I have alluded, and departed in wrath and disgust. We soon found that there was that in and about Niagara which

6*

was not to be marred by busy man and all his petty schemes for convenience and self-aggrandisement; and I may truly say, with regard to both our first and second visit, and stay within its precincts, that we were under the influence of its spell.　While within the sound of its waters, I will not say you become part and parcel of the cataract, but you find it difficult to think, speak, or dream of any thing else.　Its vibrations pervade, not only the air you breathe, the bank on which you sit, the paper on which you write, but thrill through your whole frame, and act upon your nervous system in a remarkable, and it may almost be said an unpleasant manner.

You may have heard of individuals coming back from the contemplation of these Falls, with dissatisfied feelings.　To me this is perfectly incomprehensible, and I do not know whether to envy the splendid fancies and expectations of that class of travellers, to whom the sight of Niagara would bring disappointment, or to feel justified in doubting whether they have any imagination or eye for natural scenery at all.　How blank the world must be to them of objects of natural interest.　What can they expect to see?

As to expectations, ours were excited and warm, and I shall never forget the real anxiety with which we looked out, on our ascent from Lewistown, for the first appearance of the object of our visit.　The broad fathomless blue river, streaked with foam, which, deeply sunk in a colossal channel, hurried to our rencontre, and appeared at every fresh glimpse as we advanced, swifter and in greater commotion, was to us a guarantee that the scene of its descent from the upper country could be no common one.　When about three miles from the village on the American side, you gain your first view of the Falls, together with the river, both above and below,—the island which divides them,—and greater part of the basin at their feet.

I will not say but that the impression of that first glance was heightened afterward by our nearer and reiterated survey of every portion of the cataract in detail; yet we all agreed that we could even then grasp the idea of its magnitude, and that all we had seen elsewhere, and all we had expected, was far surpassed by what was then shown to us. And when, the following year, two of us turned aside by common consent to pay a second visit to Niagara, after having, in the interval, visited many of the great falls of Lower Canada,—cataracts in comparison to which all European Falls are puerile; and we felt our curiosity excited to divine what impression a second visit would make—far from being disappointed, we felt that before Niagara, in spite of its comparative inferiority of elevation, all shrunk to playthings.

It is not the mere weight and volume of water that should give this far-famed cataract the first rank. Every surrounding object seems to be on a corresponding scale of magnificence. The wide liquid surface of the river above, with its swelling banks, contrasted by the deep blue floods below, as, boiling up from their plunge, into the unfathomed basin they shock against one another, and race down toward the distant lake; the extreme beauty of the forested defile, with its precipices and slopes; the colouring of the waters, which in the upper part of its descent, is that of the emerald; the mystery and thick gloom which hide the foot of the falls, and add to their apparent height, and the floating clouds of vapour, now hurried over the face of the landscape, as though urged by the breath of a hurricane, and then slowly ascending and hovering like a cloud in the blue sky, all combine to form a scene in which sublimity and picturesque beauty are enchantingly blended. There is here none of that stiffness either in the scenery, or the form and appearance of the particular object of interest, which engravings too frequently give you the idea of.

Among the innumerable points of view, that from the precipitous shore of the river, about the distance I have alluded to, is the most satisfactory, if not the most striking. In the immediate vicinity of the Falls, the points of interest are so various, that if you would

require a sketch, I should not know which to select.
The grandest, doubtless, is from the Canadian shore,
near the Horse-shoe Fall; but you pass from one to
the other, and everywhere the picture presented has
no compeer or rival in nature.

Many things combined to make us prefer choosing
the village on the American shore, for our halting place,
in preference to the garish hotel on the opposite side.
The greater monotony of the right-hand division of
the cataract was counterbalanced by the grand distant
view of its more varied neighbour, and by the practicability of a near approach to both from Goat Island,
to which an easy access is afforded by a boldly-con-
structed bridge over the rapids.   Besides, we agreed
that the position of that village and its inns, was not
only more rural and secluded, but that better taste was
exhibited in its details.

What a glorious scene!   To sit upon the summit
of the impending precipice of the island, and see, as
we did the morning after our first arrival, the summer
mist begin to rise and disengage itself from the heavy
white cloud of spray which rose from the depth of the
boiling basin of the Great Fall beneath us.   By degrees, the curtain was partially removed, revealing the
wall of slowly-descending water behind, now dimly
descried,—as, confounded with the floating sheets of
foam and spray which the wind of the mighty cataract
drove backward and forward over it like innumerable
clouds of thin floating gauze,—it mocked us with its
constantly varying shape and position; and then appearing unveiled with its sea-green tints, brilliantly
illuminated by the passing sun-beam.   An hour after,
and the mist had disappeared; the Falls were sparkling in the bright sunshine; and a brilliant Iris was
resting on the body of vapour which the wind carried
away from the face of the descending columns.   The
scene at sun-set, day after day, was no way less majes-
tic, when the sun, glancing from the Canadian side of
the river, lit up the precipices and woods of Goat
Island, and the broad face of the American Fall, which

then glowed like a wall of gold; while half the Fall of the horse-shoe, and the deep recesses of the curve were wrapped in shade. Morning, noon, and night, found us strolling about the shore, and on the island, which is an earthly paradise.

I remember the quiet hours spent there, when fatigued with the glare of the hot bright sun, and the din of the Falls, with peculiar delight. We loved, too, to escape from all those signs of man's presence, and busy-bodying to which I have alluded, and, burying ourselves in the fresh, dark, scarce-trodden forest still covering a great part of its area, to listen to the deadened roar of the vast cataracts on either hand, swelling on the air distinct from every other sound.

There, seated in comparative solitude, you catch a peep, across a long irregular vista of stems, of the white vapour and foam. You listen to the sharp cry of the blue jay, the tap of the red-headed woodpecker, and the playful bark of the squirrel; you scan the smooth white boles of the beech or birch, checquered with broad patches of dark-green moss, the stately elm and oak, the broad-leaved maple, the silvery white and exquisitely chiselled trunk of the cedar, or the decaying trunk of the huge chesnut, garlanded with creepers; but you will hardly ever lose the consciousness of the locality. The spell of Niagara is still upon and around you. You glance again and again at the white veil which thickens or grows dim beyond the leafy forest :—the rush of the nearer rapids, the din of falling waters, the murmur of the echoes answering the pulsations of the descending mass, fill your ears, and pervade all nature.

Every thing around and about you appears to reply to the Cataract, and to partake of it, none more so than the evergreen forest which is bathed from year to year in the dew of the river. These noble trees, as they tower aloft on the soil, are sustained from youth to age by the invigorating spray of the mighty Falls. Their leaves are steeped, summer after summer, in the heavy dew, their trunks echo the falling waters, from the day

they rise from the sod, to that in which they are shaken
to the ground ; and the fibres of the huge moss-grown
trunk, on which you sit, prostrate and mouldering on
the rich mould beneath, bedded in the fresh grass and
leaves, still vibrate to the sound of its thunders, and
crumble gradually to dust.   But all this proves nothing
—as a matter-of-fact man might say—but that I am
Niagara mad.   We have much before us and many
sublime scenes, though none may vie with that, before
which we have been lingering :—*allons!*

On our departure from Buffalo, the thriving port
at the eastern extremity of Lake Erie, an important
change was effected in the previous plans of our little
party.   These had in some measure threatened a separation from our friend Washington Irving, to whom
the Canadian provinces, which Pourtales and myself
had intended to take as our next step, offered no particular interest.   He therefore meditated a return to
New-York by the Ohio.   Divers and kindly meant
were the attempts repeatedly made to bring each other
to adopt unity of plan, yet without success, till most
fortunately, a few hours before the separation was to
take place, an unexpected circumstance was the means
of re-uniting us in one common scheme.   We had
taken our passage on board a steamboat, bound for
Detroit, but touching as usual at the intermediate
ports, at one of which, on the Ohio shore, Mr. Irving
proposed landing, while we accompanied the vessel to
the end of the voyage.

It was our fortune to meet on board with a gentleman, the communication of whose business and plans
instantly reconciled us to any modification of ours
which might be necessary to enable us to adopt the
same.

The General Government had at this epoch determined to send out certain gentlemen as commissioners,
to arrange various matters connected with the Indian
tribes newly congregated on the western frontiers.
Prior to this, experience having shown the insurmountable inconveniences and the evils consequent upon the

existence of bodies of men in their savage state in the centre of civilization, a resolution had been taken by the people of the United States to extinguish the claims of the Indian tribes to lands east of the Mississippi, by the gradual purchase of their lands or reservations, and to remove beyond that river. This project was now in the course of gradual execution, and divisions of many of the tribes were already ranged along the western boundary of Missouri and Arkansas. Others were on the point of removal. The commission to which I have alluded was to be stationed at the frontier-post of Fort Gibson, about eight hundred miles up the Arkansas river, and thither our new acquaintance, Judge E. of Hartford, one of the three commissioners, was proceeding by way of St. Louis, and the State of Missouri. We learned from him that from this point it was contemplated to dispatch expeditions to various parts of the unexplored region to the West, to examine the surface of the country, and report upon the practicability of any portion of it being set aside for the occupation of the Indian tribes still to be removed. To the solicitation made that Mr. Irving would join company, and connect himself with the commission, so far as he might find it agreeable, a prompt acquiescence was yielded on his part, as so doing merely entailed an extension of his plans; and as far as my comrade and myself were concerned, the frank promise of hearty welcome, if we would also form part of the expedition to further our own projects, offered too much temptation to be resisted or rejected.

So the tour in the Canadas was relinquished for the present, and it was now—hurra! for the Far West!

No certain intelligence as to the movements of others connected with the Commission could be gained, till we should reach Louisville in Kentucky, and landing at Ashtabula, we had to repair thither with all becoming speed by way of Cleveland, Newark, Columbus, and Cincinnati.

LETTER VII.

In a recent letter I referred to the circumstances attending the early settlement of New England. Those which distinguished the first colonization of these rich regions of the West beyond the mountains, carry with them a yet greater degree of interest. Neither the history of the English colonists in Virginia, nor of those in the Eastern States, despite their fierce struggles with the red proprietors of the soil, can be said to be distinguished by an equal air of romance. The posts of the advancing column of civilization in these instances, were ordinarily pushed forward with a degree of caution, and seldom so far, as to be totally beyond the reach of co-operation and support. Here however the case was different. We see small companies of men, and even single individuals, impelled by a spirit of adventure, and the love of a free unshackled life, venturing some hundred of miles in advance, over a difficult and elevated mountain barrier, planting themselves fearlessly in the wilderness on the other side, and remaining, without the hope of aid for months in utter solitude, in a region, where nothing but the most sleepless caution could secure their lives against the merciless and wily savage.

It might be asked by some of the tame gentlemen of Europe, what was the object of these half-savages, and where the utility of encountering such a perilous state of exile. Were they criminals flying from the punishment of misdeeds which imperatively obliged them to get beyond the pale of orderly society? No. Was it sheer necessity? No. Was it lust of gain? Not altogether. Love of glory? No. Love of science? Still less. Were they young and ignorant of the perils? No, Boone was forty years old. More fool he! would answer many a one, who never would comprehend the motives and impulses of such vagrants. Yet even in the best regulated, most orderly, and most civilized state of society, in which the prevailing temper is to pursue and to love a quiet state of existence, in which the variations and even extraordinary incidents are so commonplace and so gentle, as hardly to ruffle the monotony of its course, and where any departure from the ordinary boundaries is rather set down as a crime than a virtue,—even there will be found individuals in whose bosom there is a fire of restlessness which cannot endure a life of monotonous regularity. In Europe, in olden time, chivalry with all its romance, war, knight-errantry, minstrelsy, love, and nonsense, provided what was then a legitimate channel for those of this cast; and the temper of the times increased their number.

Till lately, war served the same purpose, drawing off the humours from the body politic ; and the restless spirits of the times found an asylum and occupation in arms. However, in time of peace such excitement no longer exists, and little remains but the discipline, which is wormwood to the young and impetuous.

It is from among those possessed of this restlessness of body and mind, that you may, in looking over the records of human actions, cull the greatest number of great men of all countries and ages,—men who dare attempt what others dare not ; at the same time, for one individual, who, forsaking the beaten path, has, by striking fortuitously into a more noble one suited to his talents, left a name and a character for high deeds to posterity, thousands, nay, tens of thousands, have only left the hackneyed road to disappear in the swamp, and fall into oblivion or ignominy.

At the present time, the doors of the temple of Janus remain shut; chivalry is out of fashion,—ay, not only its absurdities, but many of its noble, generous, courteous, and Christian graces. The increase of population has glutted the professions; modes and methods of distinction for the restless, which a century ago would have allured them, are now worn out. Travelling, the love of locomotion, that great resource for the changeful spirit, is no longer made of distinction. It is no longer a solitary being toiling forward in doubt and peril, and earning the right to be the sole narrator of the earth's wonders, but whole squadrons pouring down every European road. Ladies' maids and bandboxes are seen at the cataracts of the Nile, and our wives and sisters make the over-land passage to India. As to forging and highway robbery, there are now so many ways found out of cheating your friend with perfect safety to your person, that it is not worth while to run the risks of either, alluring as some of the pictures lately given to the public might be.

One consequence of the present state of things appears to be, that the quantum of restlessness, formerly absorbed by a few comparatively, is now thrown into the composition of the whole mass, and, though diluted, produces strange effects.

Hence these shoals of travellers; the overcrowded watering-places ; those new lights in politics, religion, and education ; the innumerable speculations and consequent bankruptcies ; the general impatience of government, and of moral as well as physical control. Hence this golden age of roguery and radicalism, cant and *charlatanerie ;* disunion, disloyalty, want of faith. Well might we say, Alas, for the times of chivalry.! How many men of the present day, had they been born under its star, might have had their restlessness satisfied by giving or receiving many a hearty thwack and bang on the head, instead of doing the mischief to society which they threaten. How many might have run a better chance of honourable mention as stalwart knights and jousters, than they promise to do as politicians and reformers.

But to return from what may well be called a digression. To this spirit of restlessness, more than any other passion, it would seem that the early settlement of Kentucky and the West is to be ascribed. The

hap-hazard and in some measure precarious existence
of the Virginian and Carolinian frontier settler, was, as
you will imagine, particularly favourable to the devel-
opment of this restless feeling.

The French, who were the greatest pioneers of the
country of the Lakes and upper Mississippi, had about
the middle of the last century erected a fort at the
junction of the Alleghany and Monongahela rivers, where
Pittsburg now stands, for the protection of their
trade on the Ohio, and the facility of making outfits ;
yet up to the defeat of General Braddock, or even
ten years after it, nothing seems to have been known
to the Anglo-Americans of the country to the west of
the mountains and the south of the Ohio river.   It is
difficult for one, who, like myself, has seen the teeming population of the West at the present day, to believe, that two thirds of a century ago no white man
had crossed the mountains of Virginia, to discover
what lay on the other side.   Yet such was the case !
However, the time was coming when this vast extent
of country was also to be brought under the dominion
of the white man, and be added to that rich heritage
which he should leave his children.

Ample as the country might seem to be on the
eastern side of the Blue Ridge, and other lines of the
Apalachian chain dividing the waters of the West
from those of the Atlantic, it was beginning to be too
crowded for some of the settlers.   In their eyes, the
country was becoming too thickly settled ; the operation of the law, gentle as it might be, was too severe ;
the forests, from the increase of population, had become two scant of game—they had lived too long in
one place.   They knew nothing of the unexplored
regions beyond the mountains ; but, that from that
quarter descended the bands of savages, which occasionally harried the higher settlements on the upper
waters, from the Susquehanna to the Peedee.

In 1749, a lunatic, wandering as was his wont
during his paroxysms, crossed the dividing ridge
beyond the great valley of Virginia, and on his return
asserted that he had been upon streams whose waters

ran to the West. No great public notice seems to have been taken of this discovery. Yet it is upon record that a reconnoitring party, crossing the mountains in the same direction, in the year 1751, and falling upon the waters of what is now Green Brier river, a tributary of the Kenhawa, found two solitary white men, natives of New England, living on its banks, though some hundred yards distant from each other. Even in that wilderness, human passions and pertinacity of opinion had wrought disharmony, and there they had lived apart from the world and from each other, nothing passing between them but the morning salutation, as the one came from out the hollow tree which served him for a shelter, and the other from his log hut. The Virginians subsequently made a small settlement there, which was utterly cut off in 1763 by an incursion of the Indians.

It was in 1767 when the first adventurer from the banks of the Yadkin, in North Carolina, a man of the name of Finlay, came back to his family, after a long absence, with accounts of the marvellous beauty and riches of the country beyond the mountains. He subsequently returned thither the same year, with a party of which the celebrated Daniel Boone was one ; and from that time forward, adventurers from among the restless inhabitants of the outskirts of civilization were occasionally seen to quit the vicinity of the ' clearings' with their rifles, blankets, and dogs, and, entering the forests, disappear for a while in the direction of the mountains.

One thing is not to be lost sight of—the experience of one hundred years and upward had not been thrown away, and the hardy backwoodsman of this day had that in his favour which the New England settlers had been without. The modes and resources of Indian warfare were perfectly known to him. He had been cradled in the forests, and had been brought up amidst the alarms of Indian incursions. From his earliest youth he had been taught the value of the rifle, the most powerful and convenient weapon in the world for

the use of a single arm. He knew the nature and resources of the country, and unshackled by the education or the prejudices of the Old World, the forest was now his home.

Still the hardihood, presence of mind, patience, and invincible resolution of these pioneers cannot be too highly estimated. I can conceive the feelings of wonder and delight of these first solitary adventurers, when, surmounting the several ridges covered with their splendid vegetation of rhododendron, azaleas, and laurels, they looked down upon that wilderness of fertility and rich vegetation to the westward; that beautiful region, which, though it now appeared to them as the land of paradise, was soon to verify its Indian appellation of 'the Dark and Bloody Ground' to them also; and by these fearful epithets was it subsequently long known and stigmatized.

The early descriptions extant of the original state and appearance of this portion of the vast valley of the Mississippi, and the impressions they suggested, though recorded by no practised hands, have in them a truth and nature more suited to the sublimity of the subject than the attempts made at a later day with all their labour and finish. Truly, he who would portray the West must use other pallet and pencil than that of a miniature painter. It would appear that while the regions to the north of the Ohio afforded a home to divers Indian tribes, the wide tract of country stretching on the southern shores toward the Cumberland mountains and the great river Mississippi, watered by so many noble streams, was claimed by none in particular, but formed a kind of hunting ground, in which innumerable herds of wild animals found food and covert, and the bands of hostile Indians met to pursue alternately war and the chase.

It is easy to conceive, that the sight of those immense herds of bison, an animal hitherto unknown to the settlers, the troops of deer, elk, and bears with which the land abounded, should strongly stimulate men, whose subsistence and gains had hitherto in a

7*

great degree depended upon the fruits of the chase. But beyond this the productions and forms of external nature seem to have struck the early adventurers with wonder, when compared with those to which they were familiar on their side of the mountains.

The unexampled growth of the ordinary forest trees; their frequent disposition over the soil in open woods, unencumbered with brushwood; the interminable cane-brakes, broken only by the narrow pathways trodden down by the bison and deer; the luxuriance of every form of vegetation, as it sprung from a virgin soil, whose fertility was as exhaustless as its depth was extraordinary—all these things might well excite surprise. Then the fruits, the flowers;—the magnitude of single trees of the poplar or sycamore species, as their mighty shafts rose a hundred feet into the air, bearing with them their gigantic parasites; the numerous 'salt licks,' frequented by game of every species; the abundant springs and streams, and the extreme beauty of the sward in the more open country; and the discovery in the depths of untrodden forests of huge artificial mounds and fortifications, covered with the growth of centuries, and the extraordinary relics of a race of enormous animals buried under the soil— all combined to produce a species of unwonted excitement, and had their effect in nerving these men to the endurance of their perilous situation, as in small parties, or even singly, they sat down to spend days and months in the wilderness, totally cut off from all communication with their race. Such was the lot of Finlay, Boone, and others of the same stamp and mould, whose names will be for ever identified with the discovery and settlement of the West. From the pertinacity with which these men would cling to their discovery, it would almost seem as if their hearts misgave them, that the whole might prove a delusion, and that if they returned over the mountains, they would never be able to find that rich, and pleasant, and fruitful land again.

However, the news soon spread among the frontier

settlements of Virginia and the Carolinas.   Stronger parties ascended and traversed the ridges of the Alleghany.   The singular breaks, called Gaps, so frequent in them, were explored ; and within five or six years after Boone's first passage of the mountains, during which he and his companions had repeatedly made fearful experiences of the terrors of this terrestrial paradise—a colony, in which his wife and children were included, was settled in the newly discovered region.   From this time up to the victory of General Wayne, on the Miami, over the western savages, the country lay open to a steady tide of immigration from the east.   But this interval of twenty years, and especially the earlier part, was one of infinite trouble and disaster to the new colonists both in Kentucky and Tennessee.   That species of security which was consequent upon the first adventurers on the western side of the mountains being few in number, unexpected by the savages, and without any fixed place of abode,—a security which had in many instances failed after a short time to be available, from the naturally observant and practised eye of the Indian in following any uncommon trail ; this was, of course, altogether at an end, from the moment that parties of any number crossed the frontier, and commenced permanent settlements in the West.   Self-defence was, therefore, the first object of the intruders.   The new settlers had decided to live beyond the arm and government of the parent State, and they were consequently also beyond its protection, and had to depend entirely upon the goodness of God, and the vigilance of their own character and courage.   Their little assemblage of log cabins was accordingly surrounded by a tall strong stockade, to serve as a place of retreat and defence.

And in such isolated positions, open to the guile of the implacable Indian, exposed to famine from the destruction of their crops in the neighbourhood,—worn out with sickness and constant watching,—frequently attacked, and never sure of the duration of a time of apparent quiet,—murders and burnings on every side, did the mothers of Kentucky brood over their little ones. Many of the infant colonies were exterminated root and branch, more were deserted, and the panic-struck inhabitants retraced their steps from the 'Dark and Bloody Ground.' To single combats, and skirmishes between the colonists and small marauding parties of the Indians, followed conflicts between larger parties, gathered together for the attack and defence of a given post; and more than once the numbers of the savages prevailed over the whites, and the strength and best defence of the colony seemed to be cut down to the ground. Prior to the year 1790, it was calculated that not less than three thousand persons were murdered, or carried into captivity in the west. Yet they struggled on. They were a peculiar race, and seemed to be fully nerved to their task. The pliancy of the female character, and the facility with which woman, despite her softer sex, will rise superior to the weakness of her nature, when circumstances imperatively demand sacrifice and exertion, were never more strikingly displayed. She watched and learned to read the signs which betokened danger, and to aid in repelling it. The very horses, dogs, and cattle scented the Indians, and gave warning of their approach by their signs of mute terror.

Still, numbers poured into the country, allured by the known fertility of the soil; and where one settlement had been abandoned or destroyed, many sprung up. Wagon after wagon was seen climbing up the eastern steep; the proprietors cast their last look upon the steril hills and exhausted fields of the old States, and then passing down the laurel-covered ridges to the land of promise, with slaves, children, and cattle, chose their ground, and fixed themselves in the wilderness. The parents, perchance, might look back in the hour of difficulty to the land where they had lived, hardly, perhaps, but in security, with something like longing and repentance; but the children grew up in the midst of the excitement of their position, with increasing fondness for the soil, and attachment to their new homes. Thus, farm after farm was brought into cultivation, and the Indian receded, till from their numbers and position, those farthest removed from the hostile lines began to taste the blessings of peace and security ; hamlets succeeded to single houses ; villages to towns; roads were made, and magistrates appointed, and the infant country taken under the wing of the parent State.

Still it was not till toward the close of the century, that there was peace on its borders. The Ohio, which formed the principal highway of the immigrants, was for many years the scene of the most horrible tragedies, the Indian still making his incursions from the northward, and using every art to harass the intruders. Open tracks, and decoys, in which the miserable whites already in their power were constrained under pain of death to allure the passage boats by piteous appeals to their compassion, and outcries for assistance, to approach the shore and fall into certain destruction, were alternately resorted to, till the strength of the Indian confederacies was broken by signal defeat and dispersion to a distance.

As soon as the country found peace and repose, the claims of the young for education, and that of all classes for the regular protection of the law, and for religious instruction, were felt to be urgent.

Hitherto the want of some power to repress irregularities and punish the crimes, which could not fail to spring up with the increase of inhabitants, and under circumstances which allured, not only the enterprising, but the vicious of the parent States to settle beyond the mountains, seems to have given origin to a compact which was made occasionally among the more sober of the male inhabitants of each district, by which they assumed the power both of deciding upon the crimes of individuals and of awarding punishment. The regulators, as they were called, I have every reason to believe, were an eminently useful race of men, and, it may be maintained, in most instances just withal ; though it must be owned that the summary

mode in which cases were disposed of, and even capital
punishment administered without legal form, is a little
startling to the sticklers for fixed laws, judge, and
jury.   As to religion, though many of the fathers of
Kentucky seem to have been very far from immoral
characters—their code seems to have been more that
of the Indian whom they dispossessed, divested of
gross superstition, than that of the Christian;—and
for that matter, Indian religion is of far greater diffu-
sion through Christendom than might be imagined.
The fashionable religion of the day is neither more
nor less.   Yet no sooner were families united, than a
call for something higher was heard.   The want of a
more settled provision for the spiritual guidance and
instruction of the people, and their scattered position
over such a vast extent of surface, gave origin to
the 'Camp-meetings' of which you have doubtless
heard.   That mode of engaging in social worship was
not only irreprehensible, but in every way praiseworthy, considering the purpose for which it was in-
stituted, and the temper in which it was attended.
But it is with that as with every thing human; and
what was good and perhaps necessary at the time, is
now, under a very different state of things, decidedly
bad in most cases.   Instead of the simple gathering together of a number of families under the thick shade
of the forest, from every quarter of the compass, to one
common centre, to listen to the word of God, offer Him
their common supplication and thanksgiving, and have
the sacraments administered in sincerity and sobriety;
you may now see, assembled under the same name,
and often in parts of the country where you would
suppose that such a proceeding was wholly unnecessary, a crowd of thousands, most of whom, it may be
said, without being accused of uncharitableness, meet
for any purpose but that of devotion.   Even the devotion that is seen in such assemblages, takes the air
of religious excitement; and as to the rest, intrigue,
dissipation, electioneering, chaffering, and cheating,
hold their festival at the modern Camp-meeting.   In

fact, that arrangement as little suits the present settled state of the country, as the system of the regulators would. I need not tell you that these self-appointed judges have long ago made way for men of worship and learning, who show reason for their authority, whatever they may do for their decisions. I am aware however, that something akin to the regulators still exists in certain out-of-the-way corners of the Mississippi valley.

As to the fine race of backwoodsmen, of whom Boone seems by common consent to have been considered the patriarch, they were evidently raised for a special purpose, and that purpose accomplished, the country was two narrow for them.

We see him, the battle fought, and the country gained, entangled in the snares of war, driven from that small portion of the rich heritage he and his fellows had secured to his countrymen, which he claimed as personal property, and in his old age, disgusted with the forms and hollow nature of society, once more shouldering his axe and rifle, turning his back upon the thickly peopled region, and followed by his wife, who, thirty years before, had been his companion in his first removal, seeking an asylum in the Far-West, beyond the Mississippi, where he died full of years in 1818.

LETTER VIII.

I now resume the thread of our personal adventures. Our stay at Cincinnati was only of two days' duration. We found the good citizens of that rising and flourishing city busily ruminating over the first edition of a well-known picture of their domestic manners, which the English press had just sent forth for their especial benefit. Whether the compote was justly and wisely compounded, I was in no way enabled to judge at the time, but it was very evident from the wry faces on all sides, and the aroused spirit of indignation, that the bitter herbs predominated over the sweet. For the rest, such was the crowded state of the only large hotel in the place, two having been burnt in the course of the spring, that we deemed ourselves fortunate to fine a speedy opportunity of departure in one of the splendid steamboats with which the landing place was crowded.

Our next halting-place was Louisville, another large and thriving city, situated on the Kentucky shore, just above the Falls of the Ohio. Its position on one of the great bends of the river, with the islands and rapids below, forms one of the most striking among all the beautiful scenes with which the Ohio abounds. Here we immediately took our passage for St. Louis on the Mississippi, seven hundred miles distant, on board another steamboat, but were ultimately detained two or three days by some disarrangement in the machinery.

The Ohio truly merits the title of '*La belle Rivére*,' which was bestowed upon it by the first French setlers. Whether you see it from the summits of the little bluffs, through which it has delved a deep broad bed in this upper part of its course, filling the vale with its expanded waters, and laving the edge of those rich patches of alluvial ground on which the hand of man has spread the sunshine of cultivation among the overshadowing woods, or from the deck of the floating palace, which bears you with marvellous rapidity from basin to basin, and point to point, it is always 'the beautiful river.' Its current, at the time we descended it, was gentle, and comparatively clear, the waters being very low. Yet six months earlier, the whole of the valley of the Ohio, from Pittsburg to the Mississippi, had been the theatre of such devastation and distress, from the extraordinary floods, as to be almost incredible to those who, like ourselves, only saw the river flowing gently within its ordinary bounds. It was difficult to conceive, that such a wide broad bed, sunk thirty or forty feet below the edge of the perpendicular banks of the levels should ever be insufficient to contain its water. But in the month of February of this year, after the fall of excessive rains on the mountains, at the head of the Alleghany river, the junction of which with the Monongahela at Pittsburg forms the Ohio, the waters rose foot by foot, and hour by hour, till the whole country was inundated. The flood attained its height at Pittsburg on the 11th, and at the Falls on the 19th, moving at the rate of about one hundred miles each day, and bearing forward the accumulated produce of a thousand farms, mills, and villages. At Cincinnati the waters rose sixty-four feet perpendicular above low water mark. A still greater flood is on record as having happened in the year 1772, before the settling of the country, but none since. The fertility of spring and summer had done much to remedy and conceal the devastation caused by this terrible visitation, yet many convincing signs remained of its power.

The time of our detention was as pleasantly spent as circumstances admitted of, but we were anxious to proceed, having much in prospect in another region before the close of the year. The shallowness of the water in the rapids not admitting the descent of even the smaller steamboats, we were constrained to pass through the newly constructed canal, which, by the aid of three noble locks at the lower end, secures the uninterrupted navigation of the entire river for vessels of moderate burden, without the delay of unloading, portage, and reloading, which was formerly necessary. All obstacles overcome, we found ourselves once more fairly afloat on the bosom of the river, and straightway proceeded on our voyage. At the lower extremity of the canal, and before the small towns in the immediate vicinity, we left thirty or forty of the most splendid steamers of the first class, waiting for a rise in the water.

The changes which the successful adoption of navigation by steam has operated in a very limited space of time upon the face of the wide regions watered by the Mississippi and its tributaries, are doubtless among the most extraordinary ever achieved by human agency.

Many things combined to make the year 1811 the annus miribilis of the West. During the earlier months, the waters of many of the great rivers overflowed their banks to a vast extent, and the whole country was in many parts covered from bluff to bluff. Unprecedented sickness followed. A spirit of change, and a restlessness seemed to pervade the very inhabitants of the forest. A countless multitude of squirrels, obeying some great and universal impulse, which none can know but the Spirit that gave them being, left their reckless and gambolling life, and their ancient places of retreat in the north, and were seen pressing forward by tens of thousands in a deep and sober phalanx to the south. No obstacles seemed to check this extra-ordinary and concerted movement : the word had been given them to go forth, and they obeyed it, though multitudes perished in the broad Ohio, which lay in their path. The splendid comet of that year long continued to shed its twilight over the forests, and, as the autumn drew to a close, the whole Valley of the Mississippi, from the Missouri to the Gulf, was shaken to its centre by continued earthquakes. It was at this very epoch, in which so many natural phenomena were combining to spread wonder and awe, that man, too, in the exercise of that power with which his Creator has endowed him, was making his first essay in that region, of an art, the natural course and further perfection of which were destined to bring about yet greater changes than those effected by the flood and the earthquake ; and at the same time that the latter were agitating the surface, the very first steamboat was seen descending the great rivers, and the awe-struck Indian on the banks beheld the Pinelore* flying through the turbid waters.

From the time of the battle of the Miami, to which I

* The Choctaw name for the steamboat, literally 'fire-canoe.'

alluded in my last, up to this epoch, the number of inhabitants in Kentucky, Tennessee, Ohio, and the adjoining States, had gone on increasing with astonishing rapidity, and swarms were pressing forward from the new settlements even beyond the Mississippi. The banks of the Ohio and its tributaries were covered with innumerable farms; and rafts, and flat-boats, and barges of every description, laden with the produce, floated upon its wide surface, toward the general market of the West, New Orleans.

Besides the barges and vessels of heavy burden, which made their long annual voyage to and from that city, the river was covered, particularly in time of flood, by thousands of whimsical machines, for boats they could hardly be called, most of which have now disappeared.   The greater part of these rude constructions were broken up, sold, or abandoned when the end of the voyage was attained, and the produce which they bore down to the general market disposed of; after which the settler returned to his farm, a thousand or fifteen hundred miles off, as he could.   From seventy to eighty days were consumed in thus effecting the long and monotonous voyage from Pittsburg to New-Orleans.   But now a change was to be wrought in the facilities of communication between countries so far apart, upon which no one could have calculated, and the vast results of which are not yet fully developed.

Circumstances gave me the opportunity of becoming acquainted with the particulars of the very first voyage of a steamer in the west, and their extraordinary character will be my apology to you for filling a page of this sheet with the following brief relation.

The complete success attending the experiments in steam navigation made on the Hudson and the adjoining waters previous to the year 1809, turned the attention of the principal projectors to the idea of its application on the western rivers; and in the month of April of that year, Mr. Roosevelt of New York, pursuant to an agreement with Chancellor Livingston and

Mr. Fulton, visited those rivers, with the purpose of forming an opinion whether they admitted of steam navigation or not.   At this time two boats, the North River and the Clermont, were running on the Hudson.   Mr. R. surveyed the rivers from Pittsburg to New-Orleans, and as his report was favourable, it was decided to build a boat at the former town.   This was done under his direction, and in the course of 1811 the first boat was launched on the waters of the Ohio. It was called the ' New Orleans,' and intended to ply between Natchez in the State of Mississippi, and the city whose name it bore.   In October it left Pittsburg for its experimental voyage.   On this occasion no freight or passengers were taken, the object being merely to bring the boat to her station.   Mr. R., his young wife and family, Mr. Baker the engineer, Andrew Jack the pilot, and six hands, with a few domestics, formed her whole burden.   There were no woodyards at that time, and constant delays were unavoidable.   When, as related, Mr. R. had gone down the river to reconnoitre, he had discovered two beds of coal, about one hundred and twenty miles below the Rapids at Louisville, and now took tools to work them, intending to load the vessel with the coal, and to employ it as fuel, instead of constantly detaining the boat while wood was procured from the banks.

Late at night on the fourth day after quitting Pittsburg, they arrived in safety at Louisville, having been but seventy hours descending upward of seven hundred miles.   The novel appearance of the vessel, and the fearful rapidity with which it made its passage over the broad reaches of the river, excited a mixture of terror and surprise among many of the settlers on the banks, whom the rumour of such an invention had never reached ; and it is related that on the unexpected arrival of the boat before Louisville, in the course of a fine still moonlight night, the extraordinary sound which filled the air as the pent-up steam was suffered to escape from the valves on rounding to, produced a general alarm, and multitudes in the town rose from their beds to ascertain the cause.   1 have heard that the general impression among the good Kentuckians was, that the comet had fallen into the Ohio; but this does not rest upon the same foundation as the other facts which I lay before you, and which, I may at once say, I had directly from the lips of the parties themselves.   The small depth of water in the Rapids prevented the boat from pursuing her voyage immediately; and during the consequent detention of three weeks in the upper part of the Ohio, several trips were successfully made between Louisville and Cincinnati. In fine, the waters rose, and in the course of the last week in November, the voyage was resumed, the depth of water barely admitting their passage.

When they arrived about five miles above the Yellow Banks, they moored the boat opposite to the first vein of coal, which was on the Indiana side, and had been purchased in the interim of the State government. They found a large quantity already quarried to their hand, and conveyed to the shore by depredators who had not found means to carry it off, and with this they commenced loading the boat.   While thus engaged, our voyagers were accosted in great alarm by the squatters of the neighbourhood, who inquired if they had not heard strange noises on the river and in the woods in the course of the preceding day, and perceived the shores shake—insisting that they had repeatedly felt the earth tremble.

Hitherto nothing extraordinary had been perceived. The following day they pursued their monotonous voyage in those vast solitudes.   The weather was observed to be oppressively hot; the air misty, still, and dull; and though the sun was visible, like a glowing ball of copper, his rays hardly shed more than a mournful twilight on the surface of the water.   Evening drew nigh, and with it some indications of what was passing around them became evident.   And as they sat on deck, they ever and anon heard a rushing sound and violent splash, and saw large portions of the shore tearing away from the land and falling into the river.

8*

It was, as my informant said, ' an awful day ; so still, that you could have heard a pin drop on the deck.' They spoke little, for every one on board appeared thunderstruck.   The comet had disappeared about this time, which circumstance was noticed with awe by the crew.

The second day after their leaving the Yellow Banks, the sun rose over the forests the same dim ball of fire, and the air was thick, dull, and oppressive as before. The portentous signs of this terrible natural convulsion continued and increased.   The pilot, alarmed and confused, affirmed that he was lost, as he found the channel everywhere altered ; and where he had hitherto known deep water, there lay numberless trees with their roots upward.   The trees were seen waving and nodding on the bank, without a wind ; but the adventurers had no choice but to continue their route.   Towards evening they found themselves at a loss for a place of shelter.   They had usually brought to under the shore, but everywhere they saw the high banks disappearing, overwhelming many a flat-boat and raft, from which the owners had landed and made their escape.   A large island in mid-channel, which was selected by the pilot as the better alternative, was sought for in vain, having disappeared entirely.   Thus in doubt and terror, they proceeded hour after hour till dark, when they found a small island, and rounded to, mooring themselves to the foot of it.   Here they lay, keeping watch on deck during the long autumnal night—listening to the sound of the waters which roared and gurgled horribly around them ; and hearing, from time to time, the rushing earth slide from the shore, and the commotion as the falling mass of earth and trees was swallowed up by the river.   The lady of the party, a delicate female, who had just been confined on board as they lay off Louisville, was frequently awakened from her restless slumber by the jar given to the furniture and loose articles in the cabin, as, several times in the course of the night, the shock of the passing earthquake was communicated from the island to the bows of the vessel. It was a long night, but morning dawned and showed them that they were near the mouth of the Ohio. The shores and the channel were now equally unrecognizable, for every thing seemed changed. About noon that day they reached the small town of New Madrid, on the right bank of the Mississippi. Here they found the inhabitants in the greatest distress and consternation ; part of the population had fled in terror to the higher grounds, others prayed to be taken on board, as the earth was opening in fissures on every side, and their houses hourly falling around them.

Proceeding from thence, they found the Mississippi, at all times a fearful stream, now unusually swollen, turbid and full of trees, and after many days of great danger, though they felt and perceived no more of the earthquakes, they reached their destination at Natchez, at the close of the first week in January, 1812, to the great astonishment of all, the escape of the boat having been considered an impossibility.

At that time you floated for three or four hundred miles on the rivers without seeing a human habitation.

Such was the voyage of the first steamer. The natural convulsion, which commenced at the time of her descent, has been but slightly alluded to, but will never be forgotten in the history of the West ; and the changes wrought by it throughout the whole alluvial region through which the Ohio and Mississippi pour their waters, were perhaps as remarkable as any on record. We hear less of its effects, because the region in which they occurred was of such vast extent and so thinly peopled. That part of the alluvial country which is contiguous to the point of junction of the two rivers, and especially the vicinity of New Madrid, seems to have been the centre of the convulsion. There, during the years 1811 and 1812, the earth broke into innumerable fissures, the church-yard, with its dead, was torn from the bank, and engulfed in the turbid stream. To the present day it would appear that frequent slight shocks of earthquakes are there felt ; and it is asserted that in the vast swamp at the back of the town, strange sounds may at times be heard, as of some mighty caldron bubbling in the bowels of the earth. Along the banks of the river, thousands of acres with their gigantic growth of forest and cane were swallowed up, and lakes and ponds innumerable were formed. The earth, in many parts, was observed to burst suddenly open, and jets of sand, mud, and water, to shoot up into the air. The beds of these giant streams seemed totally overturned ; islands disappeared, and in many parts the course of the river was completely changed. Great inundations were the consequence. The clear waters of the St. Francis were obstructed ; the ancient channel destroyed, and the river spread over a vast tract of swamp. In many places the gaping earth unfolded its secrets, and the bones of the gigantic Mastodon and Ichthyosaurus, hidden within its bosom for ages, were brought to the surface. Boats and arks without number, were swallowed up ; some buried by the falling in of the banks, others dragged down with the islands to which they were anchored. And finally, you may still meet and converse with those, who were on the mighty river of the West when the whole stream ran towards its sources for an entire hour, and then resuming its ordinary course, hurried them helpless into its whirling surface with accelerated motion toward the Gulf.

Six days were now employed by the steamboat on which we had embarked in reaching St. Louis. For many miles below the rapids, the river scenery continued fine but monotonous : the shores were often hilly and always forested, but never rose to any prominent outline : while every object on the banks was diminished to the eye by the vast breadth of the stream. The lowness of the water, the great changes effected in the channel by the spring floods, and occasionally morning mists, all conspired to interpose impediments to a very continuous progress. Besides, the boat we were in was only a third-rate. However, there was so much novelty in our position, that we bore all the misfortunes that fell to our lot with equanimity and fortitude, as became gentlemen 'travelling for pleasure and instruction.' We used to sit for hours in a little group on the high roof of the cabins, far removed from the heat of the fires and the boilers, the chatter of the passengers, or the jar of the engine; while the lapse of each second was marked by the sonorous rush of the white puff of steam from the pipe above our heads. Each little settlement we passed had its own peculiar interest, and each tributary stream no less— and there were scenes incident to the river which were always pleasing. The frequent landing-places, overshadowed by fine aged sycamores; the relics of ancient and whimsical craft still met with here and there —now a square, or oblong box, floating along with the current, with the outline and the party-coloured vestments hung upon the shaft of the rudder or brightly reflected on the water;—then the broad-horn of an emigrant family, lying in some sheltered cove, while the heterogeneous crew of all ages and colours was passing an hour of activity and relaxation on shore.

Though greatly diminished in number you still meet with many an ark, for the transport of goods, built as a broad flat-boat with a deck of two or three feet elevation above the level of the water. They have generally a small window fore and aft, and a door in the middle, a peep into which will show you a goodly store of pots, pans, or flour barrels. A narrow ledge runs round them for the convenience of poleing. A small chimney rises above; raccoon and deer-skins, the produce of the hours spent on shore, are nailed on the sides to dry. The larger are generally propelled by four oars, and I have occasionally seen them surmounted by a crooked mast and topmast. Here you will meet with one fitted up as a floating tin-shop, gleaning many a bright dollar from the settlers. Others again are of a still more simple construction, and have merely a temporary deck supported upon rails, through which the sheep and other live stock may be descried. Hay for their consumption will be piled above, and cabbages stowed away in the compartment behind.

Of the large barge, upon which the greater part of the valuable goods in request on the river were formerly transported, few are now seen in the lower waters. They required twenty hands to warp them up against the current at the rate of six or seven miles a day, and were frequently of one hundred tons burden. The lighter keel-boat is still in use.

Farming seemed to be mere pastime,—the seed thrown upon the soil producing a thousand-fold with but little attention and labour, while the forest nourishes the cattle and swine of the backwoodsman without the expenditure of a cent.

On the earlier part of the voyage, occasional halts at the wood-yards were agreeable to all, as affording an opportunity for a half-hour's stroll: but when we descended below the Wabash, our opportunities of going on shore became a little too frequent. The high wooded bluffs ceased to border the stream after we had advanced one hundred miles below Louisville ; and we were now following the river as it flowed in an expanded bed through that rich alluvial region in which it mingles its waters with those of the Mississippi. The villages were farther apart, though we seldom paddled many miles without descrying the tops of Indian corn, and the fences, roofs, and smoking chimneys of some backwood settlement.

The ' Illinois' was certainly not a fortunate boat, in spite of the horse-shoe nailed to the capstan. After many scrapings and bumps upon the sand-bars and shoals with which at low water the Ohio is becoming more and more impeded, from the vast quantity of alluvion washed down into it since the partial clearing of the forests, it was our lot, somewhere above the remarkable cavern called the ' Cave in Rock,' to share the fortune of two other steamers, and get so irreparably shoaled about sunset, that after many hours spent in attempting to extricate ourselves, by carrying out anchor after anchor, the use of the lever, and furious press of steam, it was decided, that whether the prospect were agreeable or not, the vessel must be partially unloaded, and for this purpose lighters were procured from the nearest settlement. After a glorious moonlight night, finding that many hours must elapse before there was any possibility of moving, we went a shore, and passed the morning in the forests of Illinois; and it was not till after a detention of twenty-four hours that we got in motion again. Two more serious detentions, from a like cause, occurred at the mouths of the Cumberland and Tennessee rivers, after which we finally reached the mouth of the Ohio on the night between the 10th and 11th of September, and entered the 'Father of Waters.'

Our progress was now proportionably slow; that mighty river pouring downward toward the Gulf, a turbid and rapid torrent, in spite of its great breadth, and the low state of its waters.

By God's providence we escaped all the perils of the navigation, whether in the shape of sawyers, snags, planters, or sand-banks,—also a more sudden and unpleasant peril, from having been run foul of by a descending steamboat in the night, without, however, suffering much injury, and arrived safe at St. Louis on the morning of the 13th.

I have found two reasons for hurrying over the details of much of our proceedings hitherto. The difficulty of a choice among a mass of recollections and materials, which, however interesting, might not be altogether novel, may pass for the first; and as to the second, we have not yet done with the West, and opportunity and humour may be found at some future time for the introduction of such entertaining information as I have hitherto held back. I might give you twenty more reasons, and wind up by saying, that I have had neither time nor patience, which would remind you of the forty reasons given by a notorious gentleman why he did not make a certain purchase,

the last of which was—that he had no money ; or what
may be considered more pertinent, of the many reasons, philosophical, physiological, zoological, and osteo-
logical, said to have been given by Mr. Peale of the
Philadelphia Museum, why, in opposition to the opinion of the learned, the great tusks of the enormous
fossil mastodon appeared therein with their points
turned down ; the last of which was, that the ceiling
of the said museum was not lofty enough for him to
place them with the points up.

I must also procrastinate with regard to St. Louis,
for upon our arrival there the commissioner found
that he had been long expected by several of the gentlemen more or less connected with his purpose of
repairing to the westward ; and with the exception of
a morning which was set apart for a visit to Jefferson
Barracks, to see the Indian Chief, Black Hawk, every
hour of our brief stay was fully taken up with a variety
of arrangements and preparations.   By the defeat of
the Indians at the Bad Axe river, and the capture of
Ma-ka-tai-me-she-kia-kiak, and his sons, together with
the Prophet and other Chiefs, the war carried on by the
tribes of the Sauks and Foxes with the borderers of Illinois had been shortly before terminated.   The Chief
and his party were then in prison, and though kindly
treated by his victor, he was an object of interest and
pity to us.   The fine old warrior was then seemingly
near his end, and drooped like the bird whose name
he bore, when caged and imprisoned.   Little did I
then think that six months after I should see him alive
and in freedom, on his ' progress' through the Atlantic
cities after being set at liberty,—wondering at all, and
wondered at by all.

Too many friends and advisers we found to be productive of great embarrassment, and after much, and
to us most unnecessary palaver, it was finally déter-
mined that each should travel as it best suited his convenience or fancy, to another point of rendezvous up
the Missouri, namely, the small frontier settlement of
Independence, three hundred miles off.   This was to

be our ultimate point of union before turning south into the country occupied by the Osages and other Indian tribes. Colonel C. who had joined us here as our guide to the main seat of the commission at Fort Gibson, made choice of his own mode and time of travelling with his domestics. The Commissioner with a medical gentleman attached to the party, decided to wait for a steam-boat which was expected to leave St. Louis for the Missouri in a few days; and as for Mr. Irving, de Pourtales and myself, we at once determined to purchase horses and a light wagon to transport our baggage, and travel as a trio, as heretofore, by easy day's journeys to the place of rendezvous. Accordingly we furnished ourselves from the American Fur Company's stores, with bear-skins and blankets—after endless trouble procured horses, and pronounced ourselves ready to start. We had secured the services of a French creole, accustomed to the country and mode of travelling, who was to serve us in the several capacities of guide, groom, driver, valet, cook, interpreter, hunter, and jack-of-all-trades; and as he became consequently a prominent character, you shall not have to complain of his being kept in the background.

There are always some last words to be spoken, and some last things to be done at every departure of consequence. So it was with us, and as soon as one hole was patched up another was found; the horses had to be shod when they ought to have been on the road; and the wagon, though according to the custom of the times, warranted in good repair by the veracious seller, was no sooner put in motion, than it had to be mended by the purchaser. At length, on the evening of the 15th, we got fairly *en route*, and travelled about twelve miles over a horrible road to the Missouri, opposite St. Charles, where we found a shelter for the night in a little French inn, which, with its odd diminutive bowling-green, skittle-ground, garden-plots, and arbours to booze in, reminded us more of the Old World than any thing we had seen for many weeks.

LETTER IX.

THE following nine days were spent by us in
steadily travelling westward, toward the place of rendezvous, through a country but sparingly inhabited by
emigrants from the older states.

Previous to our departure from St. Louis, we had
only just caught a glimpse of the face of our future
guide and attendant, Antoine, or Tonish, as he was
called by his familiar acquaintance. After his services
were secured, he pleaded sundry indispensable preparations, and the natural desire to take leave of his family,
for his immediate departure for the small village of
Florissant, promising faithfully to meet us on the banks
of the Missouri, opposite St. Charles, at daybreak the
following morning. But it was not till after passing
hour after hour at the little French auberge, to which
I brought you at the conclusion of my last, in vain expectation of seeing him arrive with a horse which we
had agreed to purchase of him, upon strong recom-
mendations from impartial people, who knew his super-
excellent qualities, and testified to his being an
undaunted buffalo-hunter,—and finally losing all patience, we had crossed the river about noon, that
Tonish made his appearance, fully equipped, and gave
us the first specimen of that dexterous effrontery with
which we became at a later period extremely familiar.
However, our party was now complete, and turning
through the outskirts of St. Charles, we struck into
the western road and pursued our journey; Tonish
having charge of the wagon which held our small
stock of necessaries; by which arrangement the three
travellers were left at perfect liberty to saunter, halt,
hunt, or do what they would. The tent, blankets, and
skins, which formed the main bulk of our baggage,
were of no use to us in this earlier stage of our autumnal tour, as up to the point of rendezvous at Indepen-

dence, we found that we might always depend upon reaching one or another of the scattered farms, both at the approach of night, and our noon-tide halt. Upon an average, we advanced about thirty miles a day, which was as much as our steeds,—which, to tell you the honest truth, were none of the best,—could well achieve, and a few general sketches of our journey may suffice.

Our route for the first week led us wide of the river, over an undulating country, the lower parts of which were thickly covered with forest, and the upper spread out into open prairie. Over these the decline of the year was beginning to shed those gorgeous and brilliant hues, which none can fancy or form an idea of, but those who have beheld them. The forests were fine, but not to be compared with the gigantic growth of those on the Ohio. I confess that at this time, their frequent interchange with the prairie was always welcome, as, after the novelty afforded by the peculiar character of the scenery of the latter had passed away, its monotonous, unvarying outline and bright colours were alike fatiguing to the eye and the fancy. We had not then conceived that admiration for this great feature of the West, which we afterward did : indeed, we had not, during this early period of our western travels, any conception of the great variety and sublimity of the scenes, which they elsewhere exhibited.

We had every reason to admire the hearty hospitality of those, upon whose kindness and attention we were daily cast-for entertainment and shelter. As the constitution of Missouri sanctions the possession of slaves, it was a matter of course that the settlers were for the most part adventurers from the central and southern states of the Union, and principally Kentucky and Tennessee, and that in their buildings and family arrangements, they should imitate those of their fathers. The farms were ordinarily reclaimed from the forest, that being the richest soil. The dwelling-house usually appeared built substantially of round or square logs, all the interstices being neatly filled with white plaster, and they presented two quadrangular apartments, distinct from each other, with a wide open space in the centre, all covered by one common roof. In the better farms, one of the rooms was set apart for guests, and was clean, and furnished with three or four beds. The central division of the dwelling formed the ordinary sitting apartment of the family, and from its being open at both ends, was a pleasant cool retreat. As is the invariable custom of the southern states, the kitchen premises were in separate log-huts in the rear, the whole clearing being surrounded by a zigzag fence of chesnut rails, beyond which might be seen many an acre of tall Indian corn, rising under the girdled trees of the forest. Here the settler apparently lived in peace and plenty; cattle, swine, poultry, being abundant, and costing little or no toil or expense in raising, and that was indeed a poor farm which did not enable the good woman, with half an hour's notice, to spread before her guests a plentiful meal of ham, fried chicken, eggs, milk, honey, delicious butter, boiled maize, and hot wheaten bread. For the rest, venison and turkeys were plentiful in the woods, besides innumerable squirrels, upon which we made war as we rode along.

There was one thing, however, connected with our daily repasts, which gave us some concern. The moment we signified our wish to be provided with a meal, was an evil one for the poultry; for as the arrival of travellers, though not an uncommon, was a very uncertain event, every preparation for their entertainment, even that of catching and killing the birds, had to be performed after arrival. The consequence was, that as soon as the black Clorinda, or blacker Juno, in the kitchen, received her orders, a strong detachment of the little woolly-headed urchins of every hue, who swarmed like musquitoes in this land of corn-bread and pumpkins, was upon the alert to secure two or three of the long yellow-legged cacklers within the fence. They were generally aided by a big dog, and not unfrequently backed by one of those noisy, garrulous, busy old ne-

groes, who are to be met with every where, as privileg-
ed inmates of the family, in consequence of having
known and cared for the master or mistress when a
child, and followed his or her fortunes from the old
states. The scene of confusion and the uproar consequent upon this hunt were indescribably ludicrous ;
although we had not yet become savage enough to
gaze, without some qualms of pity and sympathy, upon
these fugitive portions of our breakfast or supper, as
they scudded from one corner to another, followed by
a flight of missiles, or the nimble fingers of the grin-
ning children. The devoted birds after flying here and
there, would often as a last resort get under the house
—the flooring being generally raised upon stones or
logs about a foot from the ground—but no place was
safe, for there the dogs would ferret them out, and it
was really a relief to hear that they were relieved from
their misery and terror.

The expectation of this scene often damped our
ardour, while advancing cheerily through the forest to
the place where we were to break our long fast : and
we used to fancy, that, from the poultry having become
aware by long experience of the fearful perils consequent upon the arrival of hungry travellers, we could
sometimes, when just in sight of the farm, spy the whole
flock, cocks, hens, and chickens, scudding off in a
crowd as quietly as might be, into the tall maize-field,
or among the brushwood. Our sleeping quarters were
frequently of the roughest description, but we travelled
merrily and happily together day by day, and were
conscious that we had yet rougher living before us.

As we proceeded, we began to observe many things
which were new to us, such as the large flights of par-
roquets, frequent salt springs, and a sensible change in
the productions of the forest. Among these the papaw
tree, with its heavy luscious fruit, was the greatest
curiosity.

The fourth day we crossed the 'Thirty Mile Prairie,'
and on the fifth, passing almost wholly through interminable forests, reached the town of Franklin, near

the Missouri.   We here made a diversion from the usual road to Boone's-Lick, a large and productive salt spring, discovered many years ago by old Daniel Boone.   Here he was accustomed to repair in his old age, when his strength would no longer bear him through the fatigues of the chase, to lie in wait, and shoot the deer as they approached near the spring.

The Missouri was subsequently crossed at Arrow Rock Ferry, and our line of route than lay wholly to the south of the river.

I recollect with delight our escape from a hot and crowded log-cabin, where we had been compelled to halt after dark and pass a restless night, and the following morning's ride over the open prairies.

I should despair of being able to convey any idea to your mind of the glories of the autumnal Flora, covering these immense natural meadows, like a rich carpet.   God has here, with prodigal hand, scattered the seeds of thousands of beautiful plants, each suited to its season, where there are no hands to pluck, and but few eyes to admire.   After the early grass of the spring begins to shoot up through the blackened surface of the scorched soil, it becomes spangled with a host of flowers, the prevailing colours of which are white and blue.   These, as summer advances, give place to a race in which red predominates: and when the yellow suns of autumn incline over the west, their mild rays are greeted by the appearance of millions of yellow flowers, which, far statelier and of ranker growth than their predecessors, rise over their ruins, and seem to clothe the undulating surface of the prairie with a cloth of gold.   The great predominance and variety of the *heliotrope* and *solidago* species, give this tint to the landscape, while at the same time there are many showy and beautiful plants, products of the same season, of less glaring colours.   Such are the *asters*, from the large and beautiful species which displays its rich clusters of blue and purple flowers in the brake, to the small delicately-leaved varieties seen on the more open grounds.   You observe whole districts covered with the tall and striking flowers of the red or white *eupatorium*, and every where among the long grass, the *liatris*, or rattlesnake's-master, shoots up, and displays its spike of red flowers. Then there are the exquisite varieties of the *gentiana* with their deep blue, and a thousand other flowers which I cannot undertake to describe. At this season, the dwarf sumac, in hollows and on such parts of the prairie as have remained untouched by the autumnal fires, becomes a striking feature of the open grounds from the blood-red hue of its leaves and fructification.

The greater part of the road to Lexington, after traversing the river, lay over wide prairies.

When we were within a few miles of that town we met the long train of trappers, which annually crosses the great western desert toward New Mexico, returning from the Rocky Mountains and Santa Fe; their mules laden with the skins for which they had dared that long and perilous pilgrimage. They were about seventy in number; men worn with toil and travel, bearing in their garb and on their persons evident marks of the adventurous passage of those immense prairies which lie to the westward. Seven of their number had fallen in combat with the Indians on their return. These expeditions, however, hold out the expectation of such enormous profit, that adventurers are never wanting to fill the ranks.

Having heard nothing of the steam-boat, we were not surprised on our arrival at Independence on the afternoon of the 24th, to find that we were the first at the place of rendezvous.

LETTER X.

THREE days yet elapsed before the members of our party were all assembled. The Colonel arrived the

evening of the same day with ourselves, but the Commissioner and Doctor proved themselves the laggards
of the party, and did not join us till the close of the
third.   They had met with ' moving accidents by flood
and field.'   You may remember they had resolved to
ascend the Missouri in a steam-boat, and loss of both
time and patience was the consequence.   The waters
of this mighty river were low ; they stranded again
and again, and finally had been obliged to leave the
boat aground, about one hundred miles below Independence, and get forward through the woods as they
might.   Judging from the querulous tone which per-
vaded their remarks, we concluded that the journey
had been far from agreeable.

However, such misfortunes are soon forgotten, and
finding that we had not been idle in the interval, but
had got pretty well advanced with the variety of new
arrangements deemed necessary, it was resolved to
prosecute our journey into the Indian country without
delay.

But before we quit Independence, a few remarks
upon our proceedings and occupations while there may
be acceptable.

The town of Independence was full of promise, like
most of the innumerable towns springing up in the
midst of the forests in the West, many of which, though
dignified by high-sounding epithets, consist of nothing
but a ragged congeries of five or six rough log huts,
two or three clapboard houses, two or three so-called
hotels, alias grogshops ; a few stores, a bank, printing
office, and barn-looking church.   It lacked at the time
I commemorate, the three last edifices, but was nevertheless a thriving and aspiring place, in its way ; and
the fortune made here already in the course of its brief
existence, by a bold Yankee shopkeeper who had sold
sixty thousand dollars' worth of goods here in three
years, was a matter of equal notoriety, surprise, and
envy.   It is situated about twenty miles east of the
Kansas river, and three south of the Missouri, and was
consequently very near the extreme western frontier of

the state. A little beyond this point, all carriage roads ceased, and one deep black trail alone, which might be seen tending to the south-west, was that of the Santa Fe trappers and traders.

I have felt a momentary temptation to give you a sketch of a deer hunt, in which we were engaged with a number of the sporting inhabitants of the settlement, but recollecting that, though very animated and exciting, it was unsuccessful, and that we have more hunting in prospect, I will let it pass.

It is advantageous to feel that you are a philosopher, even though you may be a sportsman, and that, whether your position be that of a solitary individual, strolling for hours with his gun, or the member of a party, the excitement is reward enough. As to myself, whether I return laden or empty-handed, I always return gratified.

On the morning of one of the days spent here in expectation of our friends' arrival,—mounted on Methuselah, an old white horse of the innkeeper's, and followed by a ragged water-dog, called Cash, I left my comrades and our horses to their repose at the town, partly for a morning's pigeon shooting, and partly with the purpose of going down to the ferry on the Missouri, to inquire if any intelligence had come up the river with reference to the expected steam-boat.

After missing the path, and an hour's rough scramble in the thick forest, during which I found means to insinuate my steed, gun, and person, through many a tangled jungle of rope-vine, brush, and creeper, much to my own astonishment and that of the grave old quadruped which I bestrode, I descended the bluff which here rises precipitously from the bank of the Missouri, and reached the ferry. I met with no intelligence, but with an acquaintance from the town above, who proposed to me that we should ride together six or seven miles down the river, and call upon one of his friends, whose 'clearing' was situated at a point where the current is unusually narrow, and of difficult navigation. To this I readily acceded, as it would give me a better opportunity of observing the phenomena connected with this stupendous stream, than any I had hitherto enjoyed. Though, geographically considered, I believe Mr. Flint is right in insisting upon the claim of the Mississippi to be considered the main river of the western region, in spite of its inferiority of length, yet, considered as a river, without reference to the peculiar geological formation of the continent through which it flows, there is no doubt of the pre-eminence of the Missouri.

The 'Father of Waters,' with his clear bright expanse and gentle current, is, in fact, swallowed up in the turbid and boiling volume of the 'Mother of Floods,' as she comes rushing in at right angles, upon the central valley, a few miles above St. Louis; and though it must be allowed that the southerly course of the Mississippi is preserved even after the point of junction, and the breadth of the latter is three times that of its mighty tributary—yet the attributes of the Lower Mississippi are in fact those of the Missouri.

No European can form an adequate idea of either of these great rivers, expanded like lakes, while their waters are seen rushing forward through the rich forested country like mountain torrents, tearing down the banks, changing their beds, and from their turbid colour, and the quantity of mud and slime with which they are heavily charged, having all the appearance of rivers in a state of extraordinary flood :—yet so they have boiled on from year to year, and from age to age.

The turbid character of the waters of the Missouri has been frequently attributed to the volumes of earth and sand brought into it by the Yellow Stone, one of its largest tributaries ; but it is ascertained to have the same character to the very gates of the Rocky Mountains, where it comes rushing through deep and perpendicularly walled defiles toward the great plains ; and the fact seems to be established, that in those distant regions the unprotected surface of the earth is undergoing a gradual change, and is gradually being washed down by the action of the rains and ten thousand streams.

There are phenomena connected with the Missouri, and indeed all the great western rivers, which would appear at first consideration almost inexplicable. Among these, none is more remarkable than that presented by the comparatively small volume of water which they appear to contain at the points where they disembogue themselves, after a course of thousands of miles in length, and the reception of so many tributary waters. Take the facts connected with the Missouri. At the Mandan villages, two thousand miles from its sources, and sixteen hundred from the Mississippi, it is said to be as deep and as wide as at St. Charles, a few miles above its mouth. Yet within these points it receives a number of large tributaries, among which we may name the Platte and the Kansas rivers, the former of which brings down from a computed course of two thousand miles, a volume of water as large as that of the Missouri itself. River after river pours in its floods ; yet however great, they appear to produce no effect on the main stream. Various causes are alleged in explanation of this, besides that of great evaporation. The whole bed of the Missouri appears to be a loose shifting sand, through which vast quantities of water are supposed to filter. Farther, it is urged, that the wide alluvial tracts, in connection with the river, are based on a porous soil of sand and loam, which absorbs much of its volume ; conveying large portions into the main valley of the Mississippi by subterraneous channels. In the same way it may be argued that the small quantity of water visibly entering the Gulf by the Mississippi, may be accounted for, by the quantity drawn into that great general reservoir, by many concealed drains of the same character.

The upward navigation of the Missouri by ordinary boats may be conceived to have been always a most perilous and arduous task, and even since the introduction of steam-boats, it is found more uncertain and hazardous

than that of any other western river. The vast length
of its tributaries, and the distance of its sources, render
it liable to frequent floods, of which three are always
confidently looked forward to at certain intervals in the
course of every year. The first rise that takes place is
in the early spring, when the lower tributaries give
forth their surplus waters in concert with the Upper
Mississippi and her northern tributaries. A month
later the Platte and other streams rising in the spurs of
the Rocky Mountains, send their tribute to the eastward; and the greatest and most regular rise takes
place in the course of June, when the accumulated
snows on the Rocky Mountains yield to the influence
of the sun, and the floods come pouring down from the
' head-waters ' of the main river, over the Great Falls,
and joining those from the Yellow Stone, they swell
the torrent, flowing through fifteen hundred miles
of prairie, and advance day by day, till they gain
the frontier of Missouri, and finally pour into the Mississippi. The rise of water in the latter river, at this
time at St. Louis, is generally between five and fifteen
feet.

During this latter period of flood, the navigation of
the river, by steam, is safe and uninterrupted; and the
American Fur Company's steamer, the ' Yellow Stone,'
takes advantage of it to make its yearly trip to their
factory at the mouth of the river of that name, eighteen
hundred miles from the Mississippi. The duration of
the voyage has ordinarily been from eight to ten weeks
in ascending, and ten to fifteen days in returning.*

It is impossible to note the facts which I have just
alluded to, with regard to the distinct periods at which
the waters from the several streams connected with
both the Missouri and Mississippi are poured into the
great valley of the west, without being struck with the
great and compassionate providence of God, which by

* In the summer of 1831, the ' Yellow Stone ' ascended the Missouri,
1400 miles, but could not reach its destination. In 1832, they were
more successful, and reached the factory, and in 1833, succeeded in
ascending yet 300 miles farther, being 2100 miles from the mouth.

so dispersing the rivers which drain that vast extent of
open country, over such various degrees of latitude,
secures the valley from the yearly visitation of an overwhelming deluge. If all these mighty rivers were so
situated, by similarity of length and position, as to
break up simultaneously, there is no doubt that the
whole of the extended region, occupied by the alluvial
lands, would be uninhabitable. But the deep snows
of the Alleghany have sent their tribute to the ocean
by the Ohio, before the icy chains which bind the
waters of the Upper Mississippi are loosed; and the
floods caused by these and the lower waters and tributaries of the Missouri and Mississippi have subsided
many days, before the streams of the great Western
Chain can, from their vast distance, arrive with their
contribution.

Resuming my narrative : Having rounded a noble
and expanded bend of the river, in about an hour's
time, we heard by the barking of dogs, and the chat-
tering of many voices, that we were approaching the
farm in question. The tall leafless boughs of a few
girdled trees then appeared, and as we entered the
opening on the bank of the river, we descried the
rough log huts forming the usual habitation of a
squatter or backwoodsman. From the prominent
appearance of a long table covered with dinner apparatus, which appeared arranged in the open air, a few
steps from the door, a number of dogs whining and
snuffing around it, and the unusual bustle among the
negro dependants toiling about a small fire in advance,
we suspected that something extraordinary was going
on. A young negro took our horses with that affecta-
tion of extreme politeness and good breeding, which is
so highly amusing in many of his colour, and which
inclines me to think that they appreciate the character
of a ' fine gentleman,' more than any other part of the
community. The principal log hut was built on a
little level, half way up the steep bank impending over
the swift and turbid river below. In immediate proximity to it, I noticed the broad, solid stump of a mag-

nificent oak, which had been just felled, and lay prostrate, with his crown of foliage hanging over the bluff,
a piece of labour which appeared to me so gratuitously
unnecessary and wanton, that I could not avoid making
a remark expressive of my regret, as its position was
not only picturesque, but, I should have thought, of
real utility to the huts under its shade. The reason
given was characteristic, amounting to this, that it
might one day fall on the dwelling.

We were met by the settler with the frank un.cere-
monious bearing of his race. He informed us that his
wife had got a number of her neighbours with her for
a 'quilting frolic,' and made us heartily welcome. The
interior of the log hut presented a similar scene. A
square table was seen to occupy a great part of its
floor. It was surrounded by a compact body of
females, whose fingers were occupied with all diligence
upon the quilt which lay stretched out before them, and
which, though neither the smartest nor costliest, promised, judging from the quantity of cotton or wool
which I saw stuffed into its inside, and the close
lozenge-shaped compartments into which the latter was
confined by rapid and successful gobble-stitching,—to
be of real utility and comfort, during the coming
winter, to the matron who presided. A life in the
woods teaches many lessons, and this among the rest,
that you must both give assistance to your neighbour,
and receive it in return, without either grudging or
pouting. Accordingly, among other usages current
among the back-settlers, the necessity and comfort of
which each has learned in turn, that of lending a free
helping-hand in the spirit of kindness, is both a laudable and a natural one ; and hence arises the custom of
which I have given you a specimen, with others of a
like character. A family comes to sit down in the
forest,—they must have a shelter ; and giving notice
far and near, their neighbours for many miles round
lay down their employments, shoulder their axes, and
come into the ' log-rolling.' They spend the day in
hard labour, and the evening in good-humoured

hilarity, and then retire through the forests, each to his own clearing, leaving the new-comers their good wishes, and a habitation. They frequently render one another the same service in rotation at harvest ; and in the case under our eye, the outcry of the good woman for a quilt, had not failed to call together twenty of her neighbours, young and old ; and many hands made light work. Like the generality of women brought up in the backwoods, they were reserved and silent before strangers. I should have said stupidly so, and that there was more harshness in manner than belonged to the sex under any circumstances ; but I had before my eyes a proof that they were at least good neighbours, and therefore thought their manners in this respect of little consequence. The meal which followed was plentiful and homely, and was dispatched first by the female and then by the male visitors, with that marvellous rapidity which is generally observable in the West; and, as I sat apart till our turn should come, I was very much amused with the bustle of the scene. I watched the plates run the gauntlet from the table to the washing-tub, among a set of little negroes of all shapes and sizes, who all strove to act as preliminary scourers, much to the disappointment of the dogs that whined, whimpered, scratched, and pushed their sable competitors, and not less to the annoyance of the fat negress who acted as cook, and who, with lustrous visage and goggle-eyes, flourished her dish-clout over the tub in a fume of impatience.

The settler had, in the course of the preceding spring, bought three hundred acres of land of the state, at a dollar and a quarter per acre. He came to work upon it in the month of April, at which time the sound of the axe had never been heard in these forests. During the course of that month, he girdled the trees on ten acres—built himself a log hut—and brought his family out from Independence. At the close of May, after burning the brushwood, and slightly breaking the surface, he sowed the ten acres, upon which the sun now shone freely, unobstructed by the dying spring foliage, with a bushel and a half of gourd-seed maize; and at the time of my visit in September, he showed me a crop upon the ground ready to harvest, of fifty bushels to the acre—the whole return being, consequently, five hundred bushels for the one and a half sown.   At the same time the fodder, yielded by stripping the tall stems of the maize of their broad and redundant leaves, amounted to a thousand bundles, sufficient to afford winter-food for fifteen head of cattle, which, during the summer, had lived and fattened in the forest, with their compeers, the swine, without being a charge upon the owner.   Besides this produce, the field had yielded fifty wagon-loads of pumpkins, of which great use is made, both for the family, the negroes, and the stock.   Such are the amazing fertility of this region. and the facility with which the necessaries of life may be procured!   I have given you this single instance out of many of which I took exact and particular note.

When I add that the whole tract purchased was of the same inexhaustible richness of soil, covered with the most exuberant and noble forest, many trees which I measured being six yards in girth, abounding with excellent water and limestone, situated at a point where there would be no difficulty in transporting any quantity of produce to a market, you may well suppose that the owner cannot but become wealthy.   There are reasons why many who are in equally favourable situations do not.   Loss of health is very frequently the lot of those who occupy these teeming lands, and I have ordinarily observed, that the ease and little expenditure of labour and anxiety with which men of this class find themselves enabled to gain food, and even superfluities, seem to unnerve their bodies, and unstring their minds.   Many become listless and unenterprising, and lose that energy which can alone secure riches.

To return to the village, which I re-entered in the course of the evening, and our proceedings there:

At this time, (with all humility be it said,) I held the perplexing but honourable offices of commissary-

general, and minister of finance to our mess. I could
never rightly divine whether this was owing to the discovery which my comrades, Irving and Pourtales, had
made of my superior skill and activity,—I certainly
slept less than either of them—or whether their impo-
sition of these dignities and duties on me proceeded
from the simple and pure intention of sparing themselves extraordinary trouble of mind or body. Such,
however, was the fact : and I was fully empowered to
take care of our outward affairs—to buy and sell—
higgle and haggle—chaffer and cheat; and be cheated,
for the public good. In Independence, I had my
hands full. I purchased bacon and knives and forks,
salt, sugar and flour, coffee and camomile flowers, pep-
per and potatoes, and a multitude of sundries, according to my own judgment, or their fancies and wants.
But all these matters were trifles, compared with the
strain upon the mind and conscience consequent upon
the purchase of horses. Though I confess to you that
this part of a gentlemanly and classical education had
been strangely neglected in my case. I had already
learned to look wise in the faces of those brought for
sale—to speak knowingly and positively about their
age—and though, after having had my fingers snapped
at in St. Louis, I had grown rather chary of peeping in
jockey style into the mouths of unknown steeds, yet I
contrived to keep up my credit as horse-dealer after
all ; and now, for your benefit, I will give you a lesson
how to choose a horse for the desert. We will presume that a dire necessity exists for the purchase, and
that time admits of no longer delay, and that this necessity is a matter of notoriety to every rogue for ten
miles round. Not an old nag or irreclaimable horse
can exist within that distance, but he will be straightway brought in from the forest, where he may have
been scouted even by the wolves, brushed up, rubbed
down, renovated and endowed with every marketable
quality and virtue. Suppose yourself standing before
Captain Warner's Hotel, in the rising city of Independence, and up comes a Yankee settler, Mr. Elisha
10*

Pike, with a horse to dispose of. You are perfectly aware of two things—first, that the animal must have grievous faults, else Mr. Pike would have sold him long ago; and secondly, that however great or grievous these faults are, you have now no choice but to purchase the animal. Your only object must be to save your credit as horsedealer. You see at a glance that whatever bargain you may contrive to make, it cannot fail to be a bad one. After the ordinary preliminaries, I advise you to place yourself for a few moments in speechless reverie (the less you speak the better,) about three yards in advance of the animal, and look him in the face. Then move slowly round him, muttering something about ' heaves'—' staggers ' —' spavin '—and ' wall-eyed.' As you advance to your first position, you may hazard a question. ' Does he trot or break?' ' *Ere a thing what you please,*' is the ready answer of Mr. Pike. ' Mr. Pike,' you proceed, ' I think his left eye waters.' ' *A mere touch of the whip,*' responds the seller.

The price is asked and named. ' Too much by half, Mr. Pike.' ' *Times aint now as they used to was,*' is the prompt rejoinder of the undaunted horse-jobber. After a moment's hesitation, if he looks tame, you may venture to stoop down and peep at his knees and his fetlocks, always trusting that he will not incontinently spring on your back. You may always safely mutter something about 'coming down ;' or if you see he turns his toes out, express your fear that he is a ' speedy cutter.' The next thing is to desire the seller to bare his teeth. If he happens to have none, I should hardly know what to advise you to think, as there is no knowing with some of those Yankee steeds whether the deficit is to be ascribed to extreme age or extreme youth ; perhaps you had better not hazard an opinion, and resort to the main trial, which we generally had recourse to in despair. This is to take your gun and jump on his back. Then put spurs to him, and dash forward for half a mile at a hand-gallop over one of the rough, broken, stump-bestrewn roads leading through the forest, discharging your piece in mid-career; and depend upon it, if he neither comes down with you as he scrambles among the stumps, nor swerves at the report, you may after all venture to strike the bargain; hazarding no very decided declaration as to your reasons for so doing, and maintaining such a demeanour as may give Mr. Pike the impression that he has only overreached your pocket and not your judgment.

But, *plaisanterie* apart, as the last operation here, we exchanged or swopped for old Methuselah, value five dollars, the gallant steed sold to us by our worthy Tonish for forty-five dollars, but which we discovered to be so lame that the very day after the purchase no one could ride him. The only positively good quality of our new acquisition was, that he was so deaf that the discharge of a piece of ordnance would never have made him start, and his negative plea to be considered a horse of price, was founded upon his having belonged to the family of old Daniel Boone, in consequence of which Pourtales took a fancy to bestride him.

In the evening of the 27th I accompanied the Commissioner alone to the Shawanese Agency on the frontiers; and the following day we struck across the wide prairies to overtake our companions, who had meanwhile left Independence, cutting the Santa Fe traders' trail, and, finally, bending more to the southward, hit upon that of our own party, which we followed till we found them encamped in the twilight in a low skirting of wood, under the edge of the prairie.

LETTER XI.

THE following morning, by the time the gray dawn was brightening into daylight, our lengthened train might be seen issuing from the hollow in which we had passed the night, and proceeding over the rolling surface of the prairie beyond. The appearance of our cavalcade was far from being unpicturesque, and had I Chaucer's wit or Stothard's pencil, I might contrive to furnish you with a picture of almost as much interest as the 'Pilgrimage to Canterbury.' It is to be hoped that you will agree with me in accounting the time spent in the Far West, both this and the following year, as the most interesting portion of my late travels. I cannot suspect you of longing, like my other very sensible correspondent, to win me back from the sketches of character and natural scenery to which my own inclination and temper led me, to the purlieus of alms-houses, the prices of beef and coals, and converse concerning parish beadles and overseers. If you should, the sooner you tell me the better,—in the meantime take a sketch of a day on the Missouri frontier.

Our cavalcade consisted of the Colonel and his two servants, viz. a black boy William, and a little thin lack-a-daisical Frenchman named Prevôt, who generally took charge of our two wagons while on the march ; then the Commissioner, the Doctor, Washington Irving, Count Pourtales, and your humble servant, and lastly our scape-grace Tonish, together with another half-breed, whose services were principally required to care for a number of led horses.

Slight traits may suffice to delineate the principal personages.

The Colonel, whom we considered for the time being the head of the party, generally led the van ; a fine, good-humoured, shrewd man, of French descent, with claims both to fortune and family in Missouri. As our conductor, we were all beholden to his courteous manners, and extensive information on every subject connected with the country and its red inhabitants, for much of our comfort and entertainment. In the pursuit of his profession of Indian trader, he had often dared captivity and death. Among the Osages, whose principal trader, and organ with government, he had long been, he was supposed, and I believe justly, to possess the greatest influence. In fact he had been brought up from his early boyhood, more or less in their camps; had hunted, feasted, fought with and for them, and was considered by them as a chief and a brother. From him we were glad to take our first lessons in hunting, camping, and backwoodsman's craft, and enjoy our first peep at that kind of life, which, judging from his fine vigorous person, and the health shining on his sun-burnt features, was, with all its hardships, congenial to health and good humour. He was to be our guide to the Western Creek Agency, about three hundred miles to the southward. The Commissioner, with whom we had long become intimately acquainted, was worthy of the respect which all entertained for him. His kindliness of spirit won our regard; and we all did justice to the singleness of purpose with which he, a happy husband and parent, and truly a lover of quiet, had left his family and the comforts of an Eastern home, to become a peacemaker among the rude tribes and inhabitants of the West.

The Doctor was, I am happy to say, quite an unnecessary appendage, and I believe he would have felt no disappointment, had his lot been cast otherwise, as this kind of adventurous life was not consonant with his tastes. He had not made up his mind to all those petty troubles which are unavoidable beyond the pale of civilization, and you will always find that such men are sure to meet with more mischances than their neighbours. As to our trio, I need say nothing here, but pass on to the domestics, a far richer field for description.

The black boy was only distinguished by his good-nature, and by his sleeping like a racoon, while he held the reins and pretended to drive. The Colonel's little French retainer, Prevôt, was the scape-goat of the party. He had certainly been born under some very unfortunate aspect of the heavenly signs, and seemed unable to shake off their malignant influence. Nothing could be more diverting to others, than the composed melancholy which seemed to reign in his features and sentences, as his weak nasal voice was heard in the brake, or at the camp-fire, deploring his unhappy lot. Did a horse kick—Prevôt's shin-bones or fingers bore testimony to the fact.   Did it happen that the passage of a rivulet was difficult for the wagon,—look but back, and you might be sure that the legs and skirts disappearing in the brushwood, as the possessor tipped back from the inclined seat, were the appurtenances of little Prevôt : and so to the very end of the journey, when we left him on the Neosho with a terrible catarrh.

These worthies, however, will all be forgotten ere long, and probably you may hear no more mention made of them, but Tonish will not so soon sink into oblivion.   Light, active, in the prime of life, no horse could take him by surprise ; no inclined plane could throw him off his balance.   He was a man of no mean qualifications.   Full of make-shifts, and unspeakably useful in the woods, they were his home.   A house was an abomination to him, and he was at a loss what to do with himself when he got within one.   He possessed, however, a wife and family at Florissant, to whom his visits would seem to have been ' few and far between.'   He was garrulous to excess, in spite of an impediment in his speech, in the form of a barrier, which it was necessary to break down by an effort, after which the words composing the meditated sentence came tumbling out headlong.   He was a weaver of interminable stories, all about himself and his hunting exploits.   We soon found out that he was a determined and audacious braggart ; but it was sometime before we all came to the unanimous conclusion, that, for lying effrontery, none of us had ever seen his equal.   In fact, such was the ingenious and whimsical way in which he would bring a host of little lies to cover a big one, that it became a matter of amusement with us to watch his manœuvres.

Following our march as fancy dictated, or stowed away in the rear of the wagons, we had a train of eight dogs, all belonging to the Colonel, who was something of a humourist, and accordingly they all had appropriate names, dictated by love, hate, and political feeling, among which note Henry Clay, a greyhound ; Jackson, a bulldog ; and Mrs. Trollope, a hound with a number of whelps.

In the south-westerly course which we now followed, the farms or clearings were few in number, and of rare occurrence ; the general character of the country being that of wide open prairies, with long lines of timber trees skirting the course of the creeks and rivers, many of which rose in this elevated corner of the country. The road was merely a track over the natural sod of the prairie, and though practicable in the dry season for such light four-wheeled vehicles as those in our train, the swollen state of the streams often rendered it impassable for weeks.

Our mode of proceeding was pretty uniform. We struck the tent early ; travelled about fifteen or twenty miles at a sober pace, after which we made halt for an hour, allowing the horses to pick up a little food, and then proceeded ten or twelve miles more, till about an hour before sun-down, when we sought a convenient camping-ground, affording wood, grass, and water. This was the general order of the day's march. If a suitable spot was found in the neighbourhood of one of the scattered farms, it was well ; if not, no one lamented it, for we were much more comfortable and at home in the forest, than under the crowded roof of the settler. We had always egregious appetites, plenty of provisions, absence from care, and sound sleep on a bear-skin ; and what more could we wish ?

Many of our encampments were eminently picturesque, but as I may have subsequently much of this kind of life to describe, I will not now allude to any in particular.

You may suppose us drawing toward the close of a day's journey, and the sun sinking fast down the western horizon. The broken line of the cavalcade, the great intervals between the horsemen, the wagons toiling far in the rear, and the difficulty of keeping the spare horses on the track, as they seize upon every opportunity to diverge from it, to feed upon the rank grass, all betoken the propriety of making choice of our night-quarters.

The streams and creeks, meandering among these vast prairies, are generally deeply sunk, and bordered by a belt of rich forest, of greater or less breadth, and upon such our choice always fell, as we had here wood, water, shelter, and fodder for our steeds. If possible, we halt before the sun is down, that we may get every thing comfortably settled before night-fall, choosing an open space among the trees, within a stone's throw of the water.

The spot being fixed upon, we drive and ride in among the tall grass and dismount : each unsaddles his steed, hobbles it, as the term is, by tying the two fore-feet close together, and sends it hopping into the forest like a kangaroo, crashing and scrambling through the gigantic and entangled brushwood, which rises under the heavier timber. Here, at this season, they feed upon the pea-vine, a very nutritious plant which abounds in all the wooded alluvial grounds or ' bottoms' of the Western Prairies.

As soon as this first duty is performed, we think of ourselves. While the half-breed and the black cut wood, Tonish makes a fire against some fallen tree or log, and flits to and fro in the smoke, like a goblin, while preparing his poles and spits for cookery. Mean-while other hands are employed in pitching the tent, and laying down the bear-skins and blankets within or without as suits convenience.

By the time this is all fairly arranged, and our arms and accoutrements are carefully hung around, night has closed in ; and the fire gleams bright and cheerily upon the huge trunk of the oak, butter-nut and beech, which rise from the tall jungle of towering weeds springing around us far over our heads. Tonish is now by far the most important personage, and we, in common with Henry Clay, Jackson, Mrs. Trollope, and the rest of the lick-lip fraternity, await the result of his operations.

Now and then Clay advances his sharp nose too near certain tempting spits, which, stuck into the earth, and leaning toward the bright embers, support slices of savoury venison, the plump prairie-hen, or squirrel, and gets a sudden knock upon it from Tonish's knife handle. Jackson stands doggedly under the tail of the nearest wagon, with goggle eyes sparkling in the fire light, in eager expectation of the coming feast; and Mrs. Trollope keeps up a constant snarl at her four whelps, as, incited by the maternal example, they push their noses from underneath the saddles, and from behind the great log, toward the point of general attraction.

At length the Colonel's sonorous voice is heard, ‘ *Messieurs, le soupé est paré !*’ and each rousing himself to the willing toil, contrives a seat around a tent cloth, and partakes of the banquet. And banquet it was; for we lived at this time like princes, as coffee, biscuit, and bread, were plentiful in the camp, in addition to our other luxuries, among which I would recount that despised dish, fried pumpkins.

Then follows the second table, at which the dogs think themselves entitled to partake, and the half-breed and the black are kept busy in alternately bestowing right-handed morsels to their own mandibles, and left-handed thumps to Henry Clay and company.

The table withdrawn, we sit half an hour round the fire, listen to each other's tales, and, between whiles, to the distant howl of the prairie wolf, the shriek of the owl, the chirp of innumerable grasshoppers and crickets, the cry of the bustards going to sleep in the neighbouring marsh, or speculate upon some odd nondescript out-of-the-way noise in the deep forest; till in fine, growing gradually sleepy, we steal off to rest.

I cannot say that silence always held her sceptre over us, even when sound asleep, for little Prevôt and the black snored so loud, that the dogs would sit up and bark at the noise.

Long before daybreak there was generally a wakeful spirit among us; the fire was stirred up—the breakfast prepared—the horses caught and brought into camp, and before sunrise we were on the road again.

———

LETTER XII.

THE character of the country, over which our whole journey from Independence to the Arkansas river was effected, with the exception of a few casual settlements where cultivation had changed the natural face of the soil, was that which distinguishes the whole of that immense territory between the Mississippi and the Rocky mountains. We skirted for several days the eastern limits of those boundless plains which know no settled inhabitants, and over the other extremity of which, at five or six hundred miles distance, the gigantic summit of Mount Pike serves as a landmark to the scouting Indian or trapper.

The scenery exhibited by these vast grass-covered prairies, with but the occasional break afforded by a wooded creek, is monotonous to a certain degree; yet as all those over which we passed belonged to the class called 'rolling prairies,' where a constant gentle elevation and depression of the soil gives some variety, besides inducing a variety in the character of the vegetation, we did not find our journey wearisome. You may have some idea of this class of open country, by recollecting the general outline of our higher and more extensive moorlands—allowing your fancy to clothe them with a deep rich soil, instead of dark peat, and with a carpet of the brightest flowers and grass from six inches to six feet in height, according to circumstances, instead of monotonous purple heather.

The creeks were abundant in this part of the country, so that we were rarely out of sight of trees at a greater or less distance from our line of route, but as much as thirty miles were passed without seeing any. Here and there the country swelled up into a higher level than ordinary, into singular ranges of lime-stone hills, surmounted by what are called 'flint knobs,' which rise not unfrequently some hundred feet above the general level of the country. Over such a chain, called the Mounds, we passed on the last day of the month, and were greatly struck with the regular form and mould of the southernmost excrescence in particular, which rose up in the exact form of a truncated cone. No feature of the western country has been more striking and embarrassing to me than its natural and artificial mounds, of which there exists a regular chain, from such as this just mentioned, about which we feel convinced, in spite of its singular position and regular form, that God was its only artificer, to those whose immense size and shapelessness are attended with incontrovertible proofs that they are wholly the work of human hands.

We made a halt of half a day in the mission settlement of Harmony, an establishment under the direction of the American Board of Missions. It is situated on the banks of the Great Osage river, about seventy-six miles from the village of that division of the Osage tribe known by the name of the band of White Hairs. In both this and the sister settlement of Union on the Neosho, which we passed a week later, it appeared that the ends aimed at by the missionaries were chiefly the establishment and maintenance of a school for the Indian children, and the introduction of a taste for agriculture, and that their views of usefulness were limited to these objects.

At the time of our halt the settlement was surrounded by a number of strolling Indians of the Piankashaw tribe, and these excited the more interest, as they were the first of the children of the forest we had seen in the vicinity of their own settlements, and in their own guise. Among the men there were many fine picturesque figures; but the mixture of Indian and European costumes was strikingly grotesque. The apparel of three warriors, whom curiosity attracted to us during the morning, may give you an idea of Indian taste and coxcombry. The oldest, Big Fish, appeared clad in the usual Indian leggins and moccasins or shoes, of tanned deer-skin, and his smoke-stained blanket was thrown negligently over a soiled cotton shirt, furnished with a superabundance of frill, while his head was enveloped in a shawl-turban of gaudy colours. The second of the group wore a fanciful green cotton shirt under his blanket, his lower limbs being clothed like those of his fellows; but he depended on the paint lavished upon his dark features to win the hearts of the squaws in the train, having adorned himself with bright blue and vermilion in two irregular square patches, the one on the left temple, and the other on the right eye. The third was really a handsome fellow, with a bunch of stained eagle feathers on his crown, a dark blue shirt, blanket, and red cloth leggins. Their squaws were hideous to behold.

The day after we passed Harmony, our route, which had hitherto lain within the Missouri line, crossed the frontier by bearing more to the west, and we entered the country then appertaining to the Osages. As we advanced, the surface of the prairies became more and more stony.

My general custom during this portion of our tour, was every morning, as soon as I had saddled my horse, a duty which each took upon himself, to shoulder my gun, and leave the encampment on foot, both for the sake of varying the mode of travel, botanizing, and the chance of meeting with game, before the noise of our advancing train should have driven it at a distance from our path. At this early hour the sweetness and freshness of the air were indescribably delicious; and though the gaudy Flora of the declining year was in a great degree void of perfume, yet it seemed as if every sense partook of enjoyment. It is just at this time when the sun's level beams begin to warm the dank surface of these wide meadows, that the air is filled with the mournfully sweet and glassy notes of the yellow-breasted meadow-lark, as she rises from her covert in the tall grass, and flies, as you advance,.from one tuft of wild indigo to another. It is then that groups of that fine species of grouse, the prairie-fowl,* are to be seen sitting upon the trampled sod of the track, sunning themselves, while with outstretched neck and expanded ruff the watchful cock-bird gives careful notice of the approach of a human foot. It is then that the deer may be met with, bounding to covert; and that the white and black autumnal moths are seen fluttering among the flowers and grass in myriads.

As the sun gets higher, the falcon may be observed on the alert, with his level wing and piercing eye, slanting along the trail, peeping into every rut, and prying into every tuft of grass for the grouse, who instantly bury themselves in the wilderness of plants, and thus escape his rapacious gripe. At the same time the moths disappear, and in their place numbers of winged grasshoppers, yellow, green, and red, rise from the side of the road, take their short flight of half a dozen yards, play the butterfly for an instant, and then drop heavily among the flowers.

I believe it was on the afternoon of the second of October, that we arrived at the limit of a long swell in the country of greater elevation than ordinary. An old Osage warrior of the Gray Hairs' band, whose name was '.the Destroyer of Cities,' alias ' the Burner of Wigwams,' then attached to our party, and acting as our guide, was riding at the head of our small column. When he arrived at the brink of the ascent, he paused, reined in his pony, and turning half round as he beckoned us forward, spread his arms, signifying to us the wide expanse that burst upon his sight; and that this broad extent of country, dimly descried in the deep red haze, was the present domain of his tribe.

Tetrao pratensis.
11*

And truly that apparently illimitable ocean of meadow, wreathed in the smokes ascending from a hundred burning tracts, with its numberless lines of forest, stretching like capes and promontories into it, mingling with the dun and misty horizon, toward which the sun was sinking like a glowing ball of fire, formed a sublime scene.

His tribe had broken up from its summer residence on the Neosho; the warriors forming the great hunting party had gone off with their chief toward the Buffalo-range and the great Salt Plains, many days' journey to the westward, for their autumnal hunt; and the rest of the band were dispersing to their several hunting-grounds within the limit of their own territory.

The following day, as we proceeded southward, we saw ourselves surrounded by the smoke of their fires. It rose on every hand, over the level horizon of prairie, or through the forest along the creeks. About noon many groups appeared in sight, pursuing their way in long files, or in single small bodies over the country, with squaws, papooses, and laden ponies.

With the exception of a blanket and a few ornaments, there was little European clothing observable among the males. The warrior was generally seen marching first, with his firm straight step and upright bearing, burdened with nothing but his rifle. Many of them were good specimens of the North American Indian 'brave,' and wore the head shaved, with the exception of the scalp-lock on the crown, and painted vermilion. In general they were tall, and in a certain degree martial in gait and bearing: yet, though straight-limbed, too spare to be handsome. The countenances of the squaws, on the contrary, after true savage fashion, were bent toward the earth, from the burden of skins or other articles imposed upon their shoulders, and secured in its position by a strap of leather over the temples. The Indian ponies had also their burden of baskets and utensils; and the round head and glistening eyes of many a little papoose bobbed up and down among the motley bundles of which the load was composed;—the boys and elder children brought up the rear.

At this time, our encampments were continually surrounded by this tribe. The moment the Indian proclaimed a halt to his family, he drew to one side—grounded his rifle—twisted his blanket closer over his attenuated person, and looked on with listlessness and apathy at the labours of the squaws, who meanwhile were busily employed in bending the twigs of the underwood into a skeleton hut—covering them with mats and skins—making their fires, and cooking. In every thing they seem to be the drudges of the males. As to personal appearance, with very few exceptions, I can only specify three degrees,—horrible, more horrible, most horrible!

Of all the Indian tribes at which we got a glance, this and the following year, the Osage came nearest to our idea of the North American Indian. The Southern Indian struck us as being more effeminate; and the more northern tribes, though I own they were in appearance far finer specimens of manly beauty, yet wanted much of the dignity of march and demeanour of the poor Osage. He is truly the child of the desert; and while the Creek and the Cherokee, whom circumstances have brought into his neighbourhood, are in some degree showing an inclination to bend to their circumstances, and cultivate the ground, and may attain to a certain degree of civilization, the Osages still scorn the alternative of labour to famine. Their Great Father at Washington sends them milch cows, draught oxen, and farming utensils, and delegates to instruct them in their management and use. The Missionaries provide schools, and by labouring themselves, attempt to show that labour and freedom are compatible with each other. The squaw is cajoled to send her son to school; but what is the consequence of all these well-meant attempts to civilize them? The cows are killed to get the milk—and the oxen are killed because the Indian cannot see the wisdom of starving while so much food is walking about. The Indian attempt at ploughing, which begins with seven able-bodied warriors assisting the coulter in its operation, ends with the machine being broken or thrown aside in disgust. The agent, who, seeing the impossibility of getting them to do any thing when the object is not manifest and of speedy fulfilment, encloses a large tract, sows it with maize, keeps it in his own hands till ripe, and then, summoning the band, says— 'My brethren! your village is composed of twenty lodges—here are twenty acres of ripe corn—take it, and divide it justly.' The chiefs grunt their approbation—' It is all good—very good !' The satisfied agent goes to bed, and when he gets up at sunrise the next morning, sees three hundred hobbled horses eating, fighting, and trampling the corn into the earth: one of the joint proprietors having had the bright idea that by hobbling his horse and putting him into the field, the share appertaining to him might be gathered without any manual labour or mental exertion on his part ; a felicitous idea, which is soon hailed and followed by the rest. This is a fact ! Again—instead of feeling under an obligation for the instruction offered to their young, the Osage father thinks the boy ought to receive wages for going to school. Even in the case when the Missionaries, through circumstances, have contrived to keep a young Indian halfbreed (for a full-blood Indian can hardly ever be detained beyond childhood) for a few years, and given him some insight into the most common laws and uses of agriculture ; the only consequence is, that when he goes back to his tribe, he is worth nothing—he is neither able to subsist in the manner of the Pale-faces, nor to hunt with his red brethren, and frequently becomes an outcast. Yet, though this seems to be the unsuccessful issue of most attempts to civilize the Osage —I am aware that there is one trial making on the Neosho, by a person of great tact, prudence, and Christian principle, where he has a fine fertile tract under his own cultivation, and the control of a small

band of Osages, which promises well. But few of his
Indians join the great spring and autumnal hunts, or
the war parties of the tribe—and that is certainly a
proof of success ; for, in general, you might as soon
expect the young wolf, whom you bring up from a cub,
in apparent gentleness and attachment to your person,
to remain so, when, having come to his full strength, he
has once strayed beyond his chain—seen the round
moon—snuffed the night air—and heard the howl of
his compeers in the mountains, as you can that the
young Indian should lie by and labour the earth with
the spade and harrow, when he sees his brethren dance
the buffalo-dance, and turn their faces to the broad
desert—or hears the war-whoop of his tribe. For the
rest, the life of the Indian is well known, and I need
not dwell upon it.

I have noticed elsewhere the determination entertained by the government of the United States to
remove all the scattered remnants of the Indian tribes
dwelling on their reserved lands in the different parts
of the Union east of the Mississippi, to the country
west of the same great river. At the time of which
these letters treat, this had been in a great measure
effected, and by the sale and cession of their lands to the
east, many tribes found themselves dispersed upon the
frontier, from about the 91st to the 95th degree of longi-
tude, in the Missouri and Arkansas Territory, while
yearly additions have since been made to their number.
Thus, portions of the Creeks, Cherokees, Choctaws,
Quappaws, Delawares, Senecas, and Shawanees, with
many minor tribes, were ranged along that parallel ; the
Osages forming, as it were, the advanced line. The
Seminoles of Florida, by this time, have left their homes
on the waters and barrens of the Peninsula, and have
gone to sit down on the edge of the great desert, by
the side of their brethren the Creeks. The three first-
named tribes certainly hold out a promise of the gradual
attainment of civilization—many not only cultivating
large tracts, but holding in their own persons many
slaves, and living altogether by agriculture. They

may become permanent possessors of the soil they now cultivate.   The recent invention of written characters, by a full-blooded Cherokee, consisting of eighty-four signs, expressing all the dominant sounds of that language, and the great number of half-breeds among them, are both favourable to this change of life.   The best proof that they are advancing from their savage state to a higher grade, is that their numbers increase; while almost all other Indian tribes spread over the American Continent, far and near, are known to diminish in number so rapidly, that common observation alone enables any one to predict their utter extinction before the lapse of many years.

There are certainly causes operating to produce this ultimate disappearance of the red tribes of America, which are not fully understood.   It is pretty well ascertained, that at the time of the discovery of this continent, their numbers were diminishing, and the same is observed at the present day of tribes as yet far removed from either direct or indirect influence of the white man.   However, we need not seek for hidden causes why those in contact with European blood should wither and eventually pass away, leaving no vestige behind them.

The gifts which the Pale-faces brought to the Children of the Forest have indeed been fatal ones, and by them the seeds of misery and death have been sown to a terrible extent.

I do not believe that at the time they first saw the vessels of the discoverers and their followers come over the Great Ocean, they were either a happy race or one of simple habits.   The life of fierce extremes which they were even then found to lead; the close acquaintance with all the extremities of war, disease, and famine, which even then they endured; the uncontrolled sway of violent passions; the degradation of their women, all tend positively to contradict the supposition that this might be or was the case.   Whatever may have been written, said, or sung, they were never the rivals of the Arcadians.   Their system of religious faith was, it is true, perhaps in itself, the purest that has anywhere been found among savages, and eminently distinguished them from their neighbours to the southward. Their faith did not, perhaps, like that of many heathen nations, aggravate and stimulate the force of their animal passions ; but it does not seem to have had the power to check and chasten them.

What the influence of their contact and intercourse with the European has been, we all know. Where he found them poor, he left them poorer ; where one scene of violence and vengeance has been seen, there many have been acted ; where he found one evil passion, he planted many ; where one fell disease had thinned their ranks, he brought those of his blood and land to reap a more abundant harvest. His very gifts were poison : selfish and inconsiderate in his kindness, he was very bitter in his revenge and anger : he excited the passions of the savage for his own purposes, and when it raged against him, he commenced the work of extermination. He then read that the day of the aboriginal inhabitant of the soil had come, and that the white man was destined to take the place of the red, and perhaps he divined well and truly ; but he had no right to presume upon it, or that he was to be the active instrument in forwarding that mysterious dispensation of God.

We read the history of the conquest of the provinces in the southern division of the Western Hemisphere and the Islands, and execrate the bloodthirstiness of the Spaniard, who exterminated whole tribes at once by the sword, under the banner of the blessed Cross ; and yet the conduct of the Pilgrim Fathers and their children towards the aborigines of the North is hardly less culpable or less execrable. Like the Spaniard, the Puritan warred under the banner of his faith, and considered the war as holy. No one who reads the history of these countries since their first settlement, can draw any other conclusion, than that the white man secretly, with his grasping hand, selfish policy, and want of faith, has been, in almost every case, directly or indirectly the cause of the horrors which he afterward rose openly to retaliate.   How often did he return evil for good ! That the wrath of the Indian, when excited, was terrible, his anger cruel, and his blows indiscriminate, falling almost always on the comparatively innocent ; and that defence, and perhaps retaliation, then became necessary, to save the country from repetitions of those fearful scenes of murder and torture which make the early settlements a marvel and a romance, is also to be allowed :—but the settlement of the various portions of America, with but few exceptions, is equally in the north and the south a foul blot upon Christendom.

But the evil is now done, and unfortunately irreparable, in that part of the continent of America in which I am now writing to you.   The Indian tribes have melted like snow from before the steady march of the white, and diminished in number and power, beaten back, they first gave way and retired beyond the Mountains, and then beyond the Great River and to the westward of the Great Lakes.   If you ask, where is that noble race whom Smith found in Virginia, the race of Powhatan, which then overspread that fair country between the Alleghany and the sea ?—where the powerful tribes of the East,—the posterity of Uncas or Philip,—the white man's friend or the white man's foe, —or the tribes that clustered round the base of the White Mountains?—the same answer suits all ; they are gone ! —and scanty remnants scattered here and there, hardly preserve their name.   We shall hear no more of the Indian patriot or the Indian statesman.   You seek for the scions of that famous confederacy, the Five Nations, the Romans of the West, as they have been termed. In the depth of a narrow wooded vale, retired from the flourishing settlements of the whites, in the western parts of the state of New-York, lingering on the spot where the Great Council-fire of the confederacy burnt for centuries, I have seen the handful of degenerate children who call themselves Onondagas.   A few of the Oneidas still occupy a small reservation in the same neighbourhood.   The sweet vale of the Mohawk has long ceased to call that tribe master. Queen Anne's Chapel, built for their especial use, never sees an Indian within its walls. A scattered remnant of their tribe and of their confederates has settled down in Upper Canada; and as to their powerful antagonists, the Delaware, with its branches, so celebrated for their oratory,—and the Shawanees, the tribe of Tecumseh, what a feeble and scattered remnant are now distinguished by those lofty names!

It is my conviction that the government of the United States, as well as the population of its settled districts, are very sincere in their desire to see justice done to the remnant of these tribes, and, as far as is consistent with the general welfare of the community, to favour and succour them. The main difficulty is, how and by what means these ends are to be attained. The measure now generally adopted, of buying their various lands and reservations, where surrounded by the population of the States, and principally those of the east of the Mississippi, has met with much condemnation from Europeans, especially from those who know the secret of these purchases. The only valid apology which can be made for it, is that of stern and absolute necessity. If the existence of that be proved, the policy may be defended, however many things may seem to cast doubt on the expediency or the justice of thus expatriating the wrecks of these tribes from their small heritage of the land of their forefathers; for though the land is virtually bought, and the tribe to a certain degree well remunerated, it is still expatriation. This plea I have, however unwillingly, been led at length to admit. The white man and the Indian cannot be near neighbours. They never will and never can amalgamate. Feuds, murders, disorders will spring up; mutual aggression among the dissolute and ignorant of both classes will give rise to yet greater evils. If the Indian turns his back upon the alternative of civilization, he must recede; and were it not even advantageous to the white, it would be mercy in the latter to

12

attempt by all lawful means to arrange matters in such a way as to avoid the possibility of collision.

Yet, granting that this policy is sound because imperious, no one can look upon the state of the Indian, struggling for existence on the frontier, without commiseration. He is perhaps removed from an impoverished country as far as the game is concerned, to one abounding in it, and of greater extent and richness of soil than that which he relinquishes. The annuity granted by government, the provision made for schools and agricultural instruction, would seem to place him in a more enviable situation, even though he were removed a thousand miles from the graves of his fathers. Yet here he is, if any thing, more exposed to oppression; from that portion of the white population with whom he is in contact being in general the most abandoned. And it is in this that the Indian system pursued by the government is yet defective. I would ask, are the majority of the agents appointed by government to live among the Indians,—to carry its benevolent designs into execution, just, honest, and good men—men of character and probity—above profiting by the defenceless state of the tribes, and superior to the temptations held out on every hand for self-aggrandizement? I think I might answer without fear of contradiction in the negative. The Indians are surrounded by bad men, as the hungry wolves of the desert surround a troop of horses. The government of the United States shows by its conduct to these agents that it does not put confidence in them; and the hard measure which it deals out to them is but a bad apology for much of the iniquity practised by them. The position of both Indian agent and Indian trader is one of overwhelming temptation to a man of lax principle.

As long as matters are so, and the Indian tribes are not put under the inspection of irreproachable men, this difficulty of essentially benefiting them, must be felt by the well-meaning and honest-hearted people of the older States. Men of character are sent out, it is true, from time to time, to see for themselves, and

report upon this or the other question ; but they seldom
know any thing of Indian affairs from personal experience ; and those that do, and the only men who can,
instruct them, are the very Indian agents and traders,
few of whom, for very evident reasons, are to be trusted.
Such are the great impediments in the way of obtaining
correct information of the real state of affairs, as those
best informed are for the most part inclined to be influenced by private views, and those best intentioned
least likely to arrive at the truth. The system con-
demns itself.

What check is there upon an unprincipled agent,
who knows that for a bottle of whiskey an Indian will
sign or say anything, and at the same time that his
testimony is not valid in a court of justice ?

As to the Missionaries on this frontier, my general
impression was, that they were worthy men ; rather
upright than sound in their views for the civilization
and moral improvement of the tribes among whom
they were sent to labour ; and, like many of their
brethren all over the world, far too weak handed and
deficient in worldly wisdom, to cope effectually with the
difficulties thrown in their way by the straggling but
powerful community of traders, agents, and adventurers
of every kind, with whom they must be associated in
their intercourse with the Indians. Their work must
be a work of faith and humble dependence on God, for
by their own strength and wisdom they will achieve
nothing. He can effect what men would pronounce
impossible. In the lawless, licentious conduct of most
of the nominal Christians connected with them, the
Indian finds sufficient excuse for not quitting the faith
of his fathers, as that proffered in exchange seems to
produce such evil fruit. But I must bring this long
letter to a close.

On the 6th of October we reached the Neosho, or
Grand River, a tributary of the Arkansas. We found
the great village of the band of Grey Hairs deserted
and despoiled of all its contents, as we had been given
to expect ; we paid a short visit to the small settlement

of Osage Indians, under the care of Mr. Riquois, the gentleman alluded to above, and then pushed on to the Saline.

This was an estate situated on the romantic bank of the Neosho, about fifty miles above Fort Gibson. It was the property of the Colonel, whose welcome home amid a crowd of Negroes, Indians of divers tribes and of both sexes, dogs, pigs, cats, turkies, horses, ducks, all looking fat and happy, was an extremely amusing sight.

We were his guests for a day or two, long enough to see that we were on a fine estate, producing but little surplus after feeding the biped and quadruped ' varmint' living upon it ; and to witness the coalition formed between the squadron of new dogs and the old retainers, who behaved with great urbanity and kindness to the new comers. We then proceeded, by way of Union, to the Western Creek Agency on the river Verdigris, not far distant from the fort.

LETTER XIII.

I MIGHT have mentioned in my last, that on our arrival at the Saline, the Commissioner and Mr. Irving had pushed forward in advance of us, to Fort Gibson, the former being anxious to reach his future head-quarters, to learn whether his coadjutors had found their way thither from the eastward. Both the Neosho, upon which the fort was situated, and the Verdigris at the agency, upon whose banks Pourtales and myself had halted at the close of my last, discharge themselves into the Arkansas within a few rods of one another, the posts mentioned above, being four or five miles from the points of junction, and in the line about six from each other.

The original idea of my comrade and myself had been to attach ourselves to one of the two great bands of the Osage tribe, the Grey Hairs or Clermont, and to accompany them on their autumnal hunt. This project was however eventually defeated, and you would hardly be interested by my going into the history of the disappointment, which, in truth, was a grievous one, especially to my companion. Both bands had already raised camp, and gone off to the westward, and we were glad to accept the invitation we received on our arrival at the agency, from our companions at the fort, to join them in overtaking, and subsequently accompanying, an armed expedition to the westward, which had been despatched a day or two previously in that direction, by the commander of the cantonment. An Indian runner had been sent after the body of rangers composing it, with orders to the officers to halt till the commissioner and his party should come up with them.

The intimation of this new plan was conveyed to us on the afternoon of our arrival at the agency, and as the next morning was appointed for departure, the interval was one of great hurry and bustle of preparation.

The excursion we were upon the eve of commencing, differed from that which we had but just concluded in many ways. It was to carry us beyond all human habitations, white or Indian, into a tract of country but imperfectly known even to our guides. It was out of the line of the usual Indian trails, and the luxury of a baggage-wagon was out of the question. The party in advance were all men inured to the semi-savage life of the backwoodsman, and carried their whole stock of conveniences and necessaries on their saddles : and as to ourselves, a few spare saddle-horses, and three or four beasts of burden for the transport of our tent, cooking apparatus, and little hoard of luxuries, were all that it was deemed advisable to be added to the train.

Of all our former company, the indespensable Tonish alone was retained ; the others having reached the point of their destination. None of the gallant steeds we had brought from St. Louis and Independence were

12*

thought in a condition to undertake this fresh campaign in their state of exhaustion, with the exception of those hitherto used for the wagons, and these were now pressed into the service as sumpter-horses, and furnished with pack-saddles.

So here was a grievous duty again : and fresh calls for the display of jockeyship and cunning. The worst was, that all the rogues about us, and they were many, knew that we were in a cleft-stick. They knew, as I have described elsewhere, that horses must be had, and as is usual in such cases, showed their sympathy by fleecing us without conscience. However, bargains were concluded, letters written and despatched on their long journey to our European friends—provisions bought and packed—the indispensable buck-skin leggins, moccasins, and hunting-shirts procured — the thousand and one odd jobs which always imperatively claim a man's attention when he has hardly time to turn himself, disposed of somehow or other—arms cleaned—ammunition looked to—balls and buckshot provided in sufficient quantity for a regular battle— horses shod—and saddle-bags stuffed to repletion. Besides our ordinary saddle-horses, we contrived to procure two excellent steeds for extraordinary service ; and as matters turned out, you will see how much we stood in need of them. In fine, imagine us ready just in time to join our two friends, who arrived from the fort at the hour appointed, and finally, about noon, October 10th, under the escort of an invalid lieutenant, and twelve or fourteen invalid rangers, setting forth with our beasts of burden in quest of the party some fifty or sixty miles in advance. Imagine us sleeping in the court yard of one of the frontier farms on the first night, passing through the Creek nation and by the very last white habitation at noon of the second day, and finally, relinquishing the hope of falling in with the Osages, bending our steps with our companions undauntedly toward the unknown desert region before us.

The setting sun! You may have remarked how

steadily for nearly the whole of this year we turned
our faces toward that glorious spectacle ;—how spring
found us day after day with our hopes and wishes
directed there at the hour of eve, while we listened to
the songs of the emigrant on the bosom of the sea ;
how evening after evening, we saw the purple and gold
of the summer sky reflected upon the vast liquid surface of the rivers of the New World ; and now, when
autumn was spreading its gorgeous hues over the forest
and prairie, we still pressed forward toward the glowing sky, and camped with our faces to the west.

Practice makes perfect, and by degrees the disorder
which almost always accompanies a hasty departure,
was succeeded by something like order in our train
and its details.

Every article, however ill adapted for packing and
transportation on the back of a horse, seemed after a
while to get accustomed to the position allotted it by the
sharp-witted Tonish and his coadjutors, of whom more
anon.

I recollect one exception, however, and that was an
odd boot, (a yet more melancholy spectacle than an
odd glove,) which was a complete eye-sore as it
dangled hour after hour from the crupper of one of the
pack-saddles. We were perfectly at a loss to know
what had become of its fellow for some time, till on
the arrival of the commissioner's new attaché as guide,
hunter, and interpreter, who had lagged in the rear,
we heard, that many miles back, he had descried a
Creek Indian with a moccasin on one foot, and my friend
Pourtales' fashionable boot on the other, very patiently
hunting about in the long grass for the fellow.

I have named the guide, Beatte, and as he will, perhaps, figure on divers occasions on my paper, you
shall here have his character. In consequence of the
arrangements made by one or other of the party, he
and another half-breed, named Antoine, had been
added to the number of personal attendants. In the
character of the latter, indolence seemed to be the prevailing feature. It was depicted in his heavy, sleepy,

dark eye; and the Indian blood evidently predominated over the French. He was willing and active
enough when excited, but it was no common occasion
that would incite him to action. For an hour together
he would stand at the camp-fire, with his cloak tightly
twisted round his body, his arms motionless within,
and gaze upon nothing with a fixed glance, in which
there was neither life nor speculation. In form, he
was an object of admiration to us all, and I suspect to
himself no less. His body and limbs were most symmetrically moulded. His bust was that of an Antinous.
Indeed, I may here observe, that the finest living
models of the human figure I ever saw, were among
the Indian half-breeds.

Beatte was the son of a French Creole, by a Quo-
paw mother. He was of medium height, and of a
light compact form and good features. His clothes,
poor as they might be in quality, always appeared
well draped on his person, and there was something in
his whole character and manner, which answered to
the picture my fancy paints of Robin Hood. Wayward and distant till he became attached to our
persons, we were all inclined to misjudge him at first;
but before we had been a week together in the wilderness we found his value. He was by far the best
hunter of the whole party engaged in the expedition.
The very reverse of Tonish, who used to spread the
tidings of his own going forth to the chase throughout
the camp, with huge predictions of extraordinary success, which were very rarely fulfilled; Beatte, seeing
that the horses were hobbled, and his services not in
immediate demand, took his rifle, stole forth quietly,
and seldom came back empty-handed. Further, he
was the only one in the whole company who had any
knowledge of the country, and his information and
guidance might in general be depended on; moreover
there was that feeling about him, that he would be true
to you in a strait, and stand by you either in a bear-
fight or an Indian skirmish; and that was not to be
undervalued. That he had met with rough adventures

enough in the course of his chequered existence was
proved by the state of his limbs and ribs, most of
which had been broken or dislocated again and again.
In short, when the time of parting came, we all looked
upon Beatte as a friend, and Tonish as a scaramouch.

The objects proposed by the expedition were to
penetrate into the country lying between the river
Arkansas, eighty or one hundred miles above the
Neosho, and the Great Canadian to the southward.
The idea had been entertained of reserving that part
of the country for the ulterior occupation of the tribes
on the point of removal from the southern states of the
Union, and for this purpose it was necessary to ascertain its real character. The course of the intermediate
streams, principally that of the Red Fork, and the
tributaries of the Great Canadian were but indifferently
known, few besides trappers and hunters having hitherto
visited their banks.

An ulterior project of reaching the Great Red River
by pursuing a southerly course after gaining the bank
of the Canadian was included, but you will find that
the expedition failed to accomplish this, from the lateness of the season and other causes.

On the evening of the third day after quitting the
Agency, as we carefully followed the trail of the party
in advance, chiefly through the wooded belt of country
a little north of the Arkansas, we came to the bank
of that river,—a mighty stream descending from the
highest summits of the Rocky Mountains, through salt
and grassy plains, upwards of two thousand miles, to
join the 'Father of Waters,' of which it forms the
largest tributary, with the exception of the Missouri.

We passed at the same hour an Osage encampment,
learning by the way that the Rangers had been seen
some miles ahead. Yet we were unable to come up
with them before night-fall; and had, in fine, to encamp
in an indifferent spot for that night. The following
morning, however, we joined them after a ride of an
hour, and found them snugly posted in a rich well-
timbered level, about two miles from the river. They

had halted here already two days, awaiting our announced approach, and here the officer in command of
our escort gave his charge up to his superior officer,
Captain B.

The body of men to which we were now attached,
formed a company of eighty Rangers in the pay of the
government, enlisted for the service of the frontier,
among the young backwoodsmen of Missouri and
Arkansas, for a given time; each providing, however,
his own horse, rifle, and clothing. Food and ammunition were furnished to them; the nature of the service being of the roughest, uniforms were dispensed
with, and each appeared garbed as his fancy or finances
dictated. Among them there was an amusing variety
of character, and I have a suspicion that, intermingled
with some very sober and worthy members of society,
allured to enlist by a desire to see the world, and to
lead a holiday kind of life away from their farms for a
twelvemonth, there was a very large sprinkling of
prodigal sons and ne'er-do-weels.

As aids to the Captain, who was an experienced
backwoodsman, two or three Lieutenants, of like
qualifications and credit, were added; and a medical
man,—the very reverse of our scientific querulous
companion in the former part of our tour,—being a
man of a thousand; of sound mind and body; and
moreover an excellent marksman, and fully accustomed
to the life of hap-hazard and adventure we were prose-
cuting. The men carried rations for a certain number
of days, after which it was expected that we should
come within the Buffalo-range, and amply provide
ourselves there with the necessary food.

The camp, on our arrival, formed a strange wild
scene. The hunters had been successful, and nine
deer were added to the stock of provisions. The bee-
hunters also had been on the alert, and eighteen bee-
trees were discovered, cut down, and rifled of their
hoard of sweets: besides, turkeys and smaller game
were plentiful in the vicinity of the camp,—so that
abundance reigned there.

Groups were seen on every hand, among the trampled thicket, and in the midst of the labyrinth of pea-vine, brush, green-briar, and other creepers, engaged in some chosen occupation; drying venison, preparing the skins, mending their accoutrements, firing at a mark, or casting balls; and, when night set in, the scene presented by the huge blazing watch-fires in the deep forest, was not the less striking and beautiful.

The reveille was sounded at early dawn, and by sunrise our long line put itself in motion, proceeding at a slow, even pace, through brake and bush, and over rocky hill and prairie. According to the usage of the country, we travelled in Indian file, one following the other, and never abreast, thus indicating our line of march by a narrow, deeply indented trail across the country. Our course was much to the north of west, and lay over a line of wooded hills, rough on the sides and summits with fragments of sandstone, and of considerable elevation above the deep bed of the river to our left. We left the Bald Hill, a notable saddle-shaped eminence, rising from an elevated plateau, about half a mile to the right; and about three o'clock in the afternoon, struck the Arkansas again. Its hue was here of a deep red, and the stream, apparently about half a mile in breadth, flowed with a rapid whirling current among shoals and sand-bars. On its long sweep of sandy beach, we noticed the track of innumerable elk, bears, turkeys, and racoons; and were glad to perceive that the flood of the preceding week was gradually subsiding. Our camp was pitched in a rich hollow in the forest, at a convenient distance from the river. Here we killed our first elk, besides other game.

It would not answer any purpose for me to sketch each succeeding day's proceedings, though I delight to retrace every step in fancy. However, the next day was too important in the history of our enterprise, not to claim a short notice. I have already alluded to the general purposes of the expedition. The more detailed orders received at the garrison, directed the

Captain to cross the Arkansas at or near its point of junction with the Red Fork, flowing from the south-ward, and then to ascend the valley of the latter river for a given distance.

As nothing was known of the ford, the attempt at crossing had been looked forward to with no small interest.

By calculating the distance already traversed, since we left the agency, up to the commencement of this day's march, it was surmised we must now be within a few leagues of the point of junction; but for a few hours we were obliged in proceeding, to keep wide of the river, over a range of wooded sandstone hills, in order to overcome the obstacle to a more direct course, which presented itself, in a very high rocky promon-tory. From the heights above it, however, we caught a view of the whole country for many miles round, including a glimpse of the river of which we were in search.

The Red Fork appeared worthy of its name, pour-ing down into the main river at our feet, a turbid bright red stream, broken by wide level sand-bars and mud-banks. We soon struck into an old Indian trail, and descending into the entangled jungle to the north of the promontory, gained the densely wooded bank of the Arkansas again. Here several halts were made for consultation, and after many trials as to the prac-ticability of effecting our passage, it was found that the river in the immediate vicinity of its tributary, was extremely turbid and deep, and it was therefore con-sidered advisable to ascend higher in search of a ford.

While we were breaking our way through the en-tangled brushwood, it happened that our approach roused a poor skunk from his noontide slumber under a fallen tree. His destruction was speedily effected by Tonish and Beatte, not however before it had avenged itself by filling the air with such a subtle and fetid odour as was almost beyond human endurance. Considerable wrath was excited among the more deli-cately-nosed portion of the party by this procedure, though the feeling was mingled with surprise on observing that after having been divested of its skin, the animal was appended to the saddle of Beatte as a welcome addition to his next supper. He was in a wayward humour, and while Tonish,—who usually arrogated to himself the credit of every valuable capture,—was exciting the appetite of my curious comrade with a descant upon its peculiar delicacy, he pushed forward to his place at the head of the line, without offering either explanation or apology. Some how or other, the skunk never made its appearance at table ; and upon inquiry it was ascertained, that in the midst of the bustle consequent upon the passage of the river, it had disappeared in a most unaccountable manner, and though hunted for by Beatte with the same eagerness as a cat will hunt for a mouse which may have escaped after having been long in her possession, was not to be found. We had a shrewd suspicion that our friend Irving, whose spite against the dead animal had been concentrated and uncompromising, knew more about the disappearance than he chose to publish. We never fairly brought him to his confession ; but from a sly twinkle of the eye, and restlessness about the muscles of the lips, whenever the subject was mentioned, I have no doubt but he was the delinquent, and that some day the truth will out. I may still mention that, as we all got considerably less refined, and more savage in our tastes, in a week or ten days' time this Indian delicacy was several times served up at our mess without raising any great disturbance.

After a farther advance of two or three miles with no inconsiderable toil, appearances being more favourable, another halt was proclaimed. The river was here about a quarter of a mile wide. Beatte made the essay, and it was seen that the passage might be effected with a swim of perhaps a dozen yards in the middle. As it was doubtful whether we should better ourselves by farther advance, the captain finally resolved to attempt the passage at this spot. The men were ordered to prepare rafts for their arms and baggage,

and to swim their horses as they might.   All the axes
were put in immediate requisition.   While the forest
was echoing to the first strokes of the axe ever heard
in this solitude, and all hands were busied with hurried
preparations for what threatened to be in the opinion
of the rangers a doubtful and laborious piece of service, Beatte, Tonish, and Antoine were occupied with
their own peculiar schemes and projects for the speedy
passage of our effects.   I might still smile at recollecting my own surprise, and that of divers of the rangers
in my vicinity, when, ten minutes after the resolution to
cross was announced, I scrambled through the brush
to the brink of the river, with my saddle and other accoutrements which I had been preparing for transportation, and descried a pile of our effects already on the
level sands of the opposite shore, while our three half
savages were to be seen swimming, whooping, and
yelling in mid-current round a buffalo skin which they
had quickly transformed into a canoe, by simply tying
up the ends, and putting light sticks athwart the opening, to make it keep its shape.   Into this clever make-
shift they continued to tumble every thing in turn---
saddles, pack-saddles, provisions, clothing, tent, and
guns, and, in fine, in six or seven crossings, brought all
dry to the opposite shore, crowning their labours
during the last two trips by seating the commissioner
and Mr. Irving in turn on the top of the load, and
landing them safe and sound on the right bank.

Meanwhile, with the exception of the captain and
the doctor, who were close at hand working doggedly upon their raft, we were left alone, for the news
having been brought of the discovery of a yet better
ford, half a mile higher up, all the rangers had repaired
thither ; thus Pourtales and myself, after seeing that
we could be of no assistance, and having confided
every superfluous article about us to the care of the
canoe party, jumped on the bare backs of our horses,
and followed their trail, eventually crossing, half
wading and half swimming, as others had done before
us.

The whole scene was highly picturesque, as you looked upon the river, gliding at the base of a range of high rocky hills, with the thick forests arrayed in the glorious hues of autumn, and saw the bright flame-coloured sands sprinkled by groups of horsemen and piles of baggage.

The day was altogether one of considerable excitement, and when, toward the close, we found ourselves snugly encamped among the trees in a most romantic dell, surrounded by precipitous rocks, which, from the abundant signs afforded of our having dislodged a number of those animals, we called the Bear's Glen, we felt both happy and thankful that this first difficulty had been fortunately overcome without serious detention or accident.

I remember strolling with my gun over the head of the hill to the left, as the sun went down, throwing his golden light over the valley of the Arkansas, and thinking our position one of uncommon beauty and romance. We seemed to be once more in a hilly region. To the north-west a deep dun smoke on the horizon betokened the burning prairies and the presence of the Indian in that quarter, while directly below me, in the twilight of the deep shaded glen, the camp-fires were gleaming red beneath their wreaths of smoke, and the voices of the rangers, and the bells of the horses, rose to the ear.

On calling the muster-roll after dark, all the human beings belonging to the party were present; but Mr. Irving's horse, one or two of our pack-horses, and a few others belonging to the rangers were missing; and as several of them were reported to have been descried in the dusk, floundering in the mud of a deep creek on the other side of the river, we were not without our fears for their safety. Whatever the morrow might betide, we knew that this day's labours were at an end, and soon terminated it by lying down on our bear-skins before the fire.

Beatte was up at early dawn, and over the river with Antoine. The former returned soon after sunrise with all the horses that were missing belonging to our mess. The latter, who had gone off in search of them in another direction, did not overtake us till the following morning. On returning to the Bear's Glen, with some of the rangers, from his fruitless quest after the horses, a few hours after we had evacuated it, it was found that the rightful possessors had begun to resume their old quarters, grumbling no doubt most heartily at the inconvenience they had been put to, to make way for such saucy and thankless intruders. Poor fellows! they were badly remunerated for the use of their lodgings, for two were straightway killed, and the laggards came up loaded with their venison.

They found us encamped in a little secluded peninsula, formed by a creek in the vicinity of the Red Fork. The stream as it strayed from one deep clear pool, over broken rock and tangled grass, to another within high banks, formed a kind of natural entrenchment for us.

From this point, a few of the party who were invalids, were allowed to retrace their steps to the Fort, from which we might now be about one hundred miles distant. From the banks of the Arkansas we had traversed a number of elevated ridges, partly open prairie, and partly covered with forest, from the crest of which we often surveyed a most extensive horizon.

Four deer and an elk having been killed the evening of our arrival, and large troops of the latter seen, it was proposed to rest a day here and hunt. So, what between our proportion of the bears' meat, and other venison, and abundance of turkeys and fresh provision brought in the following day,—messes No. 1 and No. 2 were plenteously supplied during the day of rest, (Oct. 17th) and the whole camp appeared like a kitchen. Man has been defined as a ' cooking animal,' and in that particular clearly distinct from any other on the face of the globe. There could be no doubt of our belonging to the race ; for continual trussing and spitting, drying and smoking, carving and cooking, was the order of the day of repose. We found that we all belonged to the hunter tribe, and that there was to be no medium between a feast and a fast.

My next shall give you some further sketch of the organization of our party, and details connected therewith.

———

LETTER XIV.

You will have supposed, without my having perhaps expressly mentioned it, that, when in camp, our trio, with the commissioner and our several attendants, formed a separate mess, having but little connection with the others, but such as friendly courtesy and our association as fellow-adventurers dictated.

From the moment the signal for encampment was given, to the bugle-call that gave notice of our morning departure, we were in fact as much *chez nous*, as though we had inhabited separate houses. We were dependant upon our own arrangements for comfort, and upon our success, or rather I should say upon that of our retainers, for our supplies of provisions, beyond those few necessaries, or luxuries if you will, that we contrived to carry with us. The captain and his officers formed also a mess apart, and ordinarily pitched their camp-fire a dozen yards or so from our own. The men were divided, according to friendship or fancy, into ten or a dozen parties, each having its own rations, and an equal share of the venison which the hunters, appointed in rotation, brought into camp.

You will also, perhaps, have understood, with regard to the Rangers, that, though in the pay of government, neither the officers, nor the men, were considered to belong to any class of regular troops; and that neither one nor the other had any great idea of military discipline.

To keep the file, when on march; never to leave the camp without express permission, and to obey the general orders, was all that the captain required : and considering this to have been the case, I am astonished at the almost unbroken good conduct of such a number of young men, brought together with no very definite idea of what it was to submit their will to that of a superior, or of the necessity which teaches men the value of discipline. As it was, we heard and saw nothing bordering on either insubordination or coercion. They were for the most part sons of substantial farmers and settlers, and some certainly accustomed from their earliest years to study the craft of a backwoodsman. Such was Ryan, a fine old man, who, out of love to the hunter's life, had joined the expedition and the messes of those far younger and less experienced than himself. He was a fine specimen of that race for which the frontier has been celebrated ever since Daniel Boone led the way across the mountains. He had begun to hunt and kill the deer, when yet so young that his father's rifle had to be supported upon his little shoulder by both hands ; when the paternal hunting-pocket hung far under his loins, and when he had to get upon a tree stump to ram the ball home.

A dozen of the men, perhaps, turned out really good hunters ; and, in the skilful use of the rifle, might do justice to the fame which has been earned by the backwoodsman.

The whole science of rifle-shooting, and the rifles in use in America, are so different from those of Europe, and of Switzerland and the Tyrol in particular, that you can hardly draw a comparison between the merits of the rival parties. The rifle of central Europe is a much heavier weapon, and carries a much heavier ball, —not unfrequently twenty to the pound. The grooving is deeper, and a greater degree of force necessary for the introduction of the ball. Skill in its use consists rather in hitting a man or an animal at three hundred paces, than in cutting the jugular vein with certainty at fifty feet. The American weapon is, perhaps, as long or longer, carrying generally a small ball of eighty, or of even one hundred to the pound. It admits the ball being sent home from the very muzzle by a mere rod ; and is further peculiar in there being no kind of attention paid to balancing the length and weight of the barrel by the size and make of the stock. Practice alone will teach you to hold it with ease to yourself. There is a great deal more coquetry displayed in the use of the American rifle ; and the nicety with which an object may be struck at fifty or a hundred feet by a knowing hand is undoubtedly extraordinary.

The Captain, the Doctor, and Ryan, were, perhaps, the best shots of the party. But still, a word of the Rangers. I have told you that the military duties were not severe. With the exception of the sentinels, of whom three or four were commonly posted round the camp, more for the sake of keeping up an air of discipline at this period of the expedition, than from any real necessity for such a precaution,—from the moment their horses were hobbled, and sent hopping into the adjoining forest, to the hour preceding departure, when they had to be sought for and brought into camp,—the men had their time to themselves. A large portion was spent in eating and sleeping, and the excitement incident to our position made some portion fly fast, yet sufficient remained upon their hands to render its occupation no easy matter. Books they had none ; they were neither botanists, nor humorists, nor admirers of the picturesque ; so when neither their horses, nor persons, nor accoutrements demanded further attention, they had little to do, you will think, but to lie on their backs, and look up at the sky, or at the burning logs. Far from it. We found before we had been a week in the camp, that the most decided appetite of barter, or as it was termed ' swopping,' had descended, or I should perhaps say, arisen among them ; and this increased to a perfect contagion. It was a never-failing source of amusement to the lookers-on, in messes No. 1, and No. 2, to see the daily metamorphoses that took place. Nothing but the actual person seemed to be exempt from the influence of swopping. Horses, sad-

dles, rifles, clothes of every kind, exchanged masters, and
you could never be certain of an individual till you
saw his face. There was a notable green blanket-coat
which was borne forth from the garrison on the back
of a man named Guess, whom I had hired, as orderly,
to take charge of my spare horse, and which, before
we reached the Fort on our return, had clothed the
shoulders of half the Rangers in succession.   Though
in general we were considered beyond the influence of
this epidemic, on one occasion I had it offered to me
by a Ranger, who took a fancy to my buckskin hunt-
ing-shirt, and wished to beguile me into a swop.—
Many tales reached our ears of the superior cunning
and calculation of divers among them ; but of these I
will only mention the case of one man who was continually swopping his horse, and on our return to Fort
Gibson, possessed the very animal he had started with,
and sixty dollars into the bargain. I need not indicate
from what part of the Union such a sly fox must have
come.   One or two of the older and steadier rangers
kept aloof out of the vortex, and among these Ryan,
and a comical old fellow, the butt of the troop, of the
name of Sawyer.   He was one of those strange mix-
tures of simplicity and shrewdness that you sometimes
meet with.   Dame nature seems every now and then
to turn out a few individuals made up of scraps and
leavings ; some as far as their physique is concerned,
others as to the intellect : and in the same manner as
you may have noted a man here and there whose
head, feet, and hands were evidently intended for a
personage of large dimensions, while the trunk might
be puny, disproportioned, and insignificant—in the
same manner the most inconsistent and incongruous
ingredients seem to have been thrown together to fashion the minds of certain individuals. Sawyer generally
asked for a furlough three times a day when in camp,
and was celebrated for losing himself, and spending
the night nobody knew where.   He was used as a
'cat's-paw' by the men, whenever they wished to pry
into the plans and designs of the officers.

As to ourselves, we had amusement and excitement enough without swopping. We had agreed from the outset, that as the three domestics had their hands full with the care of the general disposition of our affairs while in camp, and the charge of loading and unloading pack-horses, that each of us should continue to look to his own steed—unsaddling and hobbling him in the first instance, and when brought into camp the following morning, taking off the vile hobbles and preparing him for the start. There was no hardship in this, if I except unhobbling, as the knot with which the feet were strongly secured, during the course of a long night spent in hopping through the damp grass, became often hard as iron, and as wet as a sponge ; and many a time have I begun to lose my equanimity, and been on the point of using my knife, after five minutes were thrown away with alternate application of teeth and fingers, vainly attempting to unloose the Gordian tie. For the rest, all seemed to inspire pleasure ; and when we subsequently met in the gay saloons of the eastern cities, we often recalled those days of adventure and light-heartedness.

We had left the busy world to the eastward seething like a caldron with excitement. To the ordinary bustle and stir of a people straining with soul and body for the acquisition of wealth—that attendant upon the pending election of a President, and the presence of that fearful scourge, the cholera, which had just then reached the line of the western waters, was added. Here, alone, in the midst of the great wilderness, we moved day by day ; lay down at night, and rose in the morning in peace and quiet. We were like a vessel moored in a sheltered haven, within the breakers, and out of the reach of the tempest raging in the open sea. Those who have never moved out of the narrow sphere in which all is artificial ; where the possession of much makes the attainment of more an absolute necessity ; where luxuries appear to be necessaries ;—can hardly conceive, how little is in reality essential, not only for existence, but for contentment ; or what a pliant and easily moulded mind and body we possess. Get only over your prejudice and try, and there are thousands of so-called comforts that you can do without —and of things which you can do for yourself.

I look back with peculiar delight to our mode of life, and our intercourse with a few trusty friends, on these and our succeeding autumnal wanderings. Both were spent far away beyond the noise and bustle of the great highways of existence. Surely, without having experienced it, you can find excuse for my enthusiasm.

Our connection with the world being cut off, we enjoyed a perfect absence of annoyance from without. The year was too far advanced for insect plagues, at the same time that the season was so mild and genial that, with few exceptions, our tent was thrown aside as useless.

To quit one trampled and despoiled camp just when the morning light began to reveal its loss of beauty, and turning our faces toward the west with the assurance that, please God, though none could say where, we should find another place of repose in the day's decline in all its pristine loveliness ;—to hold our march hour after hour over the untrodden waste, or through the forest—now breaking our way through a thick grove, then breathing the free air of the open prairie, or the scented brake of mint and sumac—beguiling the hours in conversation, and losing sight of the monotony of the scenery presented for weeks to our view, in the excitement afforded by the constant lookout for game, or speculation upon the trails of the Indians now and then fallen in with—who they were—of what tribe—hostile or friendly—when they passed ;—to watch the fleet course of the startled deer over the undulating prairie—or to listen to the wailing cry of the cranes above our heads, descried like so many white specks floating in the blue ether; finally, to choose our new abode in the tall deep forest by the river side, or among those exquisite groups on the higher grounds, where the forest merges into the prairie, and forms landscapes teeming with all the charming varieties of

English park-scenery—was not all this delightful? And, when the little share of toil and care which fell to the lot of each alike was concluded; and the hours intervening before sunset, which each passed as he listed, were ended,—when each came dropping in from his walk or the chase, and the fire grew momentarily brighter and brighter, as, enjoying our hunters' repast, the twilight gloom settled down among the trees,—when the evening tale and sober mirth were prolonged, till each in turn stole to his chosen nook in the tall grass, or on the thick leaves which the autumnal forest shed—were not our pleasures equally simple and guileless?

The blessing of sound sleep seemed to be denied to none who needed it : and yet I delighted to wake in the stillness of the long night, and to rouse my spirit from its lethargy ; to open my eyes upon the deep blue sky, with its host of stars, over-head ; to glance upon the dying fires and sleeping camp; to muse upon the past and the present ; to raise my heart to heaven ; and, without taking care for the future, to bless God for a portion of those sweet and healthful thoughts which spring from a calm and contented spirit, and incite my soul to gratitude for this lull and calm in the midst of the heaving and restless sea of existence.

Previous to October 22d, when we crossed the Red Fork, having proceeded about eighty miles up the country on the left bank in a south-west direction, —our advance was rather broken, and the numbers of our company became diminished by divers among the Rangers having been obliged to return eastward, either through ill health or as bearers of despatches. Five or six of the horses belonging to the men had also taken it into their heads to hobble away from us, so that our line was often a very straggling one, and the laggards were more than once a whole day's journey in the rear.

The character of the country thus far had been more hilly than usual in these western regions.   Along the immediate banks of the river, rich alluvial bottoms were ordinarily met with ; but the greater part of the upper and open country was barren in the extreme ; nothing but a scanty soil covering the bright red sandstone which frequently protruded to the surface, and appeared strewed with pebbles of rich nodulous iron-ore.

For the first ten or twelve days of our march the horses had found a sufficiency of pasturage in the rich brakes of the lower ground, the pea-vine being still plentiful, and the grass green and sweet.   Deer were also numerous, and smaller game ; and moreover the men had been furnished with rations for a fortnight. At or before the expiration of that term, they confidently calculated upon reaching the buffalo-range, and there procuring the necessary provisions for the prosecution of the enterprise and subsequent return; so that upon our coming in contact with the herds of that animal, not only much of our anticipated gratification depended, but even the success of the expedition.

As we advanced, therefore, deeper into the country from the Arkansas, we looked out anxiously for some indications of our vicinity to the buffalo ; and to this object of constant speculation and attention, yet another was added, and that was 'Pawnee-sign.' The region into which we were now advancing might not unaptly be termed the Debateable Land of this part of the continent: an arena upon which parties of the hostile tribes of the east and the west continually scouted in pursuit of the buffalo and elk, which they accounted common property, and to earn their claim to the war-eagle's feather, the skunk-skin, and the necklace of grisly bears' claws of the warrior, by the bringing away the scalps of those whom they meet and can surprise.   Few years pass but blood is shed upon these deserts, and many a spot is marked by the scenes of Indian surprise and unprovoked murder, or by the still more fearful harvest of revenge and retaliation.   From the Osage, Creeks, and Cherokees, of course we had nothing to fear, however they might now and then shed each other's blood.   Their interests are too nearly involved with that of the Pale-face, for them to meditate further wrong than perhaps the theft of a stray horse. But with the Pawnee, who would appear to be the Arab ✓ of the West, whose hand is against every one, from their far settlements on the tributaries of the Missouri to the Great Red River,—and with the bands of the Comman- ches, who make incursions into the same plains from the Mexican border, the case was different. These tribes differ from those near the Mississippi in many res- pects ; and though, from their less frequent intercourse with Europeans, they are seldom found to be furnished with fire-arms, and are in so far less formidable, yet the excellence of their horses, the celerity of their move- ments, and their personal address and numbers, give them advantages which the others have not. In their roving existence north and south, as they follow the trail of the immense herds of buffalo in their annual migration, they are often found six or seven hundred miles from their villages ; and in seeking the one, you always run a chance of falling in with the other. It may occur to you, that even if we fell in with a horde of a few hundreds of them, a body of sixty armed men, under proper discipline, would have little to fear from their hostility ; yet, setting aside the danger of surprise, there were contingent circumstances, which, if not po- sitively as disagreeable and dangerous as losing a fight and coming immediately into their power, might even- tually prove nearly as bad. Such would be the loss of any number of our horses, the murder of the stragglers and hunters, when our very numbers would be against us rather than for us, especially at this advanced sea- son. So you may well imagine that our scouts did right to use their eyes, and that singular intelligence which is taught by a life of constant exposure to want and danger ; and that the higher we advanced up the country the more interest was attached to Indian trails, marks of Indian encampments, and any moving speck upon the vast rolling prairie around us.

As to the buffalo, our eagerness to fall in with him increased day by day. Its habits are well known, and I need hardly tell you that the vulgar name is a misno-

mer, as this animal differs in many essential points from
either the Italian or the African species of urus bearing it. The hump on the shoulders, the mane and beard,
and the form of the horns, which are short and sharp,
all distinguish the bison of America from the other
species, not to speak of anatomical distinctions. They
were now known to be moving from the north, whither
their vast herds had followed the genial growth of the
fresh grass, as it sprung up under one degree of latitude after another, and to be repairing to the southern
rivers and plains to seek their winter food.

Like the Indian, they too have had to forsake their
original domains and retire into the waste. Anciently,
they were known to have roamed over the western parts
of the State of New York.   At the time that the first
adventurers crossed the Alleghany, sixty years ago,
the rich forests and cane-brakes of Kentucky and Tennessee swarmed with them.   Now there is not one to
be found east of the Mississippi : and as man has penetrated, year by year, hundreds of miles to the westward, so the bison has fled his presence, and yearly
interposes a good hundred miles between its pathway
and the nearest settlements, in contradistinction to the
‘ white man's fly,’ as the Indian terms the bee, which is
said always to move in advance of the encroaching Pale-
face. A very few years back, and the bison might be met
with and killed in the centre of the Arkansas Terri
tory ; but we had now advanced a hundred miles beyond its remotest limit, and had not yet met with them.
Their jealousy of the approach of man is no safeguard
to them ; and their vast strength and fierceness when
attacked are of no avail against the perseverance and
means of annoyance of their numerous enemies.   The
Indians, the trapper, and the white hunter, kill thousands yearly.   The wolves hunt the straggling cows
and calves in packs.   Nearer the mountains the grisly-
bear fattens upon their flesh ; but as yet their numbers
appear undiminished and undiminishable.   Ten thousand in a single drove have frequently been seen
further west toward the head-waters of the Arkansas ;

and their trample and roaring, when pursued, is said to shake the earth long before they are seen, and to fill the air with a sound like distant thunder.

How it is, that an enterprising people like the Americans have not long ago domesticated this animal, and crossed the breed of European cattle, is to me a mystery. However frequently asserted, we never heard of a well-accredited instance of its being attempted successfully.

But to resume the history of our adventures and achievements :

Two days before we crossed the Red Fork, the recent signs of the bison, which had hitherto been very dubious, became more and more evident, frequent, and certain ; and at length the joyful report of a few bulls and wild horses having been actually seen, was brought into camp by some of the stragglers. Dung, bones, and innumerable hoof-marks, were first descried ; then hollow places in the plains, where the animals had wallowed ; then, tracts of many acres where thousands had trampled and crowded for years in their passage, allured by a spring or a salt-lick, appeared depressed far below the general level of the country. At the same time, Beatte proclaimed 'Pawnee-sign,' and for the first time, by way of precaution, the horses were tied up at night, and the sentinel began to find that he must not doze on his post, as he had hitherto done as a matter of course.

The following day, after traversing apparently interminable prairies, furrowed by the deep straight trails of the bison, which, with the tokens of mounted Indians having been on their traces, kept us on the '*qui vive*' all day, we collected our scattered party towards evening in a deep-wooded copse, and prepared to ford the adjoining river early the following morning ; passing the remaining hours of daylight in some kind of general preparation—cleaning our arms, melting balls, and listening with more than even usual indulgence to the egotistical rhapsodies of Tonish, which always ended with a huge indefinite promise for the future, couched in the words : ' *Ah, qu-qu-que vous verez !*'

It was amusing to see the effect of the life we were leading, and the company we were associated with, on the spirits of the most peaceable among us. There was the good, kind-hearted commissioner, whose career had never been stained up to the present time by act of violence to beast or bird, girding himself in his own quiet way for the expected rencontre with biped or quadruped savages, and breathing destruction to the innocent skunks and turkeys. There too was to be seen our friend Irving—the kindly impulse of whose nature is to love every living thing—ramming a couple of bullets home into a brace of old brass-barrelled pistols which had been furnished him from the armory at Fort Gibson, with a flourish of the ramrod, a compression of the lip, and a twinkle of the eye, which decidedly betokened mischief. As to my comrade, incited by the marvellous tales of Tonish, it was dangerous to hunt in a jungle with him, such was his anxiety to have a shot at the bison.

You may recollect I mentioned in a former letter, a certain double-barrelled fowling-piece which the commissioner had brought away from a government agent on the Missouri. It had kept us company ever since, going among us usually by the name of 'Uncle Sam,' such was the *soubriquet* given by the Americans to the General Government, from the usual initials U. S. or United States, affixed upon government property.

It was a piece of respectably ancient mould and fabric, about four inches across the breech, and two at the muzzle ; and, when its old-fashioned locks were at full-cock, looked sufficiently formidable, from the manner in which they appeared strained to the uttermost, lying down upon their backs previous to taking the spring. Hitherto, however, it had been the most innocent piece in the whole troop. At the time we got possession of it, it had been found to be in a most ridiculous state of repletion, being full of successive charges of powder and ball, and *vice versa*, nearly to the muzzle. Being the property of the commonwealth, nobody in particular had thought it his business to look after

it. Three weeks prior to the time I commemorate, it
had been put into my hands in order to decide what
was the matter with it ; as, in spite of every appearance
of being heavily loaded, it obstinately refused to go off.
I had found three buck-shot under the powder in one
barrel, and a roll of dogwood shavings and tow in
the chamber of the other. How they came there no
one could tell; but it appeared. that whoever had an
idle moment and nothing to occupy his fingers upon,
amused himself by ramming something or other down
into 'Uncle Sam.' Well, this evening a bright thought
struck the commissioner ; the piece was straightway
poked out from among the baggage, where he had
been accustomed to see it, projecting like a stern-chaser
over the crupper of old Gombo, one of the baggage
horses, and serious intentions were evidently entertained of using it against the buffalo or the Pawnees.
But to war against any living thing seemed to be quite
contrary to its principles. It was found again to be
heavily loaded, but again refused to go off. It was of
course without a ramrod. One of dogwood, and that
a crooked one, was manufactured for it by the patient
hands of the commissioner, which with great trouble
was inserted. It was yet with greater difficulty withdrawn, and a good hour was passed in attempting to
make it disgorge a mass of unknown contents. At
length, having been put into some kind of trim, it was
included in the sum of effective weapons in the field,
and you shall not fail to hear of 'Uncle Sam's' further
adventures.

Just before we descended to covert from the higher
grounds, we had seen a wild horse dashing across our
line of march. It was the first we had met with, but,
however its appearance seemed to excite general attention at the time, after getting to camp, no more was
thought of it. The breed of horses which are scattered in numbers over these plains, is a cross between
those introduced by the Spaniards and French, but
are, with single exceptions, rather a degenerate race
both in appearance and power.

According to his custom, Beatte, after seeing that his services could be dispensed with, disappeared, and shortly after dark returned, to the great surprise of all, with a wild horse in his lasso. He had dashed off on the trail of that we had seen; had crossed the Red Fork, and met both with horses and a troop of bison. He had run down one of the former in the dusk, noosed him, detained him while his comrades fled deeper into the wilderness, and succeeded in bringing him home in triumph, much to the astonishment of the rangers, by whom such a feat was hardly considered possible. The captive was a pretty cream-coloured animal, with flowing mane and tail, and a large full eye, beaming with terror and surprise, as well it might, at its unexpected loss of liberty, and introduction among the camp-fires to the scene of so much noise and bustle.

The next morning, when the bugle gave order to resume our Indian file, the ' desert-born' appeared in the midst of us, to begin his life of servitude. The lasso was still round his neck. His eye, naturally full of gentleness, dilated with terror whenever the fond hands of the bystanders approached him ; and this feeling seemed to be increased to agony, when the captor succeeded in securing a light burden on his back. But even to this sad alternative to perfect freedom, he yielded at last with a tolerably good grace, after a few last groans, and a roll on the ground. I believe that there was more than one amongst us who felt his sympathies strongly moved for the gentle creature, and heartily inclined to regret the capture.

Our passage of the Fork was made without delay or accident, in spite of the deep red mud which formed the bed of the river. We crossed on the trails of a large herd of bison, which seemed to have chosen the same ford, and now stood on Pawnee ground. The colour of this river I have already alluded to. The briny taste of its waters, as they poured down from a region abounding, not only in salt springs, but in masses of pure rock-salt, rendered it thoroughly unpotable.

Our direction was now to the southward, leaving the course of the river tending much more to the west than it had hitherto done. My next shall give you a condensed sketch of our proceedings to the close of the ensuing week, when we halted in the vicinity of the Great Canadian.

———

LETTER XV.

THE dark brown horizon which appeared before us as we emerged from the deep bed of the river, was known to be the Cross Timbers, a broad belt of dwarf oak forest, rarely interrupted by prairie, extending across the country, from the Red Fork to the Great Canadian, in the direction of North and South. Its mean breadth, by the report of the Indians, was twelve or fourteen miles, and it was now our object to cross it in a south-westerly direction. None of our party, I think, will ever forget that hilly stony region, with its almost impenetrable forest of the closest and harshest growth, whose low, rugged branches, black and hard as iron with the alternate extremes of frost and fire, cost us many a fierce scramble and struggle on our passage both to and from the Canadian.

During the greater part of the first day, while skirting the Cross Timbers, we appeared to be in the line of march of thousands of bison. The banks of the Red Fork were in many places perfectly broken down by their tracks, as, in long lines, one after the other, in Indian file, they had proceeded southward. From this time we continued to fall in with divers parties of the stragglers, all males. On the evening of this day, one circumstance broke in upon the monotony of our proceedings. We had pitched our camp. In doing this latterly, more attention had been paid to the choice of a defensible position. As was my cus-

tom after seeing my horse provided for, I was scouting over the country at some distance from the camp,
about an hour before sundown, when I met the captain returning in great haste.   He said he had reason
to believe that there were Indians in our neighbourhood, and urged my immediate return.   The alarm
soon spread, and the scene of confusion which ensued
was amusing enough, as, in hasty preparation for a
fight, the horse-bells were instantly muffled, fires ex-
tinguished, arms prepared, and the horses brought in
and resaddled.   An anxious uncertainty prevailed for
a few hours, till most of the stragglers came in ; and
it was believed, after comparing notes, that the captain and some of his own party had been dodging one
another in the misty haze, and thus the mistake had
arisen.   However, a night alarm ensued by a sentinel
shooting, as he said, at a wolf, and I believe the panic
was of some use, as it made all parties more watchful
and alert.

We were now employed for several days in struggling through the Cross Timbers.   At the same time
matters began to change with us rather for the worse.
The encampment became poorer and poorer, affording
neither pasture for the horses, nor even water, in any
great quantity, and the little we found was generally
bad.   We began to look after one of the thousands of
'sweet and curious brooks' which gush forth on the
Atlantic side of the Alleghany.   We found no more
deer.   The bison hitherto seen had been males only ;
and even when shot had been killed far from camp, so
that but little of the meat could be transported thither.
The supplies of fresh provision were therefore a little
irregular and uncertain.   Of course, the rations brought
from the garrison had long ago disappeared.   The
bears truly were plentiful and fat, from feeding upon
the rich harvest of acorns which covered the ground ;
but though as many as nine were seen in the vicinity of
one camp, they were a cowardly set, and never waited
to be killed ; but slunk away among the entangled
brushwood, till out of sight, and then shambled off

with their ungainly gallop, so that we had no chance of another feast of bear's venison. But the most serious matter after all, was the fact, that many of the horses began to fail. Mr. Irving's strong and handsome bay had sprained his shoulder before we crossed the Red Fork, and had been, of necessity, abandoned. One of my two steeds had been useless from indisposition for many days. Two or three of the Rangers' horses were irrecoverably lost, and among them, one, whose master, having taken a fancy to hunt wild horses, had the vexation to find himself thrown and abandoned by his steed, while the latter galloped off to the desert with the troop. In short, some of the party were already on foot, and others were speedily threatened with a like fate.

In the Cross Timbers themselves, no animal but the bear could find sustenance. They were, as I have before said, composed almost entirely of oak, of which I enumerated seven distinct species, besides varieties; from the diminutive pin-oak, bearing acorns at two years growth, to the large-cupped burr-oak. Properly speaking there was no undergrowth but a coarse grass. From this iron-bound region, we generally contrived to escape towards night-fall, and to seek for a resting-place in one of those spots of verdure in the valleys, where the fading green and yellow foliage of the cotton-wood poplar forming a pleasing contrast to the leafless oak, and held out promise of our obtaining the indispensable necessaries of wood and water.

In these little oases, we commonly found some remnant of the riches of autumn, and burying ourselves and our horses in the thicket, made our position as comfortable as we could.

Besides the above-mentioned poplar, together with hickory, walnut, and willows, and the black and honey-locust, we found a rich undergrowth of dogwood, persimmon, haws, vines with sweet and sour grapes, Chickasaw plums of various colours, sassafras, and abundance of green-brier or tear-blanket, as it is familiarly called—besides sumac, the delight of the bears at this season.

Such a camp we occupied on the evening of the twenty-fourth, and a beautiful one it was; we killed in its neighbourhood four buffalo bulls and twenty turkeys, a piece of good fortune which we knew how to profit by, and lighting our fires among the skeleton bowers remaining from a large Osage camp of the preceding year, we here spent a contented night, with the feeling, that our horses would get at least one night's good pasturage.

You will easily conceive, after the description I have given you of the Cross Timbers, that we always hailed the prospect of entering upon a tract of open prairie with delight.

It was something to breathe the pure air, and have before us one of the expanded views of the prairie, upon whose surface every object was a matter of curiosity and speculation. Their hue, it is true, at this late season, when the grass is dead, was one monotonous brown—but there were variations produced by the alternations of sun and shade, which were truly sublime and beautiful.

The morning after we left the deserted Osage camp, after two hours' most laborious struggle in the forest, we came unexpectedly in sight of the North Fork of the Canadian. The coup d'œil was one of the most peculiar I ever beheld. We saw before us a meadow of about four miles long by one in breadth, bounded towards the river by a gigantic grove of cotton-wood trees indicating the course of the river. To the right appeared a large troop of wild horses, and to the left, towards the lower end of the prairie, were seen the huge backs of a number of bison. Measures were immediately taken to encircle the horses, one division of the party proceeding up the prairie towards them, under shelter of the woods, and another, of which my companions and myself formed part, moving cautiously in a long line across towards the river. It was, however, useless to attempt to take them by surprise:

they were seen instantly to snuff the air, and burst off towards the river. Their passage was cut off in that direction, when turning southward they rushed at the top of their speed towards our scattered line, charged it unmindful of our shouts, of course broke through it, and were pursued by the whole party, pell-mell, towards the lower end of the plain ; scudding down with them, and for a moment entangled in the rout, I could not avoid keeping my eye upon the buffaloes, to see what they would decide upon doing. They seemed to have been taking a nap, for they lay very quiet in the long grass, till the tumult coming down from the upper part of the prairie was within half a mile of them : when, with more promptitude than I should have given them credit for, they appeared to have made up their minds that there was something more than ordinary in the wind, and gaining their legs, began to shamble off into the forest in such good earnest, that no one could get a shot at them. When the race was terminated by the horses gaining the wooded country, we found that two of their number had been captured ; one of the rangers having secured a fallen mare, while Tonish, mounted on my friend's racer, old Crop, had actually noosed a young foal ; an achievement which gave him a subject for self-praise and self-esteem, for the rest of the expedition. '*Ah ! qu-que je vous ai dit !*' reiterated the vainglorious Tonish !

On the 26th, we met a party of Osage warriors coming back from a predatory expedition against the Pawnees. Horse-stealing seemed to be more the object of their adventure than scalps. They gave us to understand that, as far as they knew, the Pawnees were at present more to the southward, in the vicinity of Red River ; intimating that having been unsuccessful in their buffalo hunt, they were suffering greatly from famine, to alleviate which they had fed upon many of their horses.

These thieving Osage warriors were fine looking men, and much persuasion was used to tempt them to turn back with us and be our guides, without success.

The reasons they gave for preferring to go back to their tribe, rather than repairing with us to hunt the bison on the Big Prairie, and get presents of tobacco, blankets, and vermilion, were sensible enough. They said if they did not return to their comrades, they would be forthwith supposed dead; their relations would then shave their heads; their squaws would remarry, the chiefs take possession of their gear, and all that would be a great misfortune. To this we had nothing to say; but gave them some tobacco, shook hands, grunted our adieu in Indian fashion, and saw them no more. They had directed us to bend our course more to the S. S. W. and to gain the source of the creek called the Grand Bayou, a tributary of the Great Canadian, which we did; and encamped early in a very low, damp piece of ground, just contriving to get our tent up, and our accoutrements under shelter, before the heavy rain which had long threatened, set in. Every thing seemed to bode a long continuance of it. The season had hitherto been most genial. It was at once decided by our chiefs to remain in our present position both this and the following day; to rest the horses, to send out scouts and hunters, and to arrange the plans of the party for the return. To that we were now imperatively urged to turn our thoughts. The horses wanted food more than rest; the pea-vine was dead; grass scarce, and likely to be more so, as we knew that the prairies were on fire between us and the garrison. As to pushing across the Great Canadian to the Red River, that was utterly out of the question.

It was supposed that we could not now be far from the former stream, and we confidently hoped that on the Big Prairie, on its northern bank, we should be enabled to lay in provisions for the return.

The evening and night of this first wet day, long as they were, were soon over; the former by din of hard eating and conversation within the shelter of our tent; and the latter by twelve hours' unbroken sleep, such as even a raccoon might have envied.

In the course of the evening we were vastly entertained by a visit from old Sawyer, who, by reason of his age, his willingness to give a helping hand to our half-breeds when needed, and the originality of his character, was licensed beyond his fellows.

The Rangers, as was natural, began to look to their officers for a decided change of plan, as their own common sense showed the impracticability of our proceeding much deeper into the country in the present advanced state of the season; and Sawyer was as usual pushed forward to sound the intentions of the Commissioner. Like most inordinately inquisitive people, he thought his best way was to be very open-hearted and communicative himself, and thereby to win us over to his own humour. He accordingly, without provocation, gave us the history of his whole life and former adventures:—how he had, after sowing his wild oats, been incited to turn a methodist, and remained such some time, till seeing, as he expressed it, 'the error of his way,' he had become shaking quaker, and so forth. The first change was assuredly better than the second. I am obliged to say, however, that all this expenditure of confidence elicited no sympathetic disclosures from our quiet friend the Commissioner, and Sawyer at length made a retreat to announce his discomfiture to his comrades.

The following day we opened our eyes and senses to the disagreeable certainty that we were to have yet another day of unceasing rain; and I assure you it was quite long enough, and dreary beyond any thing we had yet experienced.

Both Tonish and Beatte were sent out at an early hour in one direction, to reconnoitre the country, and to get provisions; and the Captain with a comrade set out in another with the same-purposes.

As hour stole lazily after hour, the Camp became more and more comfortless. To stir out of the tent was to get both wet and covered with mud. The fires burned without cheerfulness. The rivulet at our side became a turbid yellow torrent. The Rangers lay swopping under their blanket awnings, imitating, in the intervals, to divert ennui, the cry of the birds of the forest, the hooting of the owl, or the gobble of the turkey. Now and then a hasty stroke of the axe was heard, as one or other of their number stole out to get fresh fuel. The poor horses, instead of ranging far and wide from the Camp, as at an earlier part of the journey, with bells tinkling merrily as they tore down the succulent pea-vine, now drew near the fires, and stood nibbling and gnawing the bark of the trees. There was my poor Sorrel, with a clouded yellow eye, and a show of sharp ribs, suffering from a pleurisy—the very picture of misery!

As to the inhabitants of our tent,—we lay watching the preparations for breakfast like so many cats, and when ready, devoured it like so many tigers. Pourtales was unwell, having indulged largely in the luxuries of persimmons, sloes, skunks, and sour grapes, and refused both medicine and comfort. In the intervals of conversation, the Commisioner sat the very image of patience, and gave himself up to speculation. Mr. Irving dozed by fits and starts, or perused the only volume of which our camp library was composed; and between whiles, peeped out from the folds of the tent upon the groups around, scanning the individuals composing them with his own good-natured and humoursome eye.

As to your capricious correspondent, what between the use of pen and pencil, and to other modes of temporary occupation, the morning stole away quicker than could have been expected. I then, out of pure idleness, engaged in the praiseworthy operation of inquiry into the disposition of 'Uncle Sam,' as, after doing wonders these latter days,—wounding a dying bison, killing a turkey and a skunk, he was again reported on the sick list. And no wonder. By an overthrow he had been filled up to the very muzzle with mud; and after a good hour's work, I succeeded in extracting three inches of ramrod, and made him disgorge another load of ball, buck-shot, and wet powder.

It is hardly necessary to remark that the lateness of

the season, as well as our present mode of travelling, precluded my adding to those collections of plants and insects, which I had commenced at an earlier period, and found a source of so much interest and amusement. The only prizes now within my reach, were seeds, for the reception of which I kept a bag at my saddle bow; and crammed into it pell-mell all that came in my way, from those of the largest tree to that of the meanest grass.

As to insects, all now were mute: even the grass-hopper chirped no more,—the loquacious catydid had sung his last song,—the wood-bug was dead or asleep, and there was not even a musquito to sound his small horn in our sleepy ears.

Towards night-fall, the various scouts came drop-ing in, and at length Beatte and Tonish, loaded with real bison meat, of the superexcellence of which we had hitherto heard much, but had so far withheld our opinion; for it was not to be expected that the old pursy bull-beef, which Tonish had served up to us, was the best specimen, nor that we should sing the praises of the meat which we cou'd not masticate. But here we had the choice pieces, the hump and ribs of the fattest cows;—and into the bargain a hunter's tale of their having seen the Big Prairie, which, it appeared, was close at hand, covered with herds of thousands and thousands of bison and wild horses.

'*Ah! qu-qu-qu-que des bœufs sauvages! Ah! qu', qu-qu-vous verrez demain!*' screamed the delighted To-nish, as sharpening a stick for a spit, he set inconti-nently about preparing supper.

Had our pleasures not been consulted, necessity would have obliged us to break out from our cover the following morning, and move in search of another camp; as by this time the low jungle, in which the whole party had been lying, soaked with rain for the last forty hours, had become a perfect Slough of Des-pond, and not a blade of grass was left.

We therefore merrily took our departure, and defiled with our draggled train over the turbid stream, and up towards the higher country and the Big Prairie to the southward.

I promised you a sketch of a bison chase, and you shall now have one. I could not choose for description, the attack made by nearly the whole troop, upon seven old bulls, reposing peaceably in a swamp, at which, being a mile or two in their rear on the trail of a bear, I was not present:—nor even that on the banks of the North Fork, when, becoming entangled in a rout of wild horses, the objects of our greatest ambition got to covert, before any of the amateurs could fire a shot; but our hunt on the Big Prairie aforesaid, when we fairly overtook the rearguard of the migratory herd, affords me the desired opportunity.

It was about noon, (Oct. 29th,) when, at the head of the line, we got out of the wood, and saw before us the free and wide horizon of the prairie. A long day's journey was not in contemplation, as our main object was now to hunt and cure sufficient beef to support us on our return through a gameless country towards the Fort; and it was resolved to halt upon the first favourable spot upon the banks of one of the many tributary creeks of the Grand Bayou, arising on the Prairie, and flowing north, and there to pitch camp.

Consequently, after an hour's advance, the Commissioner, Washington Irving, Pourtales, and myself, accompanied by Beatte, agreed to draw off from the main body towards the Great Canadian, with a general idea of the quarter in which we should eventually find our companions and their camp.

We had not ridden many miles before we discovered divers groups of bison and wild horses, scattered at a greater or less distance over the wide undulating surface of the country. Beatte proposed that we should halt, while he attempted to noose a horse out of a group about two miles to the westward of us; and on the instant, laying his rifle across the saddle of the Commissioner's horse, he dashed off at a wild gallop, and soon neared the herd; when, after appearing and disappearing alternately in mad career, as they fled over the broken surface, both the pursuer and the pursued were finally lost sight of. We had m anwhile been moving quietly forward on his trail, when, coming to one of the hollows, filled with low bushes, frequent on the edges of the prairie, two old bison bulls issued from their covert and began to run up the opposite rise. This was too great a temptation for Washington Irving and Pourtales, who were a hundred feet in advance; and both, after a moment's hesitation, gallopped after them. My position was one of the most unenviable constraint, as though burning with desire to follow, I was withheld by a feeling of respect for the Commissioner, by whose side I was riding, and who, at the same time that he was no hunter, appeared burdened with Beatte's rifle in addition to 'Uncle Sam.' However, seeing my comrades disappear, my impatience got the better of my sense of decorum, and begging ten thousand pardons, I set spurs to my horse and dashed after them. I remember comforting myself with the hope that Beatte would return to him in a few minutes;— but, however excusable, had any harm come to our worthy friend in consequence of my desertion, I should never have forgiven myself.

In narrating the events of a battle or a hunt, every man is, to a certain degree, of necessity an egotist, for the simple reason that he knows perfectly well his own resolves and the part which he plays, and next to nothing about those of his comrades. So I must make the narrative of my own feelings and movements, the thread whereon to weave a notice of those of others.

A scamper of a mile over the broken surface of the plain brought me in contact with one of the bulls just mentioned, which had seemingly escaped pursuit by a sidelong course. It appeared probable that neither of my companions had as yet ventured near enough to take effectual aim; for though this powerful and terrible animal will put forth all his strength to escape the pursuit of man, yet, if brought to bay, or approached too near, he is greatly to be dreaded in the moment of savage ire and desperation; and if great caution be not

15*

used, by horse and rider, one or both may fall victims to their temerity, unskilfulness, or folly.

I am far, however, from wishing to magnify my courage above theirs—for to tell the honest truth, though my horse was both strong and generous, I had received many warnings about the possibility of his taking fright —as he had never before hunted the bison ; and besides this reason for caution, there was something in the immense shaggy head, mane, and beard of my game —the deep eye that gleamed like a coal of fire from beneath the curls, and his unwieldy bulk, that made me rein in, and rather follow than hunt him ;—nay, as often as, shambling on, he turned his head and glanced revengefully on me, I thought it might be more convevenient to be off, lest he might take it into that capacious head of his to hunt *me*. However, my blood was excited and I followed him, to watch the effect on the horse. who in fact showed that he entered into the chase with all his heart ; till the oison tumbled head over heels into a deep, red, muddy creek, and waddled through ; when I thought I might leave him without compromising my valour, comforting myself with the reflection, that after all done and said, bull-beef was very far from being palatable.

A second chase, which Pourtales and myself at first sustained in company, with laudable perseverance, in a hard run of some miles, ended alike unsuccessfully to both of us. The herd of nine bulls which we had followed, split into several small bands. My companion pursued those on the right, and I continued to gallop after a single bison which I had selected as the object of my attack. After a headlong chase up one swell and down another, over broken ground, and through hollows filled with water, and deep red clay, into which my unwieldy quarry precipitately plunged with such unhesitating goodwill, that I could not but imitate his example, however little I should have fancied it at another moment,—he led me into a deep marsh, where, spent and breathless, he was brought to bay, and turned upon me. Here we bothered one another a good deal by our several manœuvres for attack and defence, and though I did my best to kill him, I failed to do so. Two of my balls had struck him on the hind-quarters as he ran, but seemed only to act as a spur, for he merely gave his tail a flourish, glanced round at me, and scampered on. Unless you strike the animal at a given spot, below the hump and behind the shoulder, or on the spine, such is the toughness of the skin and the elasticity of the muscles, that the ball seems to be thrown away; and so all mine appeared to be. I was annoyed with my non-success thus far, and with the idea of the clumsy piece of butchery I was attempting; and in fine, extricating myself from the marsh, left him to his fate. Some time elapsed before I rejoined my two comrades, who had both hitherto been unsuccessful. Beatte had also returned from a fruitless chase. He had noosed a horse, but in some of the subsequent evolutions necessary to secure his prize, he had lost his hold on the lasso, and the animal gallopped off. At a later hour, we found he had been again in pursuit for the recovery of the lasso, which he had achieved, but at the expense of the poor animal's life. In attempting to 'crease' the animal, that is, to touch it with a ball on the back of the neck, which stuns it without materially injuring it, he did what many a hunter does in attempting that delicate operation—he shot it dead.

To follow the Commissioner was now his business; but, finding that we were bent on retrieving our fortunes, he directed our attention to a far more numerous herd of bison than we had yet seen. They were at such a distance on the prairie that they looked like a dotted line under the horizon; but nevertheless we determined to go in chase. We frequently laughed at a later day when we recalled the boyish eagerness and thirst for blood which certainly possessed the soberest and most peaceful amongst us as long as we were within the vicinity of the bison. To many, this would be unaccountable,—but all such I invite to a month's sojourn in the western wilderness, and an excursion into the Buffalo-range.

It must be recollected that none of us had been at the camp, and we had but a general idea of the position and course of the creek upon which it was in all probability to be found. We knew that it had been the intention of our companions to pitch it upon one of the streams rising on the Prairie, and running to the northward, while the Great Canadian lay about eight miles to the south of us. Fixing upon certain land-marks, and especially upon the particular aspect of the stream, by following which we hoped to come to our night-quarters, we turned our faces to the opposite point of the compass, and agreed to get if possible to the south of the herd, before we approached them, so that the probable direction of our chase to the north might bring us nearer to the camp, wherever it might be, rather than remove us from it. After a ride of some miles, we found ourselves in near proximity to the herd, and almost in the desired position, when two bulls at a distance from the rest took the alarm, and beginning to run, the whole body, which might consist of fifty head, got wind of us, and began to put themselves in motion.

The bison-bull has a most ludicrous movement in gallopping, owing to the great disproportion of the head and shoulders compared with the hind-quarters, but for all that he shuffles on at a considerable pace. The cow is much fleeter, and a horse must gallop well that keeps steadily up with her. The latter are generally killed for their meat. But to my tale. We had a fine dashing run of a mile before we neared them. It was my fortune to take the first chance for a shot, as, spurring my horse past an old overgrown bull panting in the rear, I approached the centre of the herd, and came within a proper distance of an animal, bringing it to the ground by a ball which broke the spine. There is no necessity for me to determine exactly how far my good fortune preponderated over my skill; as I agree, that to aim with precision at a time when both you and your quarry are gallopping for your lives is not the easiest matter; however, as I obtained a certain degree of credit in the west, for having killed a bison in true

Indian style, I wish to keep the same with you. **My** comrades were brought to a momentary halt at the fall of the animal, but recollecting themselves, spurred forward after the flying troop. A mile further, Mr. Irving had his short-lived hunting mania satisfied, as a ball from his gun brought down a second of the herd; and halting as was natural by his game, Pourtales was then left alone in chase, which he continued with undaunted perseverance.

I had alighted to despatch the first, and to possess myself of the usual trophies, the principal of which is the tongue. To the trample and rush of the chase, a dead silence had succeeded, and I was occupied in my labours, when a slight yelp drew my attention, and, raising my eyes, I saw at a few hundred feet distance, the head of a grey wolf pushed cautiously upwards through the grass. This apparition was followed in the course of a quarter of an hour by as many as half a dozen of a similar character, appearing, as though by magic, on the verge of a circle which they formed around me; till, having secured my trophy, and being convinced that assistance from the camp was out of the question, and that I must leave my prey where it had fallen, I rode off. I then could see them stealing forward cautiously to their meal. The hunter is the wolf's and vulture's provider on these great plains; and they know it, and follow his trail on the Buffalo-range, with the certainty of having their share of the spoil.

After rejoining Mr. Irving, whom I found standing sentinel over his spoil, we did not immediately recollect that the early twilight of a dull autumnal day was drawing on, and that we had still to find our way to the camp. But where was Pourtales? Before us were the deeply indented tracks of the herd, but they and their solitary pursuer had long ago vanished over the remotest swell of the horizon. We waited and waited, and conjectured, till we dared wait no longer; and then, having looked carefully around us, and recognised some of our land-marks, we began to move slowly northward; pausing often to scan the horizon, and ascending each elevation to look out for the two objects of interest, our camp and our young friend.

We did not find the former without very considerable difficulty, about seven miles from the place where our bison had fallen, and that long after the twilight had deepened into night. Here we found the Commissioner safe and sound; but, contrary to our firm expectation, Pourtales was absent, and had neither been heard nor seen by any of the hunting parties. The bugle was sounded again and again, guns fired from time to time, and larger fires than ordinary kept up, all without success; till tired with conjecture, and knowing that no effort of ours could avail anything till day-light, we were constrained to give up all hopes of seeing him for that night.

The day's hunt had been successful on every hand, and including our own spoil, we counted ten or eleven bison killed. Abundance of meat had been brought into camp,—sufficient, indeed, to last the whole company for a month if properly cured and stored,—and upon the Prairie lay remaining masses over which the wolves were holding their stormy jubilee. One or two of the huge animals had been killed within half a mile of the camp, and a large number of these depredators seemed to have been congregated to the feast. Such a hubbub of detestable sounds as filled our ears, that and the following night, I think I never heard. It was now a faint melancholy sound; and then the whole pack would break out into full cry. You could distinguish the sharp yell of the prairie-wolf rising over the long-continued howl of the large grey species, as they fed, and snarled, and fought together through the long dark night. I remember it well, for the absence of my companion hung heavy on me, and prevented much sleep; and as Beatte and I sat over the fire in the dead of the night, musing and planning for the morrow, that melancholy concert sounded dolefully in my ears.

LETTER XVI.

THERE were three ways of accounting for the disappearance of my friend. The first, and the most probable was, that he had pursued the herd without thought or attention to direction or distance, or the approach of evening, and had eventually been unable to find the creek upon which we lay. No one could wonder at this, as the commencement of one creek on the upper lands was hardly to be distinguished from another, and you will recollect that none of us had been at the camp previous to the chase. The second surmise was, that he had been turned upon and gored by one or other of the herd; and the third, that he had been fallen in with by some roving band of Indians. However, our duty was clear, and as soon as it was day, a party was in readiness to go on the scout, consisting of Mr. Irving and myself, twelve of the best Rangers, and our three domestics. The general orders in camp were: that the men should employ themselves in drying sufficient beef to last them for eight or ten days, and that none of them should hunt to the south or east, lest their trails might be an embarrassment to us in the pursuit of our object. We had no difficulty in leading our companions to that part of the country which had been the scenes of our chase, as we had fixed upon sure landmarks; nor yet in putting them upon the trail,—as there lay the bison over which the wolves and vultures were still quarrelling; nor did we meet any great interruption in following the track of the animals for a few miles, as the soil was soft, and it was seen that the marks of a horse's hoofs bore them faithful company.

We had proceeded perhaps half an hour in this manner to the south-east, when the appearance of a number of bison in full gallop, over a distant swell of the Prairie, brought us to a stand.

' *Qu-qu-qu'il est là*,' exclaimed Tonish, whose real zeal and anxiety on this occasion made us forgive him many of his peccadilloes,—and so we all thought, when a human figure mounted and in full career appeared swiftly passing and vanishing in pursuit. But when a second figure immediately followed, the general impression with us all was, that they were Indians, and that idea linking itself with the fate of our companion, with one impulse we set off in a mad gallop across the country towards the point where they had been seen. We soon crossed their trail; became satisfied at once that they could not be the Pawnees at any rate, as the horses were evidently shod; and after following the track a short distance, found in a hollow two of the rangers, who, by disobeying orders, had given us this unnecessary panic. We had now to detect the real trail again, and half an hour was lost in doing it.

By following it further, we shortly after came to the place where it was evident that the object of our search had given up the chase, as the deeply-indented hoof-marks of the herd had wheeled off to the northward, and the solitary footsteps of the hunter were seen to diverge south. Now the greatest care was necessary, and our anxiety was proportionably great. The trail continued good, leading us towards the Canadian, till we came upon hard stony ground, and the country gradually declined to the bed of a creek running due south towards the river. For an hour longer the search continued with increasing interest and anxiety. Our comrade seemed now to have wandered to and fro on the swell, and then down in the hollow among the thickets. We could almost divine the thoughts of the rider from the appearance of the trail. Here he was undecided, and stood to look around him; and there got a bright idea, and trotted briskly on. Sometimes the marks were altogether lost from the nature of the ground; and then our lynx-eyed half-breeds would find it again, by the mere depression of a blade of grass, or a small pebble uprooted from the soil, or a scratch upon the stones.

We had seen game enough during the morning,— bison, horses, antelopes, and deer; but having a superior chase in view, had passed them all by. However, about noon, a herd of deer, led by a noble buck, rose so near us, that Beatte could not withhold a shot. The report of his piece was followed by a distant halloo.— No object appearing in sight, each spurred his horse in the direction from which the sound came to his ears, and an instant after we saw our lost comrade galloping towards us; I need not tell you that the meeting was a joyous one, and that none could feel it in a greater degree than myself.

His tale was a simple and straight-forward one. The fall of the second bison had given him the spur, and he followed the herd, and bombarded them till he had no ammunition left. He then began to think of rejoining us, or at least of finding the camp. As had been surmised, he had been deceived by the similarity of the different creeks, and had taken one leading to the wrong point of the compass. Night came on; he became convinced he was lost, and, after divers wanderings to and fro on the broken ground, in the bushes about the hollow, and in the creek, he wisely resolved not to add to his own fatigue, and to our difficulties in trailing him, by further struggles. He therefore fixed upon a large tree within sight of the place where we eventually met, dismounted, tied the forelegs of his horse together with a handkerchief, and let him go loose to shift for himself. A fire he could not make, so he climbed up with the saddle into a commodious fork of the tree, succeeded in making himself a safe and easy seat, and, in spite of appetite, cold, and a serenade of wolves, contrived, by his own account, to get ten hours' sound sleep. The early hours of this day had been passed in comparative tranquillity of mind, as he never doubted but we should be on his trail, and therefore did not move to any great distance from his night quarters. As noon approached, and he had seen nothing of us, I believe some anxiety began to creep into his mind, when the shot was heard, and his rescue from his hungry and anxious position followed as related. He deserved and got great credit for his good sense and philosophy.

Our return to the camp was a matter of course. The Grand Canadian lay about three miles south, and some of us made a circuit in returning towards its banks. It is a powerful stream, and by far the longest tributary of the Arkansas. At this point it is surrounded on both sides by open prairies, and bounded by high sand-hills, from the top of which a large extent of its valley was to be seen, with groups of bison and wild horses scattered over it. This part of the country, as you will have gathered, still abounds in game. A small group of goats or antelopes was pointed out to me, but I was unable to approach them to give their figure or appearance with any distinctness. Large flights of starlings were everywhere seen, and numerous bands of snow-white cranes.

But, as an object of natural history, nothing diverted us more than a part of the smooth prairies near our camp, where, for the space of many acres, the surface was marked by the mounds raised by a strange little animal, vulgarly and absurdly called the prairie-dog.* They are a species of marmot, of small size, rarely measuring more than fifteen or twenty inches from the top of their nose to the extremity of the tail, with a large head, short ears, and longish body. Like the beaver, they appear to be republicans, living in large communities, in burrows spread under a wide extent of prairie. The sod within their territories was everywhere well shaven and dry, and had all the appearance of being well trodden. The opening to each burrow was seen at the top of a little flattened mound of the earth, removed in making the necessary subterraneous excavations. In these they are said to live in families. They were very shy and difficult of approach for a man on foot, while, at the same time, a horseman could ride in among them without giving half the alarm ; which was attributed to their being accustomed to the presence of the wild horses of the prairie.

It was amusing to watch their sprightly movements from a distance, and the cautious manner in which they would, on ascending from their burrows, raise them-

* Arctomys Ludoviciana.

selves upon their hindlegs like a squirrel, and make a long neck, to see if the coast was clear. If they noticed distant danger, they uttered a sharp and singular bark, and never failed to make good their retreat. I noticed that they were very apt to fall foul of each other, and squabble and wrangle together like some of their republican neighbours more to the eastward.

Their burrows, however, serve for places of retreat to others besides themselves. The burrowing-owl, a distinct species, is frequently found in them, and the rattlesnake and badger also. Our friend Irving threw light upon this singular fact, by shrewdly surmising that these strange gentry were probably the ambassadors and plenipotentiaries of foreign powers at the seat of the republic; and I believe you will hardly find a more plausible one.

Our camp was that night once more a scene of good-humour, contentment, and joyous pastime. Tonish had crowned the success of the day, by capturing another foal; and, in the best humour with himself, put forth all his cunning in the preparation of sundry delicacies, to the enjoyment of which no one had as good a right as Pourtales, after the preceding day's fast and redundant exercise. Though the barking, howling, and yelping of the wolves seemed to be yet greater on this second night of their feast than the preceding, no one complained of being disturbed by it.

The sun rose bright and clear for the season on the following day; and shortly after, the turkeys and quails, whose call from the edge of the forest would have allured us to go after them at any other period of our tour, had returned to covert; and as the morning advanced, preparations were made for a remove from our resting place. It was the last day of October, and we were now to set out on our return home. Our actual distance from the fort was not known; and, in fact, we found subsequently that we both had farther to go, and more to go through, than we expected—in good truth, that the roughest part of our expedition was yet before us. I shall compress the history of the following eight days' uninterrupted march to the **N. N. E.** The greater part of the first four we were employed in breaking a painful pathway with many a tear, scratch, and grumble, through the **Cross Timbers.** Before we reached the vicinity of the Arkansas River we had to recross the Grand Bayou, though much lower down than before,—the North Fork, and the Deep Creek, which seems to identify itself with the Little North Fork of the Canadian. It was by far the most serious impediment in our course, as its great depth and swiftness precluded all idea of fording. With a few hours' delay, however, this obstacle was also overcome;—the horses were swam across, and a temporary bridge contrived by felling two gigantic trees on either side, in such a manner, that when they fell across the stream, their top branches interlocked upon, and below the surface; so that you might, with a little care, scramble along the trunk, and from the boughs of the one into the other.

Between the two last-mentioned streams, we struck upon a good Indian trail known to Beatte; and two days before we actually arrived upon the Arkansas, we gained the edge of the hilly country, and came to a sudden break, whence we gained a view of boundless expanse over the half-burned and defaced prairies for forty or fifty miles towards the great river.

At this time our appearance was that of a discomfited host. Divers of the horses were irrecoverably lost, and the greater part of the rangers were on foot, their steeds being unable to carry them. In fact, the poor animals had nothing to eat; the grass was dead or burnt, and we met with no cane before we reached the Arkansas. Added to this, many of the men, with whom it was always a feast or a fast, had proved themselves improvident to the last degree. Some had dried no meat at the Big Prairie, trusting to find abundance for their daily consumption; others had even, as we heard, thrown away their provisions the first day of our return, to avoid the trouble of carrying it, with the same false expectation.

But the fact was, that from the day after we left the vicinity of the Great Canadian, we saw no more bison, turkeys were far from plentiful, and deer became extremely scarce; and I believe that if no absolute hunger was the consequence, there was sufficient scarcity in the camp to make the general situation far from enviable.

Our mess was also rather upon short commons, and at our last encampment in a small forest, through which a hurricane had passed and levelled many a noble tree, about twenty miles from the Arkansas, we too congratulated one another that it was our last. Our small stock of flour, sugar, and salt, was all exhausted; the bundle of ' *solidago odora*,' which we had made use of as tea, had long been expended. Two of our packhorses, Old Gombo and his companion, had been left to their fate. Pourtales' crop, Mr. Irving's generous bay, and my own gallant hunter, had each in turn been left behind through sheer necessity, and the horses which still accompanied us were so emaciated, that, at last, we could not think of riding them. As to our personal appearance, though we all enjoyed excellent health, our wardrobe had reached the lowest degree of poverty, and had I patience to describe how men of dignity and worship like ourselves were attired in each particular, I have no doubt your surprise would be excited. The commissioner's dignity was completely shrouded in a common soldier's great-coat and pantaloons. Mr. Irving was clad in a suit of shirt armour, or, to speak plainly, wore a strong holland shirt over his surtout; and one tail of the latter had been left in the embraces of the Cross Timbers. Certain of Pourtales' integuments fluttered in the wind; and as to myself, though cased in buck-skin from head to foot, there were too many signs of wear and tear in my vestments to allow me any degree of self-congratulation over my fellows.

The weather, too, had given tokens of change and of the approach of the southern winter; and as we lay round our fires at night, we heard the whistling pinions of innumerable geese and ducks, winging their way

16*

from the north to a more genial climate. The beauty of the year had indeed passed away.

Thus the sight of the first frontier 'clearing' on the Arkansas, about six miles above the Western Creek Agency, was cheering to both animals and men. We reached it about noon on the 10th of November. The Rangers and their officers resolved to proceed no farther, but commenced a fearful slaughter among the pigs, hens, and geese, with which they as usual found the log-hut of the backwoodsman surrounded; while their poor jaded horses were regaled with the first good feed they had had for many a long day. Our party, however, determined to push on to the Agency—passing the river in a canoe, and swimming our horses; and at sundown reached the Verdigris, after exactly a month's absence, during which we had made a circuit of about four hundred miles.

We were welcomed to the luxuries of maize-bread, sugar, salt, and log-huts; and to as much intelligence with regard to the great world from which we had been for a short period so completely cut off, as could be afforded by those dwelling so far from the scene of important events.

LETTER XVII.

THE object of the expedition, as far as it had extended, had been in one respect accomplished, in that the character of the country between the two great rivers had been ascertained, and found to be such as to preclude all idea of settling the eastern Indians upon it. As you may have gathered, with the exception of the rich alluvial lands of the Arkansas, and a few strips of a like character along the tributary streams, the whole district we had passed over was in fact a desert, with an ungrateful soil and stinted vegetation. The rock, wherever seen, appeared under the form of a loose friable sandstone, loaded with iron. Both the soil and the waters were generally vermilion in colour, and the latter so salt, as to be unpotable in time of flood. There is reason to believe that this is the character of the country for yet hundreds of miles to the westward.

Divers proceedings and arrangements followed our return to this outpost of civilization. Our retainers were dismissed. Indians were sent after the stray horses, and we had the pleasure to see most of them brought in after a few days' delay, and sent to live in cane and clover like their fellows. The commissioner and Mr. Irving repaired to the fort on the Neosho, six miles east of the agency. It forms an open square, surrounded by a strong log-barricade, on the high bank of the river, with two block-houses at opposite angles, and contains the usual barracks, storehouses, and officers' quarters;—many other buildings, belonging to the government, or private adventurers, lying under the protection of its guns. Circumstances made Pourtales and myself fix our quarters on the Verdigris, but frequent visits to the garrison were always a source of pleasure, from the agreeable society we there met with among the officers, many of whom had their families with them. We now heard of the dire visit of the cholera throughout the West, of the great distress it had caused on board the numerous steamboats, and more especially of the ravages made by the simultaneous appearance of both this mysterious pestilence and the yellow fever at New-Orleans; besides divers items of intelligence, domestic, foreign, and political, which, though old enough, were all new to us.

Two days after our return, a small steamboat arrived at the fort with stores, and we were sorry to see our friend and companion, Washington Irving, resolve to take advantage of it to commence his return to the East; the more so, as we were obliged, from divers reasons, to delay our departure for a fortnight.

The commissioner, finding that his two coadjutors had not yet arrived, took up his quarters for the winter

at the fort, together with Tonish, who was now taken
into his particular service, as head cook, valet de cham-
bre, master of the horse, and of course as *grand veneur*.
To aid him in the latter capacity, 'Uncle Sam' was
given into his special keeping.   The morning after our
arrival at the Verdigris, this veracious personage had
made the inhabitants of the little assemblage of log-huts
aware of his being in a state of very grievous mental
or physical distress, by uttering the most piteous cries
and ejaculations,—calling to horse and jumping about
like one distracted, while he vociferously called on his
comrade Beatte for assistance.   The words which he
sung to this most unaccountable solo were, as far as we
could understand—'*Ah! qu-que j'ai perdu ma viande!
malheureux que je suis! ma viande de bœuf sauvage!*'
The upshot was, that he professed to have lost a small
parcel of dried bison meat, which he had guarded with
uncommon care during our hungry retreat, as an acceptable gift to his two patrons, the colonel at the Agency,
and the commandant at Fort Gibson, to both of whom
it seems he had, in his usual braggart strain, made a
gratuitous promise at the moment of starting a month
before.   He was with great difficulty consoled, and prevented getting on horseback to ride back fifty or sixty
miles to seek it.   His very natural and very amiable
disappointment was sympathized with; and having been
gradually reconciled to the unavoidable and most unin-
tentional failure of his sacred promise, the sorrowful
Tonish proceeded with an air of painful resignation
with his master to the fort; when lo! on following him
there the day after, the truth comes out.   All the while
that Tonish was acting the tragic scene just described,
the meat in question was to his certain knowledge
stowed safely in the centre of the bundle which con-
tained his worldly effects, and was safely braced on the
crupper of his horse.   The simple fact was, Tonish had
eaten the greater part of the intended gift, and knowing
that what remained would not bear division between
his two patrons, he took this mode of satisfying the

colonel at the Verdigris, while he got the credit of keeping his promise to the colonel at the Neosho.

I forget whether it was precisely at this period of our intercourse that he got my companion to indite a letter for him to his lonely partner in the village of Florissant, every sentence of which began in his terse and characteristic manner, thus—' *Dis, qu-que je suis bien ! Que j'espère qu'elle ma femme se porte bien—que les enfans se portent tous bien, et que tout le monde se porte bien. Dis, que j'en ai tué beaucoup de gibier—de daims, et infiniment de bœufs sauvages !' &c.* This singular personage continued to be a study for me as long as we were in the neighbourhood. He has been hitherto described in the wilds as pert, noisy, active, and slashing. He now became an altered man. He got a fit of the horribles and rheumatism, both the fruits, as he said, of sleeping in a house. He went about wrapped up in an old gray top-coat, with the collar hoisted high over his ears, and lost both his appetite and spirits. Even his extraordinary success in shooting pigeons and prairie-hens with 'Uncle Sam,' seemed to have no power to nerve his tongue, or to re-open that mine of self-esteem and applause, which lay covered up in some corner of his brain. In the midst of plenty, he was longing after the peculiar dainties of the prairies ; and the last trait I have upon record concerning him at this time, was, his great and exceeding affection for a skunk which lived under the flooring of the ruinous log-hut, where he carried on his culinary processes. I detected him feeding it faithfully, morning, noon, and night ; explaining, however, his reasons to me aside for so doing, by saying—' *Qu-qu-qu'il devient gras ! alors je le mange !'* So much for the purity of Tonish's affections.

The Rangers went into quarters in a rich and retired nook of the shady vale of the Neosho, about six miles above the Fort, where they built themselves huts, and had, doubtless, during the course of the winter months, time enough to swop at their leisure. Two other companies, one commanded by a son of Daniel Boone, arrived shortly after, and went into similar quarters nearer the Fort, to be in readiness for an expedition, which it was proposed to send out in far greater force in the early spring towards the Red River and the Pawnee country, so that the little garrison to which they were attached, and considered as out-pensioners, now mustered eight hundred men. Doubts were entertained by many even at that time, as to this description of troops being of any real utility, or calculated to render effective service ; and these were strengthened by the experience gained the following year, with which we subsequently became acquainted. The government seems ultimately to have come to the same conclusion. They were disbanded the following summer, and a regiment of dragoons, subject to severe military discipline, organized for the frontier service. Of their adventures I know nothing, yet should be inclined to doubt whether at any season of the year, or however organized, a large body of men could maintain itself in the wide plains of the West, in the presence of hostile tribes, who, employing their means of annoyance in continually harassing them, cutting off their stragglers and hunters, and stealing their horses, might reduce those to distress whom they never could or would attempt to subdue otherwise.

The fortnight which I have mentioned as intervening between our return to the outskirts of civilization and our departure from thence, was spent by each as he listed. A fall of snow, and two or three days' cold weather, were succeeded by a fine genial season of comparative warmth and comfort. We lived in a log-hut attached to the trading establishments of our old conductor, the colonel, and there were strange scenes and sights daily passing before our eyes among the concourse of Indians of various tribes, with whom this was a point of rendezvous.

After the weather had become pleasant again, the squirrel, which had disappeared for a while, and was supposed to have gambolled to his heart's content, and to have slunk to the shelter of his storehouse in the hollow branch for the winter, was again heard and seen among the dead leaves at the foot of the hickory and peccan-trees : and those countless bands of water-fowl and flights of pigeons, which had been constantly observed passing to the southward during the prevalence of the cold wind, ceased to attract the attention.

The prairie-fowls had now completely thrown aside their summer habits. Instead of keeping apart in distinct families scattered over a vast extent of country, like our own grouse at an earlier season, they now appeared congregated in immense flocks in the immediate vicinity of the farms. I had plenty of opportunity of studying their habits, but to shoot a few brace, as they were extremely wild, required frequently hours of patient and wary exertion ; whereas, at an earlier season, a sportsman, if aided by a dog, might bag any quantity, from the pertinacity with which they will lie close till forced to fly.

It appeared that at this time of the year all the birds within an area of three or four miles square, congregated together by consent at sundown on a given spot in the rank dry grass of the unburnt prairie, to sleep. Many a time have I seen them coming at sunset from every point of the compass, with their remarkably level and even flight over the swells of the prairie ; towards the place of rendezvous, which a few days' observation enabled me to determine upon within a quarter of a mile, and twice I was on the prairie early enough to hear and see them rise, and the sight was such as might make an English sportsman's mouth water. Their number must have amounted to many thousands, and the sound of their wings might be heard a very great distance. After rising, for about half an hour, they crowd the scattered trees on the edge of the prairie by hundreds at a time, after which they disperse. Their wariness at this time is extreme ; and the slightest indication of the approach of man, even at a great distance, is noticed by the cock ; who, perched on the topmost twig, elongates his neck, and peeps first on one side, and then on another, with the most provoking caution. How often have I been foiled, when, after the most cautious approach, either in serpent-fashion like the Indian, dragging myself through the grass inch by inch, or in an upright position, striving to counterfeit a tree stump ; never stirring till the sentinel looked another way, and then by imperceptible approaches, and five more feet and five more minutes would have brought the tree within range,—the careful bird began to grow more and more doubtful and restless, and finally set up that clear tremulous crow which said: ' There's a rogue with a gun almost within shot !' as plainly as though he had spoken English. The instant and complete dispersion of the whole covey to a great distance would be the immediate consequence. The plumage of this large species of grouse is not so bright as that of our moor-fowl, though composed of the same colours; yet it is a beautiful bird. While I counted the prairie as my hunting ground, it would have amused you to see my companion prowling round the bayous and lakes nearer the Arkansas, to get a shot at the ducks and geese which covered them ; employing, by-the-way, an Indian urchin to act the water-dog, and bring them out when killed. But this and other equally trivial modes of whiling away that time which we were constrained to stay here, soon brought satiety ; and we turned our thoughts with some impatience to the manner of our return to civilized society. We had been given to understand that another steamboat would probably ascend from the Mississippi within the fortnight, provided the state of the weather and the depth of water in the river permitted it. As this period drew towards a close, however, the general impression among our acquaintance was, that none would dare to risk it. The roads to the southward, if roads they could be called, were pronounced impassable : and, as we still lingered day after day, in the vain hope that the boat might yet arrive, it began to look a little probable, that, having missed the opportunity of return which Mr. Irving had embraced, we should have to winter in the log-huts of this distant settlement. The season was now far advanced: but still there was one alternative left us, namely, a descent by canoe ; and after much contrivance, thanks to the hearty assistance of many hospitable acquaintances at the fort and the agency, we got every thing finally arranged, and on the 23d of November, repaired early to the fort to take our departure.

A good, sound, stray canoe; about thirty-four feet long, and three wide in the centre, had been picked up by some of the soldiers. This we purchased, and with the concurrence of the officers at the garrison, made an arrangement with two discharged soldiers desirous of going down the river, to act as our oarsmen and caterers.

In the afternoon we bid adieu to Fort Gibson, and took our places face to face upon our bear-skins and blankets, in the centre of our trusty canoe; while our baggage was carefully stowed fore and aft, leaving place for the two paddlers, Sergeant Waddle and Private M'Connaughy at either extremity, and put forth into the main current of the Neosho. We were followed from the bank by many a kind farewell from our worthy and respected friend the Commissioner; a grimace of utter despair, accompanied by a blessing, which sounded like an imprecation, from Tonish, and the best wishes of the little knot of gallant officers, to whose frank hospitality we had been greatly indebted.

We were soon carried down into the winding turbid stream of the Arkansas, and began our paddle of five hundred miles with good courage. Our mode of travelling had at that time the charm of novelty, and we were not long in coming to the opinion, that of all modes of water-conveyance, this was the most perfectly free from annoyance. Our light vessel glided noiselessly over the broad surface, or shot down the rapids. Custom made us perfectly at ease to move in her, and change our position without throwing her off her balance. If any thing on shore attracted our attention there was no difficulty in landing instantly. If she grounded, we either poled her off; or if the shoal was extensive, got into the water and dragged her into the main channel again. We carried a quantity of provisions with us; though in general we contrived towards night-fall to reach one of the Indian or half-breed clearings, dispersed at long intervals along the banks, and to remain there till morning. Indeed, we were only once obliged, by the approach of night, to lie in the woods.

For the rest, great were our amusement and the opportunities we had of seeing human nature under singular aspects in our descent towards the more civilized world.

At the approach of the first night we landed just at the head of the rapid called the Devil's raceground, and found shelter in a Cherokee hut buried in a wilderness of canes, and on the edge of a clearing of perhaps ten acres, covered with the most gigantic crop of maize we ever saw, the average height being twenty feet. The produce was here on the lowest calculation a thousand-fold.

On the second, no clearing appearing in sight, though we continued to glide swiftly down the current far into the twilight: we therefore landed in the belt of tall cotton-wood poplars on the river shore, secured the canoe, made a huge fire, cooked and eat our supper, and lay down to court sleep on our bear-skins. Tent we had none. I recollect, that we had no sooner got every thing arranged for the night, when we became aware, by the sounds of cattle and the barking of dogs at a distance on the opposite side of the river, that we were only a mile from a farm: and also that one of those restless nights followed, as far as I was concerned, when the mind appears to be too active to allow repose to settle down upon the body; so that listening to the strange noises from the forest and darkened surface of the river; one moment watching the glare of the fires from the burning prairies on the sky, another looking at the bright stars over-head, twinkling through the branches of the poplars, I fed the fire, pondered many sweet and bitter subjects of recollection or reflection in my wakeful brain, and kept watch.

On the following day, wild and sudden gusts of wind on the river making our advance dangerous, after persevering till about noon, we paddled to the left shore to a thriving Cherokee settlement, and took up our quarters at a half-breed's, called Frenchman Jack. Of all the odd families I ever beheld, this was surely the oddest. The father of the family—a thickset athletic figure, in whom the Indian blood predominated,—was son of a Cherokee woman by a French settler; the mother a full-blooded Indian. Of several children, the eldest was a girl of about ten, of a beautifully fair complexion, with flaxen ringlets and blue eyes, and all the others had the dark lineaments of the maternal tribe. None of the family spoke either French or English, with the exception of a negro slave girl, who acted as our interpreter. The dwelling-house was a substantial log-building of one single apartment, in which there was the strangest mixture of European furniture and Indian apparatus and contrivances. It was constructed without windows, with abundance of crockery, clothes, and saddles, all nicely stowed away on shelves and pegs. Two large low bedsteads filled up the angles on either side of the door, and the deficiency of stools was made up by boxes of various dimensions which seemed to contain the wardrobe and other treasures of the family. Five other distinct erections of different shapes and dimensions surrounded the principal hut, and served as kitchen, smoke-house, store-house, &c. besides a shed covering the room in which the ordinary garments of the family were woven. Every thing about the premises bore an air of negligent thriftiness; skins of domestic animals, or those killed in the chase, were hung to dry on one side—stacks of fodder rose on the other; cattle and horses rustled in the neighbouring cane-brake; and the fierce-looking pigs, with bristling mane, and erect, pointed ears, eyed you a moment with straddling legs, as you strolled through the forest paths, and then, grunting savage defiance, scampered away over the dead leaves. As usual, the dogs were numerous, and seemingly a cross between the dog and the wolf. Every thing had an air of half-breed, and from this the fowls were not an exception; the bodies of the hens were raised up upon long, yellow, unsightly legs to an unusual height, and a peculiar breed of ducks was not wanting to complete the picture. The whole of the premises stood on the bluff bank of the river, at the angle of a clearing, surrounded by a zigzag fence, and just above the junction of a small creek with the Arkansas. Two or three canoes appeared within the mouth of the former, which was overhung by a group of contorted but noble sycamores, the only trees that were left near the buildings, with the exception of a few tall leafless ones among the huts, which afforded roosts for the numerous cocks and hens.

The storm of wind continuing without abatement, we were content to remain here. As evening approached, our attention was rivetted to the opposite banks of the river, from the prairie beyond which a dense smoke had been driving along the horizon the whole day. It was evident that the flames were approaching the river, and as it became dark, they gained the edge of the prairie. They first got into the cane-brake, crackling like a continued peal of musketry, and then burst into the wood of cotton trees over against us. Here, urged by the wind, they continued raging for an hour with the greatest violence, producing a splendid effect on both the river and the lowering sky, till driven more to the northward, they began to fail for want of equally suitable fuel. We then slunk to our blankets, lying down on the floor of the common apartment, the crowded state of which however rendered it a perfect stove.

The following day we were enabled to proceed. We got beyond the Indian lands, and at noon reached the small hamlet rising upon the site of the abandoned Fort Smith, at which we made but a momentary halt. We were now gradually approaching a region where white settlements were more frequent; ferries began to be observable on the banks, and the site of future towns marked by the court houses. What the back parts of Kentucky were some fifty years ago, and the Mexican province of Texas is now, the country through

which we were passing had been in the intermediate
period, and indeed till within a very few years back;
namely, the sink into which the offscourings of the
more settled parts of the country precipitated themselves.

Hither came the restless man, whose impulses led
him to keep the outskirts of society, and whose interest in the clearing he had made, the soil he had reclaimed from the thick forest, and the hut he had built,
became stifled as soon as the yet distant axe of a
neighbour was heard to resound in his neighbourhood,
and the smoke of additional clearings arose from the
deep blue horizon. He felt no strong tie to the place.
His adoption of it had been capricious, his relinqnish-
ment of it was no less so; and all the more agreeable
associations connected with it were disturbed the moment others came to share the thinned game, and the
trees of the forest could no longer be felled into his
very yard. He would complain of the country becoming too crowded, because he could count upon ten
neighbours within a circuit of twice as many miles.
The sight of a surveyor, and the approach of the law
with all its concomitants, would be a source of trouble
and disgust to him. Accordingly, he would dispose of
his ‘improvement’ and his live stock to some new-
comer for a few hundred dollars; pack up his house-
hold stuff, collect his moveables, summon his wife to
follow, and, shouldering his axe and his rifle, lead his
family forth with comparative pleasure to new scenes
of labour; and interposing the mighty ‘Father of
Waters’ between him and the advancing line of civilization, dive deep and bury himself in the forests of
Arkansas. In the same wilds, the murderer, red with
crime, and branded by the laws he thus evaded, sought
and obtained a sanctuary from their vengeance. The
public defaulter; criminals of all degrees; the speculator; the loose adventurer;—all flocked to the same
shades, scattering themselves in the solitudes of the
forest, or on the edge of the turbid river; or collected
together round the Indian trading establishments,

scandalizing their white and Christian parentage by
shameless and vicious lives; oppressing the Indian,
and often waging the war of the knife and rifle upon
another in the spirit of revenge and bitter hatred.   In
the wake of these would follow a host of disorderly
folk; men whom crime, perhaps, had not forced to fly
from the precincts of civilization, but whom the hopes of
a free and unshackled life spent in impunity here, if
not that of redeeming their fortunes, would bring across
the Mississippi.   The spendthrift, the debtor, he who
had been enticed to enter into composition with his
creditors, and he that had made none.   Many a man
born and educated for better things, but who, living
badly or too freely in the old States, lastly mortgaging
his estate, and plunging irrecoverably in debt, made
over debts and property to his eldest son, stole a horse,
and off to Arkansas!

To these might be added, a goodly proportion of
the speculative and industrious scions from the ' northern hive' of New England, here represented by a
single, plodding, sharp-witted pedler; there by the
owner of a flat, advancing lazily up the river from farm
to farm, with a tempting assortment of wares; and
again, by a small knot of more stationary adventurers,
who, fixing upon a favourable locality, build a log-
store, and set up as· a respectable firm of five partners,
with a joint stock of goods to the value of a few hundred dollars, and a negro slave.   At this stage the
honest portion of the community, and it is a growing
one, feel the inconvenience of having transported themselves beyond the arm of the law.   They band together, and co-operate for their mutual security, often
under the name of Regulators, forming among themselves that rough court for the protection of the innocent, and the punishment of the guilty, to which I have
alluded in a former letter.   They begin also to dream
of glory, and to form volunteer companies.   Thus
thirty settlers will enrol themselves into a rifle company, and elect their own officers in such a manner
that every individual among them has a title to prefix

to his name. From the time the good and orderly predominate, the increase of population advances with accelerated pace. The steady operation of the law follows; the country is taken under the wing of the General Government. It is then surveyed; the authorized sale of lands succeeds, and the possessor of a tract is either confirmed in permanent possession of that which he had taken from the wilderness, by purchase at a low price; or disposing of his improvement, takes the step which I had described at the commencement of this digression. Roads are laid out, districts determined upon, court-houses built, and strong log-built jails in their vicinity: chapels rise in the middle of the woods, and hamlets thicken into villages, anticipating in their lofty sounding names their future glories, as mighty towns and cities. Then comes the land-speculator, with a host of expectant and hopeful followers, led on by a puff, advancing and fixing themselves in close contiguity, in some paradise of fertility, and in their wake hundreds and thousands of others. At the same time the views of the inhabitants advance beyond mere subsistence, and the rivers begin to be chequered by the flats and other craft loaded with the rich produce of the field and forest, dropping down with the current to the distant market: and the sonorous breathing of the steam-boat is heard in solitudes, where ten years before no craft had ever floated but the light and rude canoe. This is a state of things not genial to the views, tempers, and characters of the first inhabitants. And though the great distance between the various seats of justice and the scattered population would continue for a while to be friendly to crime, and insure it a degree of impunity in many cases, yet the country could not longer be considered an asylum for it as heretofore; and at this day, the Province of Texas has taken the place of the Arkansas Territory.

But we are still on the surface of the river, and its features may demand a few lines of description. As to our two fellow-voyagers for the time being, both were originals in their way, though the private, M'Con-

naughy, was more distinguished for his general good
conduct, and his paddling and chewing incessantly,
than anything else. As to the Sergeant, he being of
Yankee blood, had more than one iron in the fire :
and to tell the truth, loved peddling far better than
paddling. He had thriftily taken advantage of an
offer made him by a trader at the garrison, to take two
dollars-worth of goods, in return for one in cash, and
having made the speculation, he was now bent upon
improving it. The consequence was, that we were
fully initiated into the mysteries of peddling, by wit-
nessing his daily attempts to get rid of his chest of
finery to the good wives along the river. He was
honest, as times go ; but could not avoid essaying to
give his traffic a lift by many an audacious, but well-
meaning lie. I need hardly mention, that the lower
we descended, the more frequent the farms became ;
though they still continued so far scattered, that we
had more than once been benighted in our attempt to
get over the ten or twelve miles between one and the
other, at the close of a day's labour ; as, besides the
distance, it became very difficult to descry them after
dusk, as they were ordinarily a little removed from the
bank. However, necessity taught us to betake ourselves to a very simple and infallible expedient for
attaining this object, whenever we were belated ; which
consisted in our setting up a rough imitation of canine
yelping and howling, which as soon as they could distinguish it on the long reaches of the river, was instantly answered by the dogs at the farms. As we
descended, the style of architecture gradually improved,
and after a long acquaintance with nothing but log-
huts, we began to meet with frame and clapboard
houses of various dimensions, though it was not till we
reached Little Rock, five hundred miles from the fort,
that we met with anything of a yet more permanent
character. On the sixth day after the commencement
of our voyage, we reached the point called the Dardanelles, and met two steamboats toiling up the river,—
the waters of which had been on the increase ever since

the day of our departure; straining every nerve to ascend the stream, and deposit their cargoes either at Fort Smith or Fort Gibson, before the failure of the present rise should leave them aground, to calculate the balance between profit and loss.

Hitherto the scenery had been extremely varied. Our position on the deep bosom of the river, it is true, never allowed us an extended view upon the adjacent country, and was frequently bounded for many miles together, by the forests, sand-bars, and low alluvial lands in the immediate vicinity of its bed, with their green bands of cane, frequented by bears and turkeys, and long lines of sober gray poplars. Among these the river swept majestically along, sometimes in one broad channel of a third of a mile in breadth, and at others in many different currents, spread over a far greater surface, as its vast bed was obstructed by poplar-covered islands and shoals. At such time frequent breaks were observable in the banks, through which the surplus waters are discharged in the rainy months, into innumerable ponds and bayous. The bright shoals were at this season covered with long lines of ducks, geese, and brants. The extreme vigilance and trumpet voice of the latter gigantic species, rendered approach within shot an utter impossibility. Flights of these birds were seen continually winging their wedge-like phalanx over our heads. Swans were occasionally met with, and such immense flights of pigeons as I dare not describe, lest I should be accused of sharing the inventive powers and disposition of many of my class. They passed over our heads at irregular intervals, with a very swift flight to the southward; their numbers increasing greatly whenever the sky was overcast. While in America, I never succeeded in seeing one of their roosts, but met much evidence confirmatory of the singular appearance presented by the place of their retreat, where millions seem to congregate, breaking down the arms of the trees by their mere weight, and covering the ground to a great depth with their manure. In many parts of the Midland States, the crows are known to congregate in the winter season in the depth of the forest in almost equal numbers.

Whenever the river took a large sweep, we were sure to find a cut-off, or straight channel, opened in the bank, and forming a chord to the arc, by which much of the water of the river passed downward in time of flood, but at other times is mostly choked with immense quantities of rubbish; and many were our debates and arguments for or against yielding to the temptation of attempting to take advantage of these seducing short-cuts.

Huge accumulations of bleaching driftwood and timber lay piled up at the heads of the islands and on the sand-bars. Snags were abundant, but we were preserved from serious accidents.

Upon the rich alluvial soil displayed to a great depth on the perpendicular banks, we had a section-map of the different depositions for many centuries. They were dark red, yellow, or light-coloured, according to the tributary stream down which the flood, which had deposited them, had come. Thus we knew that the white lines had been deposited by a rise of the Neosho or Verdigris, and the deep red by those of the Red Fork, or Canadian, to the southward. Yet you must not imagine from what I have stated above, that the general surface of the country was level; in fact, this was far from being the case. A chain of hills, called the Ozark mountains, of considerable extent to the northward, rise in this part of the great western valley, and often abut upon the Arkansas, presenting steep wooded acclivities on either side, with a small appearance of pine-covered rocks toward the summit. At the Dardanelles, the river cuts through a spur of this chain of greater height than ordinary, and forms by far the most picturesque scene found along its course. Below this point, it holds a monotonous and rather uninteresting course for many miles. On the eighth night, we entered with the twilight a singular division of the stream, forming a long basin, broad and tranquil as a lake, with a high pine-covered rocky shore on one side, and a uniform grove of cotton-wood trees bending over the water for five or six miles in a straight line on the other; and from this point to Little Rock, or Acropolis, as the learned prefer to call it, the capital town or seat of government of the territory, twenty or thirty miles distant, the river flowed for the most part in contiguity to the hills, which here and there presented rather a picturesque outline.

We arrived at Little Rock on the morning of Dec. 9th, and, finding the common inns very discreditable resorts, were received with courtesy into a clean and decent boarding-house, kept by a respectable baptist minister.

Though we were aware that the steamboats which we had seen on their passage up the river, would shortly return to Little Rock, and that we might continue our voyage to the Mississippi by their means, yet we had become so partial to our canoe, and the perfect independence and absence from annoyance which it enabled us to maintain, that we felt inclined to pursue our voyage to the mouth of the Arkansas in her. The distance to Montgomery's Point was yet between two and three hundred miles. An unexpected obstacle to our intention, however, arose in the conduct of our paddler, M'Connaughy, who, true to the impulses of his warm Irish blood, unfortunately fell into bad company the moment he got ashore; and partly terrified by the idea of confronting the cholera, which was still reported to rage in some of the Mississippi steamboats; partly cajoled by the hope of lucrative employment, and lastly, through the incapacitating effects of whiskey, resolved to remain here.

We had therefore, whether we would or no, to wait for the first steamboat. It came down the river the following day, after we had passed a quiet Sunday in very comfortable quarters. Of Little Rock, I can say little, but that it is one of those thriving places frequently met with, where society is still in a ferment; the good and the evil being strangely mixed up together.

The 'Reindeer' made but a short pause, and early the following morning started with its freight and passengers on its downward course.

So here, in a measure, we finished our wanderings in the Far West, and that with real regret. Every species of travelling has its lessons, and this had not been wanting in such. During our journey of a thousand miles in this region, we had become acquainted with much of that species of knowledge which is the stay of the hunter, and gives him assurance in the vast solitudes of the the trackless forest and prairie. Many a secret of horse-craft and wood-craft had been revealed to us. We had been taught to distinguish the trail of one animal from another,—to steer according to the tokens afforded in sunless days by the trees of the forest and the plants of the prairie of the side from which the north wind blows, or the sun should appear,—to know the track of Indian friend or Indian enemy,—to distinguish their forsaken camps and to read their hieroglyphic signs graven on the trees. We had found that to sleep unhoused, night after night, for a month together, in the damp air of the deep forest, is not necessarily followed by colds, sneezing, or consumption; and that one may contrive to live on animal food without bread or salt, without indigestion. We had been shown how to follow the bee from the flower to his distant hive in the hollow oak; and when the tree was felled, how to despoil and rifle the gathered sweets. Whether always successful hunters or no, we had learned to be patient and good tempered ones; to provide fire under many disadvantages, and to kill and cook our supper under as many more. Lastly, we had learned to paddle a canoe; make our own moccasins, and bag a bison. Were not these accomplishments worth crossing six thousand miles of sea and land to acquire?

There was one art, however, among some others that shall be nameless, in which I honestly confess for my part, that frequently as I have tried to perfect myself in it, I never could attain the most distant success. That is the art of decoying, which is at best an evil one. As

to the mode in which the hunter and the Indian will
attract the deer to their destruction, by ' bleating ;'—
taking the gentle animal's life, by treacherously exciting
its natural sympathies,—there is something so heartless
and diabolical about it, that I trust nothing would
tempt me to practise it. Yet I plead guilty to having
sometimes tried to coax the turkeys in rather an extraordinary way. Those feelings of pity and compassion
which were easily excited in behalf of the deer, were
certainly a little obtuse in the case of these feathered
bipeds, and it seemed as though they had been without
the pale of my sympathies. The practised hunter will
induce them to approach him as he steals through the
grass, by a skilful imitation of their gobble and piping.
But often, as buried in the thick cane brake, and
watching one of those little openings where the birds
sun themselves, I heard the tread, rustle, and voices of
the turkeys around me, and have attempted to allure
them to me by an imitation of their notes, I never succeeded in a single instance. I set up, for example, a
weak, amorous, sentimental piping like the female—it
was in vain! no broad-backed, round-tailed, burly
turkey-cock made his appearance. I gobbled in the
most seducing fashion, throwing as much devotion into
my tones as I could contrive ; I essayed to compress a
thousand blandishments into the few gutteral sounds
that were permissible, but these, far from eliciting any
sympathetic response, seemed to put the whole gang to
instant though cautious flight; for I invariably observed
that very briefly, after an attempt of the latter kind,
every sound became hushed, but the beating of my own
impatient and disappointed heart. It was evident that
there was no mistaking me for a turkey, and all the
birds that I ever brought to the mess, were the fruits of
a less guileful, more straightforward and summary mode
of proceeding.

But you have now the sum of our attainments.
What use we were to make of them on our return to
civilized society, we could not tell ; but we were well
satisfied with our adventures, and the acquisitions con-

sequent upon them ; and, 1 trust, not unmindful of, or
ungrateful for, the merciful preservation we had experienced from many evils, hidden and apparent, and for
undiminished health and strength.

Though we had now determined to repair in all
haste to the Atlantic cities to pass our winter, we at this
time meditated a return for a second campaign in the
Buffalo-range the following year—but you will see, if
our patience is mutual, how that project was defeated ;
and how, though we again visited the West, we eventually bent our attention and steps in another direction, and towards another remarkable feature of the
American Continent.

Below Little Rock, the river seems to have escaped
from the hilly country, and, with few exceptions, to
roll his red waters through a comparatively monotonous region. A few pine-covered bluffs of moderate
elevation appear on the shore from time to time ; for
the rest, the eternal forest and the belt of cotton-wood
poplar bound the view on both sides. The latter tall
and shapely tree is the spontaneous growth of the soil
throughout the rich alluvial plains of the West. Whenever the earth is torn from the outer edge of the sweep,
and thrown up on the inner, they instantly spring up
in a thick and even grove, and in six or eight years
are large enough to be cut for the use of the steamboats. The beauty and regularity of the semi-circular
bends of the Arkansas are very striking. The width
does not increase proportionably, as might be expected
from its great length of course, and the volume of
many of its tributary streams,—but this, as remarked
before, is one of the singular features of all the great
western rivers. A large quantity of surplus water is
drawn off into the numerous lakes and bayous by which
the lower region is intersected. These bayous appear
covered with aquatic plants, many of them most striking in size and beauty of flower,—and they formerly
were the favourite resort of the alligator, though few
are now found as high as this latitude.

The only remarkable town below Little Rock, is

the post of Arkansas situated on the left bank, and
that, less on account of any thing in its appearance,
than for its antiquity, having been settled by the followers of Ferdinand de Soto, the first discoverer of
these southern regions, from Florida to the frontiers of
Texas, as early as 1540. He penetrated, with a thousand men, from the peninsula of Florida, across Ala-
bama and the Chickasaw country to the Mississippi.
He was probably the first white man who beheld that
river. Since that time, the town has been in continued
occupation by the Spanish and French Creoles; the
latter of whom form the bulk of its population to the
present day.

Our steamboat was of small size, but otherwise commodious, and had it not been for a large and heavily
laden ark which she towed alongside, our voyage
would have been both agreeable and speedy. About
noon on the second day, we turned out of the river into
the singular natural canal or bayou, called the Grand
Cut, which connects the waters of the Arkansas with
those of White River. It is about six miles long, and
serves in time of flood to discharge a portion of the
surplus water of either river into the other. At this
time the Arkansas was flowing into White River,
mingling a turbid stream with the pure current of its
neighbour. A subsequent descent of a few miles
brought us to the Mississippi once more, and after
stemming its current for an hour, we reached the storehouses at Point Montgomery, where we landed to await
the arrival of the first steamboat ascending the river.
'The Reindeer' then wheeled round and pursued its
voyage towards New-Orleans, six hundred miles distant.

We were detained nearly two days at the Point,
looking with anxious eyes on the broad bosom of the
mighty river, which is here of great width, casting up
immense beds of sand, in which may be seen the wrecks
of numberless boats, rafts and arks, half imbedded in
the soil between high and low watermark. Truly, this
is the 'terrible Mississippi!'

Montgomery's Point did not, at the time I speak of, rank either in fact or courtesy above a small hamlet, and was apparently merely of importance as the point where goods might be deposited; and whence the steamboats ascending the Arkansas and White River could take their departure. In this portion of the valley of the Mississippi, the settlements are yet wide apart—but if the events of the future can at all be augured by the past, many years cannot elapse before the whole of this immensely fertile region will teem with inhabitants. I remember listening in the dusk of the evening to the sounds which were borne across the wide river, indicative of the presence of man—the axe, the horse-bells in the cane,—the cry of the women following the cattle; those sounds which are the first to break the silence of the forest, and soon to be followed by the hum of crowds and the din of manufactories.

Forty years ago, there were but 150,000 white inhabitants sprinkled throughout the confines of the great valley of the Mississippi; and now probably four millions and a half, at the same time that every avenue, from the east and south is crowded with fresh accessions.

It would be utterly out of the question to compress into a sheet or two of post paper, even the outlines of those topics of interest which have a reference to the phenomena, features, and past and present condition of this great valley. Leaving you to consult Flint's Geography for a vast mass of information which the patient and worthy author has collected, I can only throw together a few hints for your present perusal.

Of all the rivers which drain that great central valley, which occupies the whole of the interior of the North American continent, from the Rocky Mountains to the Alleghany, and from the Mexican Gulf to the Icy Sea, the Mississippi is doubtless the most remarkable, both from the length of its course and that of its confluents; its individual character; the natural phenomena connected with it, and the great fertility of the region through which it flows.

The central part of the basin from which both the Mississippi, and the other great drains of the Valley diverge to the north, east, and south, you must look for in that wide extent of level country, covered with innumerable lakes and swamps, which lies to the north and west of the great lakes. There, interlocking with one another without any intervening ridges, the innumerable sources of the Mississippi, St. Lawrence, the rivers of Hudson's Bay, and those of the Icy Sea, are to be found; at first filtering, or flowing sluggishly from one wide lake to another, and through rice covered swamps,—the home of myriads of water-fowl, till the accumulated waters take a decided bed, and the direction which God has marked for each. Many of these rivers, by turning to the northward, run further and further from those temperate regions where man has fixed his main seat; and little or nothing of them is known. With the two principal, however, the Mississippi and the St. Lawrence, it is otherwise; and though, as yet, but a small part of the immense regions which they water are fully explored, and still less brought under the hand of man; yet, the day appears to be approaching when in all probability they will be the seat of millions. The idea which has been entertained by many, that the whole of these central parts of the continent were once submerged, and that the entire breadth of the region between the Alleghany and Mountains of Labrador on the one hand, and the Rocky Mountains on the other, was one unbroken sea, may appear extravagant to those who have had no opportunity of visiting the West, or viewing the phenomena which they present in detail. I can only add one to the number of those who would feel inclined to maintain the probability. The whole region through which the Mississippi flows, from the Falls of St. Anthony, which we reached, as you will find, in the following year, bears ample evidence of this having been the case, or at least such as it would be very difficult to refer to any other theory than that of the ocean having gradually retired, leaving the waters gushing out on the surface of the earth to

follow and wear themselves channels through the inclined plane, as they pursued the retiring footsteps of
their great parent to the several points of the compass.
If not to this great natural revolution, to what shall we
refer the evident proofs of the gradual descent of the
bed of the Mississippi, to be gathered from the marks
of the gentle, but long-continued action of water in the
upper part of its course, where the river has worn
itself a bed many hundred feet deep; or the regular
horizontal deposition of earthy strata. What will account for the appearances afforded by the wide open
prairies, or the vast salt-covered plains of the Far West,
and as you descend towards the Gulf to those portions
of the country from the surface of which the waters
of the ocean must have retired the latest, and upon
which time has not yet laid the same load of alluvion
which covers the country more to the north—whence
those vast collections of gigantic sea shells, on and
under the surface, to the depth of forty and fifty feet?

Leaving the St. Lawrence for the present, my subject is now the Valley of the Mississippi, which, taken
in its wide sense, comprises the whole of the region
between the Lakes and the Gulf, and the Rocky
Mountains and Alleghany, and as such, is the largest
on the globe. As to the propriety of the Mississippi
retaining its pre-eminence as the main river, in spite of
the greater length of the Missouri, I have elsewhere
remarked that it is evidently the central river of the
region.

The whole Valley is considered as lying between
two great planes. The eastern is comparatively narrow, and consequently the tributaries to the main river
on that side have a shorter course than those on the
opposite, which extends to the base of the Rocky
mountains, and over which flow the Missouri, Arkansas, Red river, &c. and their own tributaries.

Of the Mississippi, above the junction of the Missouri, I may find an opportunity and leisure to tell you
more at a future day. It may be said to be a beautiful river throughout the greater part of its upper course;

but that epithet is no longer suited to it, after its pure
waters have been discoloured by the junction of its
great tributary, the Missouri. Then, from a comparatively calm, transparent stream, flowing with a silvery
surface between varied shores, among islands and bright
sand-banks,—it becomes for the remaining part of its
course, a dark, turbid, and boiling torrent, sweeping
forward with irresistible fury; covered with large con-
vex swells and whirls, like a boiling cauldron; and in
its terrible alternations between flood and low water,
producing such sudden changes in the surface of the
alluvial region through which it flows, as no one can
have an idea of who has not seen and marked them.

In the part of the bed of the river below its junction
with the Ohio, enormous wreck-heaps, shores cut down
perpendicularly to the water's edge; vast deposits of
mud and rubbish; land-slips caused by the undermin-
ing of the banks—when the soil, with all its rich burden of cane and forest, goes headlong into the flood,
and is carried away to be deposited elsewhere,—are
throughout to be seen. Here the stranger is shown a
bed of sand and soil extending over four or five thousand acres, deposited where four years before the river
had its bed; there a ' cut-off,' where, in time of flood,
the headlong torrent had burst over the narrow neck
of land which separated the opposite points of the great
curve which it had hitherto followed. These regular
semicircular sweeps, often twenty miles in circuit, are
a common feature of the parent stream as well as of its
tributaries, and display the same phenomena on a yet
greater scale. There you see the perpendicular outer
line eating into the land, and the inner, where the new
deposits are made, with the smooth bar swelling from
the water's edge, covered by its plantation of cotton-
wood trees, rising in regular degrees, from the red scions
of last year's growth, to the gray trunks of the full
grown tree. Innumerable ponds and bayous beyond
the present course of the river, choked by accumulations
of timber and aquatic plants, mark the spots over which
it had formerly run, but which have been forsaken in its

strangely capricious movements. Man has profited by this inclination, and by the application of a little labour at the Grand Cut-off, the steamboats now pass through an isthmus of less than a mile in length, instead of making a circuit of twenty.

Like all its great tributaries, the Mississippi is as broad, a thousand miles from its mouth, as at the point where it disembogues; and even at its junction with the Missouri, fifteen hundred miles from the Gulf, it is broader than at New-Orleans. Still eight hundred miles higher, at the foot of the Falls, it is only one-third less in breadth than before that city. As you descend it, you see it receiving river after river, one broad stream after another, but you notice no accession to its width. The Missouri,—the Ohio,—the Arkansas,—the Red river, pour in their floods of waters—all seem swallowed up in a bottomless channel. The mud of the Missouri, and bright red of the Arkansas, colour its waters, and perhaps add to its impatience and swiftness, but not to its expanse. After its junction with the Red river, the Mississippi carries its greatest volume; as about two leagues below, the first important bayou opens in the right bank, which, though four hundred miles from the ocean, carries off a portion of the waters to the Gulf. This is the bayou Atchafalaya, which is believed to be the ancient bed by which the Red river communicated with the Gulf, ere it became a tributary of the Mississippi. Below this point the outlets are numerous.

The medium breadth of the river below the Missouri may be considered as a mile from bank to bank, with a current of four miles an hour in ordinary stages of the same; but it often expands to a much greater width; and seen from the bluffs of Memphis, for example, with its wide shoals, islands, and indented shores, it struck me as much more resembling an arm of the sea than an inland river.

As to insurmountable impediments to the navigation from the Gulf to the Falls, there is none beyond those which are caused by occasional low waters at the Des

Moines Rapids, fifteen hundred miles from its mouth, and the severity of the winter, in the higher parts of its course.

Those vast accumulations of drift timber, which are remarked on some of its tributaries, growing year by year, so as entirely to impede the navigation, are not found in any part of the main river. Toward the delta they indeed form the basis upon which the sand and mud subsides, and give rise to the innumerable acres of new land, by which the continent is yearly encroaching upon the domain of the ocean. By far the most remarkable accumulation of this kind in the West, I may observe, was the great raft obstructing the navigation of Red river a few hundred miles above its point of junction with the Mississippi, where, owing to natural causes, a compact body of floating timber, one hundred and forty miles long, and from half a mile to a mile in breadth, interposed, till lately, a stupendous and yearly increasing barrier to the navigation of the higher parts of the river. That this should ever decay or be cut away would have seemed a hopeless expectation, and so any one would have said in 1832; but in the course of the succeeding year, an attempt was made by Captain Shreve, who by making a few judicious cuts, succeeded in actually clearing away seventy miles of the raft, and the steamboats then ascended as far as the Caddo Agency, a point seventy-one miles higher than could be reached by them in the spring. The raft was found to cover full one-third of the whole surface of the river, with a medium depth of twenty-five feet of timber, often compact and solid to the very bottom. Seventy miles still remained to be removed, but that has been probably done by this time. In the Missouri and Mississippi, the greatest danger to navigation arising from natural causes, may be justly attributed to the position of trees deeply imbedded with their roots in the river, and called according to their fixed or moveable position, snags, planters, or sawyers; and so great has been the loss of life and property by the steamboats striking on them, that, herculean as the task may appear, the attempt has been made to free the river from this impediment, partly by destroying the snags, and partly by cutting down the timber on the banks.   For the former purpose, two steamboats of peculiar construction have been employed for some years, under the direction of the above-mentioned engineer, and much has already been done.   In the twelve months terminating in September, 1833, the two snag-boats under his direction had raised and cut off 1960 snags, and in the intervals, when high water prevented the pursuing this branch of their labour, the crews had felled ten thousand trees from the banks. But it is time to bring this letter with its various contents to a conclusion.

LETTER XVIII.

On the evening of the second day, a small cloud of white steam, seen like a star in the dark blue shade of the forests, seven or eight miles off, announced the approach of a steamboat toiling up the river.   In half an hour's time we could distinguish the sonorous breathing of the scape-pipe, and by the time that the wild song of the negro firemen reached the ear, all was bustle and preparation.   The bell on shore was rung to bring the steamer to; and jumping into a wherry, we found ourselves on board the 'Cavalier,' a boat of the second or third class, bound from New Orleans to Pittsburg, and took possession of the berths which we eventually retained till our arrival at Wheeling a fortnight after.   We found that since they had left the city, they had had no case of cholera on board, and thanked God with all our hearts.

You may imagine us then toiling for thirteen hundred miles and upwards against the rapid currents of the Mississippi and Ohio.   This, at a season when natural scenery had lost its charm, you will suppose must necessarily have proved a trial of patience. In some degree I grant that it was such, nevertheless not so great as might be argued by those who know the impatience of modern travellers; and now that it is over, I look with interest upon all that we learned or experienced.

I will not, however, present you with any thing in the form of a journal. It was the 5th of December when we left Montgomery's Point: we halted at Memphis in Tennessee on the 7th, and reached the Mouth of the Ohio on the 10th. Little did we foresee that that very day twelvemonth we should be again at the same spot on our descent from the Falls of St. Anthony to New Orleans.

We found that the Ohio was in flood, and at Louisville, which we reached on the 13th, the steamboat passed straight up the Rapids, instead of going through the canal. The 15th was spent at Cincinnati, and finally on the 21st we landed at Wheeling, and continued our route by land over the Alleghany to Baltimore. But I have still some scenes and events to record before we quit the West.

Poor M'Connaughy! He made his appearance on board the 'Cavalier' in piteous plight. A few days before, he was sober—possessed of a good character—with good prospects; home before him and ninety dollars ready money in his pocket. He was now stripped of clothes, sense, character, and cash. At Little Rock he had met with one of the numerous gangs of sharpers always lying in wait for the weak and unwary. He quarrelled with his companion for giving him good advice; and after being well flattered and then made tipsy, he became the complete dupe of the unprincipled crew. He first, as related, broke his engagement with us and wished to stay. He then suddenly made a tipsy resolve to descend the river and continue his voyage home by steamboat: but his new-found acquaintances stuck to him like blood-suckers.

The sharper, whose dupe he had principally been,

had come on board the ' Reindeer,' ragged from head to foot, half-drunk, with his head tied up in a dirty cloth, his linen sprinkled with the blood of the last broil:—but as M'Connaughy waned he waxed, and after a day spent in gaming, swopping, and debauch at Montgomery's Point, the two parties were seen in very altered guise, to wit : Private M'Connaughy, so exceedingly tipsy that he could not tell his shoulder from his elbow,—flushed,—without shoes or waistcoat, —attired in a torn blue surtout with a faded velvet collar, for which he had given twenty dollars, a pair of old drawers hanging over his heels, no hat, and pennyless.   Mr. M'Sharper, exceedingly decent and sober ; garbed in a good pair of military trowsers, an excellent blanket coat, a pair of span new boots, a pocket full of money, and a chest full of clothes.   All his backers too looked the better for this fortuitous gleam of sunshine.

The upshot of the business was that our poor tipsy paddler was left ashore, through his own carelessness, at some landing place, about three hundred miles up the river, and thus had probably to begin the world anew : and as to the principal swindler, the bandaged ruffian, he, being detected before he had been a day on board in the act of theft, was, on the whole affair being represented to the Captain, promptly set on shore on a sand-bar in the middle of the river, to shift for himself.   Prompt justice and well-earned,—almost worthy of the good old reign of the Regulators.

No sketch of mine could give you an adequate idea of the steamboat of the West.   From the epoch of the launch of that solitary Wanderer, whose first voyage I have elsewhere recorded, up to the close of 1833, it is computed that about five hundred boats of various sizes, from one to five hundred tons burden, had been constructed or run upon the Mississippi and its tributaries.   A very small portion of these were built prior to 1820, and the number of new boats launched yearly, for several years back, is stated to have been upwards of fifty.

There is a great difference between the build and interior arrangement of the Eastern and Western steamboat, and both are essentially distinct from those unadorned but compact vessels, which, propelled in the same manner, buffet the boisterous and dangerous billows of our narrow seas, straits, and roadsteads.

As to the Eastern steamboat, the whole of the hold is converted into cabins—the transport of heavy freight being no part of the speculation ; they are superior in finish and durability, but not in appearance, to those of the West, and cost much more ; being, moreover, almost invariably furnished with low-pressure engines. On the contrary, the whole of the hull of the steamboat of the West being appropriated for the transport of goods, the cabins are generally constructed upon the main-deck. The vessels consequently appear much higher out of the water, and every one must be greatly struck at the first sight of these huge floating palaces, with their double tiers of gay cabins. The boilers, which are cylindrical, and vary from four to double that number, are placed forward on the main-deck ; and behind them the machinery is arranged towards the centre of the vessel, enclosed between the huge paddle-boxes, and a row of offices on either side. The great cylinder lying in a horizontal position, the piston works on the same plane. Thus in the Western boat the whole arrangement and movement of the engine is horizontal, while in the East it is perpendicular. Sometimes a ladies' cabin is constructed on the same deck, in the stern of the boat ; but, more generally, this part is given up to the so-called deck-passengers, and the whole range of superior cabins is built upon an upper deck, extending from the stern over that part of the vessel where the boilers are situated, the portion most in advance being called the boiler-deck. Through the latter, the great chimney pipes conducting the smoke from the fires below ascend, and as the range of cabins does not extend quite so far, the open space and the view afforded by it renders it a favourite lounge. Of the disposition of the cabins little

need be said.   The ladies' apartment is aft, and opens
with sliding doors and curtains into the main, or gentlemen's cabin, which is frequently fifty or sixty feet in
length.   Both are furnished with handsome tiers of
upper and lower berths, canopied with ample chintz
or moreen curtains, and the former cabin is frequently
fitted up with state-rooms.   A gallery runs round the
whole exterior.   Between the forward end of the great
cabin and the boiler-deck, ten or fifteen feet of the
deck is ordinarily occupied by a bar, washing-room,
captain's and stewards' offices, ranged on either side of
an antechamber.   On some of the larger class of
steamers, there is yet a third deck and range of cabins
before you come to the roof, or hurricane-deck—upon
the forward extremity of which the glazed and painted
cabinet, containing the tiller, is placed, affording a lofty
and unimpeded view of the channel.

As to the question often started with regard to the
safety of the principle upon which the machinery is
generally constructed in the West, much might be said
in favour of high-pressure engines ; and in spite of my
full consciousness of the great danger attending them,
when placed, as they frequently are, under the care of
incompetent and careless persons, I think that the reasons given are good.   These are chiefly founded upon
the character of the waters navigated ; their turbid
state, their extraordinary swiftness, requiring the application of great power ; the far greater simplicity of
construction of the high-pressure engine,—all the com-
plicated condensing apparatus being dispensed with,
which is of great consequence in a navigation where a
boat must proceed five or eight hundred miles without
the possibility of repair ;—its superior lightness, and its
being calculated to work off all the steam which is
generated ; and lastly, the mud is not apt to accumu-
late so fast in the boiler of the high-pressure engine,
being blown out at the safety-valve, while under the
low-pressure system it must continue in the boiler, and
by interposing a stratum between the water and the

iron, the latter is sometimes burnt through, and explosion takes place.

Yet, though it may thus be well maintained that the high-pressure engine is better fitted for the Western navigation,—as long as the accidents upon those waters are so frequent, and the loss of human life so great as it has been for some years past, it is no wonder that great prejudice must exist in the minds of many with regard to the system pursued. It is not, however, the principle which is wrong—it is the careless use of it. The history of steamboat disaster is one of the most terrible and revolting imaginable; and the disregard of human life which is as yet, generally speaking, a feature of the West, is a sure proof that the standard of moral feeling is low.

I have seen so much during four or five thousand miles of steam navigation in this part of the country, as to believe, that there are few voyages of more evident peril in the world than that from St. Louis or Louisville to New-Orleans, or vice versa; for, leaving out of the question the casualties incident to the navigation, arising from snags, ice, rocks, fire, or being run down, in consequence of which numbers have perished,—the peril which impends over you from a tremendous power like that of steam, being left under the direction of incompetent or careless men, is a constant and fearful one.*

The sketch of a day's proceedings on board will perhaps give you a livelier idea of our position, and of the scenes connected with it, than can be otherwise conveyed.

State-rooms are not always to be had by gentlemen,

* By a published list of the steamboats lost on the western waters, from July, 1831, to July, 1833, their number would appear to be sixty-seven, viz.—Seven burnt under way; nine in port; twenty-two snagged; two sunk by rocks; five by running foul; seven by ice; and fifteen abandoned as unfit: and previous to that time, out of one hundred and eighty-two, which had been on the river, but did not exist in 1831, sixty-six had been worn out; thirty-seven snagged; sixteen burnt; three run down; four or five stove by ice or rocks; and thirty destroyed otherwise.

as they are commonly found to be attached to the ladies' cabin alone—but in case they are unoccupied they
may be secured, and your position is so far more than
ordinarily a favoured one, as you have private access
to them by the outward gallery. Otherwise it must be
conceded that nothing is omitted that the known ingenuity of this people can contrive, to render the berths
in the main cabin as tidy and ornamental in appearance
by day, and as secluded and convenient by night as
circumstances permit of. They are so arranged, that
when you retire to rest, the thick curtains with their
vallance can slide forward upon brass rods, two or three
feet from the berth itself, and thus form a kind of draped
dormitory for you and your companions.

About an hour before the time appointed for breakfast, after the broom has been heard performing its
duty for some time, a noisy bell rung vociferously at
the very porches of your ear, as the domestic marches
from one end of the cabin to the other, gives notice that
the hour of rising has arrived, and it is expected that
every one will obey it, and be attired in such time as to
allow the berths to be arranged, and the whole cabin
put in its day dress, before the breakfast, which like all
the other meals is set out in the gentlemen's cabin, is
laid upon the table. In vain you wish to indulge in a
morning doze, and thus to cut short the day; every
moment your position becomes more untenable. Noises
of all kinds proceed from without. You persevere—
shut your eyes from the bright light which glares upon
you through the little square window which illumines
your berth, and your ears to all manner of sounds.
Suddenly your curtains are drawn unceremoniously
back, the rings rattle along the rods, and you see your
place of concealment annihilated and become a part of
the common apartment, while the glistening face and
bright teeth of the black steward are revealed, with
eyes dilated with well acted surprise, as he says, ' Beg
pardon, Colonel; thought him war up: breakfast almost incessantly on de table.' He retrogrades with a
bow, half-closing the curtains; but you have no choice,

rise you must. Happy he whose foresight has secured to him all the enjoyment of the luxury of his own clean towels, as none but the disagreeable alternative of drying his person by the heat of the stove, can be the fate of him who has not done this. As to making use of the common articles, hung up for the accommodation of some thirty citizens in rotation, no one need blush at being termed fantastically delicate in avoiding that. There exist yet certain anomalies in a position, and under a state of society, like that found on board these boats, which, though they may not surprise a thinking mind, and may be accounted for, are far from being either pleasant or usual elsewhere. And the arrangements made of the above class are surely of this kind.

But I do not dwell much on these fertile subjects for a traveller's maunderings, for four reasons. First, because they are but blots on the general picture, and as blots they are considered by all those Americans whose opinions are worthy of attention. Secondly, others, more competent to the task, have contrived to make them sufficiently notorious. Thirdly, time and a sense of common propriety may have already produced changes for the better ; and, lastly, they are disagreeable both to recollect and to detail.

During the interval which elapses between your being thus unceremoniously ousted from your quarters and forced to begin the day, and the ringing of the breakfast-bell, you may walk forward to the boiler-deck, and satisfy yourself as to the progress which has been made during the hours of darkness ; or, if you choose to follow the custom of the country, and the example of a great majority of the passengers, you may linger in the antechamber opposite the bar, and take the glass of wine and bitters, which the prevalence of that common complaint of the United States, dyspepsia, finds a bad apology for. The Americans, as a people, are far from being intemperate ; if by intemperance you mean absolute inebriety, of which less is seen, as far as a casual observer, like myself, might judge, than in any country in Europe. But if by intemperance you un-

19*

derstand a habit of the frequent unnecessary indulgence in stimulants and dram-drinking, then do they richly deserve the stigma ; though the improvement and the return to sound feeling in this respect, has been so general in many parts of the Atlantic States, that the stricture can hardly be applied to them. But in the West and South, the custom prevails to a degree ruinous to the moral and physical strength of a great part of the male population. And whoever has been witness to the mode and the marvellous rapidity with which the hot cakes and viands of the plentiful tables of steamboats and hotels are cleared and consigned to the stomach, without the possibility of having undergone the natural process of preparation, which nature has indicated as advisable, both from the number and construction of the human teeth, and the original smallness of the swallow, need seek no further into the arcana of natural causes to account for the pale faces, contracted chests, and lack-lustre eyes of a great number of citizen travellers in all parts of the West. Compared with this, what are the effects of climate or sedentary life ? or even the possible hinderance to a natural and easy digestion consequent upon the internal heat generated by republicanism, and the weight of democratic cares ?

But I have anticipated breakfast by alluding to its principal feature. The table is spread with substantials, both in profusion and variety ; and considerable impatience is generally observable to secure places, as it frequently happens that the number of cabin passengers is greater than can be seated with comfort at the table, however spacious. The steward, or his assistant, after many a considerate glance at his preparations, to see that all is right, goes to the ladies' cabin, and announces breakfast—an announcement which is generally followed by their appearance. They take their places at the upper end of the table, and then, and not till then, the bell gives notice that individuals of the rougher sex may seat themselves. The meal I leave to your lively imagination to picture. I have noted its chief characteristic. You might imagine that the beings engaged in it were, for the time, part of the engine, which is sighing and working underneath at the rate of one hundred strokes in the minute, so little does their occupation admit of interruption. There is little or no conversation, excepting of the monosyllabic and ejaculatory kind which is absolutely necessary ; and instead of the social hour, during which, in other lands, the feast of the body is often found to be compatible with the feast of the soul,—you spend, in fact, an uneasy ten minutes, in which the necessary act of eating is certainly stripped of all the graces under which supercultivation contrives to shroud its sensuality, and is reduced to the plain homely realities of bestial feeding. Wo to the poor gentleman of habitually slow and careful mastication—he who was taught to ' denticate, masticate, champ, chew, and swallow !' Wo to the man of invariable habits—he whose conversational powers are the greatest during repast—the proser—the sentimental bon-vivant who loves to eat and think—or the gentleman with stiff jaw-bones and slow deglutition ! Wo to the epicure, whose eye might well else dilate at the sight of the well covered board, and its crowd of western delicacies. Wo to the hungry gallant, whose chivalry cannot suffer him to enjoy a morsel till he has seen the ladies well served and attended through the meal. Small credit gets the good-natured soul who deftly carves for all, and ever carves in vain. There is no quarter given. Many of the males will leave the table the moment they are satisfied—the ladies leave it as soon as they well can :—and then in come the barkeepers, engineers, carpenter, pilot, and inferior officers of the boat: the table again groans with its load of plenty, and is again stripped and forsaken, to be a third time the scene of feasting for the black steward and coloured servants of both sexes. During these latter scenes of the same act of the same play, I need hardly press you to quit the cabin for the seats on the boiler-deck, or still better, for the hurricane-deck above.

In fine warm weather, more especially during your first voyage in the West, both curiosity and comfort

will lead you to spend by far the greater part of your
time in the open air ; where the gentle breeze, fresh-
ened by the rapid motion of the boat, and the magical
manner in which scenes rise and disappear, will always cheer you, while with conversation and reading
you while away the monotonous hours of a long morning. Should the boat be one of the first class for power,
well commanded and carefully engineered, and the season fine, few situations could be named of an equally
exciting character.   It is possible that you may meet
with a few well-bred, intelligent travellers—that you
may be both in good health and good-humour—that
the general run of the voyage may be prosperous and
without accidents or detention.   The steamboat may
have an engine which works smoothly and without
jarring, so that the use of your pen may be easy ; you
may have contrived to keep a few books in your travelling equipage ;—the cabin may be fully adequate to
the comfortable accommodation of those having a claim
to its use.   Above all, favourable circumstances may
have given you friends in the ladies' cabin ; by occasional visits to whom at proper seasons, you may
please and be pleased.   If so, well and good—but you
may chance to fare otherwise, and for the sake of illus-
tration we will suppose that the very contrary is the
case in almost every particular ; that, heated in body
and mind by confinement and disappointment, you
are peevish as a pea-hen ; that the society is decidedly
ill-bred and vicious—that the boat jars so with every
stroke of the piston that you cannot write a line—further, that you have no books—the cabin is crowded—
the machinery wants constant repair—the boilers want
scraping.   This hour you get upon a sand-bank, the
next you are nearly snagged—drift-wood in the river
breaks your paddles—the pilot is found to be a toper,
—the engineer an ignoramus—the steward an econó-
mist—the captain a gambler—the black fireman insur-
gent, and the deck-passengers riotous.   This moment
you have too little steam, and hardly advance against
the current ; another, too much, and the boat trembles

with the tremendous force exerted by the power that impels her. To complete your dismay, the captain agrees to take a disabled steamboat, or a couple of heavily-laden barges, in tow for the next four or five hundred miles. Instead of accomplished females, such as at another time you might have as fellow-passengers, we will suppose the ladies' cabin to be tenanted by a few grotesque, shy, uninteresting beings, never seen but when marshalled in by the steward to their silent and hurried repast, and never heard, but when, shut up in their own apartment, a few sounds occasionally escape through the orifice of the stove-pipe, making up in strength for what they want in sweetness.

What are you to do in such cases? You may lounge in the antechamber, and watch the progress of stimulating at the bar—you may re-enter the cabin, and strive to get possession of a chair and a gleam from the stove; or you may ascend to a small apartment found in some steamboats, called Social Hall, in other words a den of sharpers and blacklegs, where from morning to night the dirty pack of cards is passed from hand to hand. For the rest, you may study human nature in many forms, and one thing will not fail to strike you, and that is the marvellous rapidity with which the meals follow, and the world of important preparation which passes before your eyes for an end so little worthy of it.

The time occupied by the supple-limbed black boys, Proteus and William, in drawing out the long table, laying the cloth, and other preliminary preparations, will not be far short of an hour; while a quarter of that time suffices for the demolition of the various courses,—the whole meal, as already described, consisting of a shove to the table, a scramble, and a shove from the table. Things are cleared away, and the sliding table pushed together again; William and Proteus placing themselves at either end, twenty feet apart, and straining with might and main till the ends meet. You take a dozen turns across the floor,—you read a little, write a little, yawn a little—when, before you could have believed it possible, the steward's myrmidons, with looks of infinite importance, enter again—seize on the two ends of the table, strain them once more asunder, and the work of preparation re-commences.

The mass of the society met with upon the Western boats is, as far as a transient traveller may be allowed to plead his individual experience, to be designated by the single term, bad. It is one thing to deny the truth of a statement in which, I believe, most travellers of any pretensions to education and moral feeling agree, whether they be from the Eastern or Midland States, or from Europe; and another to find palliative reasons why it cannot be otherwise for the present. A man may make up his mind to glance good-humouredly around him, and to look upon the unwonted society into which he is here introduced, with equanimity, studying neither to give nor take offence; but nothing can make him believe that what appears before him as absolute vice, is in fact virtue in disguise,—or that consummate vulgarity is, in fact, any thing else. My impression was, that in these boats we came in contact with much of the scum of the population, and in judg-ing them to be such, I was far from believing that they were a fair sample of the people of the West generally. On the contrary, it was not the uncouth and unculti-vated, but honest bearing of the people 'belonging to the river,' which was offensive,—rusticity and vulgar-ity are far from being synonymous terms—nor that of the young Kentuckian, noisy and intemperate as he might be, stunning your ears with an amusing and fanciful lingo, which, however some who should know better may attempt to dignify and perpetuate, is, after all, nothing but slang. The decidedly worst company was, I found, invariably made up of those who should, considering their pretensions to education, public em-ployment, or the sober lives and civilization of the stock from which they came, have known better. And to this class belong many of the Americans, who travel on business connected with commercial houses in the large or small towns. They are as busy as wasps in a sugar cask as long as they are about their business, and the most listless of human beings when not so employed. They have apparently no thought, no reading, no information, no speculation but about their gains—dollar is the word most frequently in their mouths; and judging from them and their numbers, the proportion of men with money and without manners would appear to be greater in this part of the globe than elsewhere.

There is one operation connected with your daily progress, which may be signalized, as it affords some variety, and breaks the monotony of your proceedings. This is wooding, or the hour's halt at one of the innumerable farms or wood-yards, for the purpose of laying in the necessary stock of fuel; the quantity of which that is burned in the course of twenty-four hours on board a steamboat of four or five hundred tons, is almost incredible.

This halt generally takes place twice a day, morning and evening, when the whole of the bow of the boat, and on either side of the furnaces, is covered with regular piles. Besides the opportunity thus afforded of going ashore, the scene is always a busy and lively one, as in addition to the crew being engaged in it, the major part of the deck passengers lend a hand, in consideration of a reduction in the passage money, which it is to the advantage of the proprietors to make, as this procedure is productive of a great saving of time. During the night, immense fires are kept blazing at the wood-yards, to direct the boats where to find them, and the scene then presented in wooding is highly wild and picturesque.

Among the beings attached to a Western steamer, there is one class too remarkable to be passed by, and this is composed of the firemen, the sphere of whose labour is directly on the bow of the boat, upon which the long row of gaping furnaces open. They are almost invariably athletic negroes or mulattoes. The labour, which would be considered pretty severe by all but

themselves, is generally performed amid bursts of boisterous merriment, jests, and songs ; and the peculiar
character of the latter has often made me hang over
the boiler-deck railing to listen ; particularly after dark,
when the scene was very striking from the bright ruddy
glare thrown upon and around them, while with a
thousand grimaces they grasped the logs and whirled
them into the blazing throat of the furnaces.   Their
ordinary song might strictly be said to be divided into
a rapid alternation of recitative and chorus—the solo
singer uttering his part with great volubility and alertness, while the mass instantly fell in with the burden,
which consisted merely of a few words and notes in
strictly harmonious unison.

As usual we were not without our quantum of Kentucky boatmen and backwoodsmen on board, that race
whose portrait sketched by himself as ' half horse, half
alligator, with a dash of the steamboat,' and filled up
by the wondering and awe-struck travellers from the
Old World, has been so often the subject of mirth and
obloquy.   I fear the genuine breed is getting rather
scarce ; at least, though I saw many boisterous doings,
and many an amusing specimen of rough manners, I
never saw any one stabbed or gouged.   Take, however, the portrait of the extraordinary ' Kentucky
Swell,' who was our fellow-passenger for a day or
two in the Cavalier.   He came up with the boat from
New-Orleans, accompanied by his father, a fine, hale,
sensible old man, clad in a suit of home-spun from the
loom of his wife and daughters.   He had perhaps also
been a ' swell' in his youth, but all had sobered down
into an independent, staid demeanour.   Every word
he spoke was full of good, sound sense—that kind
which age and experience can alone produce ; and my
slight intercourse with him added to the respect which
I feel to those of his class, in whom generous feeling,
sound practical sense, and shrewd judgment, are often
found united with unassuming manners and simple-
heartedness.   His maxim, the wisdom of which he
upheld, after bringing up a fine family of sons, was—

' I give my boys seven years' play, seven years' labour, and seven years' instruction ;' and though his youngest, whose figure will be before you anon, evidently showed that a few years more must pass, before all the good fruits of this system were fully developed, I am not at all inclined to dispute it.

They were returning from New-Orleans to their plantation. The dress of the parent I have alluded to. That of the son bore no resemblance to it. He was strong and well built, having what is rather a rarity in the West, shoulders of a breadth proportionate to his height. His countenance, which was good, with a bold aquiline nose, bore a strong resemblance to that of his parent, though it was for the present destitute of the expresssion of good sense and honest-heartedness by which the latter was eminently distinguished. His whole dress and manner were peculiar. A coat of strong blue cloth of the Jehu cut, with white bone buttons of the Jehu size, the standing collar of which was always pulled up over the ears, and concealed them beneath its shade, served at the same time, in consequence of its being tightly buttoned from throat to waist, to hide the neckcloth and waistcoat, of the existence of neither of which am I therefore able to make affidavit. This upper garment, which was certainly typical of the horse part of his nature, impended over a pair of full corduroy pantaloons. The legs of the same, though constructed by the artist of amplitude sufficient to reach the ankle, if they had been allowed to do so, having apparently been elevated to midleg in the act of drawing on a pair of half boots, remained hitched on the top of the latter during the whole of the first day of my observations, no effort having being made to induce them to descend to the ordinary position. On the second, one descended and the other did not, and in this way Tom Lavender sported his Nimrod-looking person. I never saw his hands ; as whether sitting, standing, or walking, they were always thrust decidedly to the bottom of the large flap pockets of his Jehu coat.

In the manner in which he disposed his person in the

cabin, when inactive, upon two or three chairs, basking
before the fire, with his nose erect in the air, I thought
I detected something of the alligator part of his origin ;
while in the impetuous manner in which, striding forward with outstretched limbs, he perambulated the
cabin or the deck to take exercise, alternately inflating
his cheeks, and blowing forth the accumulated air, I
could not fail to detect the steamboat, by which the
purity of the race had been recently crossed.   He was
a man of no conversation, but he made up for it by an incessant hoarse laugh, filling up the pauses in that of three
or four trusty young cronies, who seemed to hold him
in great respect and consideration.   I should not forget
to mention, that at a later period I was informed, that
the mode of wearing the pantaloons hoisted half leg high,
as described above, was premeditated, and intended to
give an 'air distingué!'

About noon on the second day, the steamboat was
directed to the right hand, or Kentucky shore, at a point
where the forest appeared cleared from the bank for
many hundred yards in front, and the long line of
fencing peered over the edge, denoting a large and extensive clearing.   As we approached the landing-place,
I noticed a little group gathering at the corner of a pile
of cut wood, ranged on the high bank above.   Over the
landing-place, inclined a single sycamore, supported by
his main, perpendicular root over the river, with all his
leafless branches surrounded by the sweeping folds of a
gigantic grape vine.   A fine handsome man stood in
advance, and upon our mooring, came slowly down towards the boat.   His resemblance to the old man on
board was too striking to leave us in doubt as to his
relationship to the parties I have described, being that
of an elder son and brother.   Our companions had then
reached their home.   While a knot of negroes and coloured men descended to the boat, with their teeth displayed in the broad grin of welcome, and laid officious
hands upon the pile of baggage which lay on the boiler
deck in readiness, I noticed the wife and daughter of the
good old man, half sheltered by the woodstack, standing

coyly in the rear, till the whole group had ascended the bank, when they all proceeded in joy and contentment to the house. The dwelling was situated a few hundred paces in the rear—good and substantial, with an open compartment in the centre, such as I have described elsewhere. I got a glimpse of it by following the party up the bank; for to tell the truth, the meeting was both a pleasant one to see, and one calculated to make travellers like ourselves, thousands of miles from our native countries, feel a little homesick; and, notwithstanding the amusement I had extracted from the 'Swell,' I could have found it in my heart to envy him the snug home and warm welcome which we saw him receive.

But I must draw to a conclusion. Through God's good providence, we escaped dangers and difficulties of every kind,—and there were many encountered before we reached Wheeling, just as the river was filling with ice. There we took a stage, and proceeded over the Alleghany into Maryland. We arrived early on Christmas-day, within a few miles of what was to be the termination of a very long and singular ramble; when we got unexpectedly overturned in descending the Catoctin Mountain, into a deep ditch; and though we all escaped with limbs and lives, I got a sounder blow on the head than ever fell to my lot before;—which was all very well; as it made me, perhaps, think more seriously than I should else have done, of the many dangers which the hand of God had led us through, in peace, health, and safety.

LETTER XIX.

It was but the other day I was in company with a
gentlemanly foreigner—a Prussian; acute, reasonable,
and polite, travelling for his instruction and amusement,
to see with his own eyes, and to hear with his own ears.
The conversation turned upon the difference of the criminal law in our respective countries, and the mode of
procedure in criminal cases. Two things had struck
him with reference to that of England; first, the weight
which we gave to mere circumstantial evidence, in the
absence of positive truth; and, secondly, the horrible
severity of our code, and the administration of it. He
stated he had been seated for hours in the court of ses-
sions in one of our southern cities, and that out of
twenty or thirty cases under consideration, not a single
prisoner was acquitted. He was quite horrified! Accusation and conviction seemed to go hand-in-hand.
The time occupied in any one case was, as he stated,
quite insufficient for patient investigation; but his blood
curdled as he heard—Guilty—guilty—guilty! pronounced again and again by the foreman of the jury,
before he had had time to make himself master of the
bare accusation. The idea fixed, by the evidence of
his own senses on his mind, was this: that, in England, every man who was accused, must be, and was
condemned. And I wish you could have seen how wide
he opened his eyes, when he was forced unwillingly to
relinquish his belief by a calm explanation of the series
of preparatory steps through which every individual
case had passed, before it had come to the point where
he had seen it arrive, for positive decision. Of the examination before a magistrate, the reconsideration of
cases by a grand jury, he of course had, till now, no

opportunity of hearing; but he was brought to confess, after a while, that, all things considered, it was hardly to be conceived that innocence, if innocence there were, would not have been made evident in the previous stages of inquiry, and that nothing but uncontrovertible evidence of guilt could be received and made the cause of condemnation.

However, something was to be learned from this, and I trust I was not myself above profiting by the lesson, which many years of travel have assisted in impressing upon my mind; namely, that a stranger in a strange land sees with strange and partial eyes, and that the difficulty of forming a correct judgment, even with close observation, and without any disposition to distort facts, is far greater than might be supposed.

Much has been said by Americans of the temper and manners of English travellers among them, and there is hardly a book published hitherto, bearing upon their social and political state, which has not been followed by a host of angry criticisms in the periodicals from Maine to Georgia. I grant it, they have had much to complain of; and considering all things, the chuckle of gratification which agitated the people of the Union, when lately, his transparency Prince Pucklar Muskau first drank our wine, and then wrote a libel on us, was such as might be sympathized with.

Their visiters are accused, and, it must be allowed, frequently with justice, of coming with minds influenced by prejudice, and carrying away, perhaps, an honest, but certainly an unlucky bundle of false estimates, false impressions, and false conclusions. Might it not be admitted, that travellers from both sides of the Atlantic have hitherto been, with but rare exceptions, of minds and characters little calculated to carry back to their own land just notions of the countries they have been pleased to visit, and further pleased to write about.

It is to be lamented, that, at the present day, when travelling forms, as it were, not only part of the education of a gentleman in our own country—the main recreation of thousands of those who have the means in the

middle classes, and almost the business of hundreds——
that so few understand anything of the philosophy of
travel. How few show, by their mode of passing
through a foreign country, and their occupations and
temper, that they are actuated by the nobler ends attainable by the survey of other countries than their own ;
and for one who will show by his conversations and
writings, on his return home, that his mind and views
have been participants in that expansion which his range
of travel has procured for his natural observation, how
many come back with confirmed prejudices and nar-
rowed souls !

And with regard to Great Britain and the United
States of America, but little has been done hitherto by
the travellers from either side of the Atlantic to do
away with that dust of angry passion and prejudice
which filled and blinded the eyes of our fathers, both
before and after the struggle which burst the ties which
till then existed between them. Still, though family
quarrels are said, and perhaps with reason, to be of a
more bitter nature than any other, it is surely time that
between the inhabitants of the British isles and those of
the opposite shores of America—speaking the same language, claiming the same literature, the same early history ; both possessing the same ardent love of liberty,
though the one may incline to the monarchical, and the
other to the democratic form of government,—wor-
shipping God after the same manner ; each containing
thousands of real Christians, united together as brethren
by the closest bonds of the Gospel, with common hopes,
desires, and ends in living ; and the one receiving yearly
accessions of thousands from the shores of the other—
should cease to deem one another natural enemies.

I am among those whose personal experience inclines
me to believe, that the impulse in America in particular,
is towards a renewal of confidence, and the return of
kindly feeling towards the country from which they
have taken the broader features of their constitutions
and character, and whose blood was the blood of their
fathers ; and this in spite of the irritation kept up by

the press on either side.   Yet how little have travellers, either American or English, done hitherto to foster this natural feeling.

Of the English travellers more anon : in the mean time I would ask, were I at the elbow of one of my friends beyond the water, who might join the general voice of his countrymen in condemning our injustice and illiberality,—whether, as Europeans, and more, as Englishmen, our position, political, moral, and domestic. had been subjected to examination of eyes and minds less clouded by self-love, prejudice, and ignorance?   I grant the overweening love of John Bull for his country— (may it never diminish!) his sober contempt for all others —his excess of prejudice,—the ignorance which he will frequently expose as to the real situation of another country ; yet is Brother Jonathan less prejudiced and less ignorant?   To judge their words by works of the Americans, are they more disposed to hear good of England than we of America?   Are their hackneyed and senseless tirades against our monarchical form of government and aristocracy more just than ours against their democracy?   From whom is the citizen of the United States to get his knowledge of the true state of society, political or moral, in England?   From the disaffected who come over to him?   From the radical or democratic prints which are the favourites, and from which most of the information given to the American public is culled?   From the novels of the present day, reprinted and spread through America from east to west with such haste and avidity,—the feverish outpourings of the flimsy philosophers and would-be 'master-spirits' of the age, which are given forth to a gaping public as true portraitures of the manners and morals of the ' best society?'   Is America to judge of the Old World from the testimony of her own citizen travellers?   Of these my limited observation has shown me three classes; besides the young merchant who takes a short run while his vessel lies in port, and comes back with the credit of having travelled in Europe.

The first is the most numerous, and consists of young

men having the wealth at command, who, either from curiosity, or for the sake of doing as others have done, or for the sake of learning the European languages, pass a few years in travel.   They visit France; breakfast at the cafés; dine at the restaurans; linger in Paris and taste its follies, till health and funds begin to fail; they run off to Italy, and scour back by Switzerland and the Rhine, taking England on their way home.   In the latter country they sneer at everything, see no society beyond the bagmen and the roué at the hotels,—a dinner at their merchant's the topmost round of their ladder.   They grumble at their consuls and ambassadors for not showing them more respect, and not dancing attendance upon them; they go out in a fuss and come back in a fume. At home they boast of having travelled—having dined at Abellard's, supped at Bery's, intrigued with some hanger-on at the operas or theatres, and sported a Stultz. Their republicanism has been preserved undiluted, or even been concentrated by the feeling that Europe had no grade of society where they could feel quite at home. They do no credit to their own country, and are little capable of communicating just notions of Europe or European society; while unfortunately these are the very men from whom the popular idea of American gentlemen has been taken.

The second class are those who come to Europe with a disposition and the means to enjoy European life and luxury.   They return in a few years unfortunately spoiled for their own country.   They complain of ennui —want of excitement.   Dazzled by the false glare of society in Europe, without the talent which would teach them to look beyond it, and form an accurate judgment of its peculiar advantages, they have become blind to the charms of their own country, and its claims upon their love and duty.   The healthy, but less polished society of the United States, is tasteless to them.   The simplicity and matter-of-fact qualities of their countrymen become odious.   They only breed and receive disgust, and by showing how little they have gained from

European travel, they strengthen prejudice in the minds
of their fellow-citizens.

The third class, hitherto a very small one, but I know
it to be increasing—equally distinct from the republican
flippancy of the first, and the mawkish pretence to
super-cultivation of the second. The individuals composing this class have not only the means, but they
have the minds that fit them for travel. Education
has sown seeds which the latter matures. They step
upon the shores of Europe with bosoms filled with eager
and natural enthusiasm, and upon that of England with
a feeling, which, if it cannot be called love, is, at least,
veneration. They may pass years abroad, revelling in
classic, historic, and poetic association; visiting many
climes; peeping into many degrees of society, the highest and the lowest; looking calmly at men and things,
and learning that God has not averted his face from the
Old World, because he has turned it on the New.
They may form many ties, and linger till it might be
prophesied, that, flattered, caressed, and accustomed to
the excitement and luxury of Europe, their thoughts
and hopes were weaned from America; and yet such
will return with panting bosoms to their own land—
their eyes will glisten so as they have not glistened for
years at the sight of their own verdant shores—and
they calmly sit down in the bosom of society, and show,
by every word and action, that their birthright and
home have never been relinquished. The excitement of
Europe has passed away; but they find sufficient in
the return to early scenes—the faces of ancient friends
—the marvels which an absentee for a few years must
discover in this land of promise, and in the glorious
prospects for the future, sufficient to fill both head and
heart. Having brought away a just conception of Europe, and of its deficiencies or advantages, they may be
supposed to have formed a just estimate of America;
and having been temperate in their use of the luxuries
of the former, their palate is not so depraved that they
cannot enjoy the more simple advantages of the latter.

They were an honour to their country abroad, they are
calculated to be an honour to her on their return, and
wherever the influence of their temper of mind is felt,
society will be essentially benefited.

. Such examples, and I could name many among those
whom I esteem as friends, make you not only honour
the individuals themselves, but the country they call
their home.

With regard to English travellers in the United
States, do not imagine that I am without a list of them
also, which I shall forthwith find and lay before you,
leaving you to detect that to which I may be supposed
to belong.   Though our countrymen are found by
swarms upon the teeming roads of France, Switzerland,
and Italy, here their appearance is rarer, and therefore
more marked.   I mention first the Porcine English
traveller, as personifying in the eyes of Brother Jonathan the identical John Bull.   A few of this class are
met with on the steamboats and railroads, and a strag-
gler or two in the interior of the country, marching on-
ward to the music of their own dissatisfied grumbling,
like a bear with a sore head.   They are seldom long
visitants.   They arrive from England on a hurried tour,
sometimes accompanied by a companion in training,
one of those who travel over the world with their eyes
shut and mouths open.   They are sure to be disgusted
with the United States, where they have neither room
nor time to do any thing.   They complain of crowded
steamboats ;   crowded   hotels   and   boarding-houses ;
crowded carriages ;   of the sharpness of people's el-
bows ;   the quickly satisfied appetites and the unre-
strained gaze of all—the impertinent inquiries of a few.
They see nothing but want of polish, want of taste, and
want of politeness.   They ask how many of the states
are included in the term Christendom.   They rush from
New-York to Saratoga ;   from Saratoga to Niagara ;
thence to Detroit ;   and then, in utter disgust, determine
to quit the land of equality, and, in a paroxysm of loyalty

and rekindled toryism, get themselves set ashore in Upper Canada; little dreaming, that the backwoods, whether of Canada or the United States, are alike devoid of convenience; and that every new country, whether under democratic or monarchical rule, presents pretty much the same phases of society, and the same natural features. We met with such a one: a decent gentleman, but in a paroxysm of despair, not knowing how to extricate himself from a position, into which a crudely conceived desire of travel had beguiled him. We had advantages over him in every way as old travellers—laughing at a certain degree of privation—and our commiseration was, I own, mingled with a good deal of amusement, the more as his case was in no way a desperate one : but his complaints of the people, and the roads, and the fare, and the morals, were unceasing. After having been squeezed in a narrow wagon with others during a whole day's journey, and hardly allowed time to eat the unwonted food set before him—he had been compelled to sleep, as all must in such a country, in a cluster of log-huts, half open to the air. He had, from his description, out of compliment, (I never had such a piece of good fortune,) been permitted to occupy a small compartment by himself; and after describing the bad accommodations, he went on to say, with a very slow mysterious intonation, as though communicating a horrible incident, 'And, sir, will you believe it, I found that in the end I had to sleep with two ladies inside of me !' Now, stout as the gentleman was, by this he meant nothing, but that two ladies, travellers like himself, had had to retire to a compartment beyond his own. This, however, was to him the acmé of barbarism. What good can be the result of such a traveller's lucubrations?

But to go on with my list. You see here the speculator, the theorist, and the utilitarian; often men who, unable to take care of their own individual affairs, begin to feel great anxiety for those of mankind in general; as you may have seen in days gone by, a tipsy gentleman, when just upon the point of losing his reason, begin to hold forth in a strain of maudlin philanthropy about his neighbours, and sigh deeply for the welfare of the whole human race; crowning his folly, by offering his services to conduct an equally tipsy companion home. Such men frequently make their appearance in America; disappointed and indigent; having lost character in their own country, and full of a newborn fervour in favour of a land and a people of which they know nothing. Their indignation at having divulged their theories in the former to deaf ears, will only be equalled by their surprise in finding that, of all countries in the world, the United States contains the greatest number of matter-of-fact men; and that neither admiration nor support will be granted to crude and untried notions. And, like the demagogue, the freethinker in politics and religion, and many a one who leaves his country in high dudgeon, after long tampering with petty treason––men of this class frequently alter their opinions and language after their arrival here, as they find a sobriety of demeanour and sentiment in the people, which ill accords with their views; and then they abuse the country with just as much reason as they lauded it before. But what good is to be expected from these, or their reports, on either side of the Atlantic?

Next comes the hasty traveller—the young officer on furlough—the young gentleman on his return home from the West India Islands, who lands at New-York, determines to take advantage of the packet to Liverpool on the first of the succeeding month, say a fortnight hence, and in the mean time to visit the most interesting points of the United States and Canada. He flies to Niagara by the canal or the road; then takes the line of Ontario steamboats, descends the Saint Lawrence to Montreal, perhaps visits Quebec, returns panting by way of Champlain and Lake George, to the Hudson, and thus to his port in the very nick of time. Something he has seen, but can carry away no very definite notion of the people, or the state of the country.

Another class—the prejudiced and pompous traveller, travelling, as he says, for information, but seeing every thing through a bilious medium, and neither pleasing himself nor others. In the cities he will grumble at the hotels ; he will say that Bunker's and the City Hotel in New York are odious ; that Gadsby's at Washington is a bear-garden,—in which by the way he will not be far from the truth, particularly during the meeting of Congress,—and that of all the sojourning places for the traveller in the Union, the Tremont at Boston is the only one that is not offensive to a degree. In the country he will be horrified by the number of badly made coats he may see, forgetful that at least he meets with no beggars, and sees no marks of penury and want. With a mind morbidly inquisitive, he will wish to persuade himself that he understands the true colours of every thing, at the same time he looks at all through a piece of smoked glass. In his observations upon the politics and government of the country, he is totally at fault, not having taken care to draw the distinction between the operations of the General Government, and those of the separate State Governments; and in his observations upon society, he will be equally far from just, because he makes his own education, breeding, and feelings, the standard of comparison, and what he does not or cannot understand, must be wrong. The very absence of beggars will be to him a proof of a low degree of civilization. He will condemn the Americans for not every where showing that cultivation to which he may have supposed we have attained, being perhaps of two lofty a temper to reflect, that some of the points appertaining to the decencies or elegancies of life, upon which he dilates with the most cutting and supercilious sarcasm, are precisely those, to an acquaintance with which we ourselves, as a nation, have been but very recently introduced, and whose general adoption dates from a yet later period. An Englishman of this cast will be thunderstruck, nay, petrified, at hearing the oft-reiterated assertion, that English is spoken better in America than in the mother country, and with some reason, as nothing but his own observation and reflection will show him what foundation can possibly exist for such an assumption.

If he stays long enough in the country, and travels sufficiently, he will grant that throughout America he will generally hear English pronounced, as he may readily understand it. Further, that the dialects which prevail in many of our counties do not exist, though in some parts of the Eastern states, a language very much approaching to a dialect is spoken; for the rest, he will find that though as far as the general pronunciation of the language goes, all may be at least intelligible, there will be a great deal which an Englishman can hardly be expected to understand; that slang, quite as incomprehensible to him as the gipsy lingo of our own hedge-sides, forms the common mode of communication in some parts of the country; and that, generally speaking, there are few ranks of society in which a certain degree of this base coin is not current. He will find from the style of conversation of Americans of a literary turn, that out of the main cities, and in remote parts of the country, it is evident that the difference between written and conversational language is scarcely understood,—which may arise from the speakers having to draw their language more from books than from the interchange of ideas with men of their own stamp; and that consequently the use of big and pompous words, such as load the newspaper paragraphs, is much more common than good taste would admit. But enough of the pompous traveller. He may do very little harm, but he will do no great good.

You may further meet here with the sentimental traveller, who having read Rousseau and Chateaubriand, and become enamoured of the image of man in a state of nature, unsophisticated and unspoiled by civilization, or of some sweet picture of savage life, dives his way through the forests to the Indian settlements, to find an amiable ' *Chactas*,' or still more amiable '*Atala.*' 'Tis a bootless errand! The bland traveller also, good-natured to excess, losing half his time in asking questions of those who cannot answer

them, and running right and left to see common places;
—the book-maker, he who comes with the purpose of
writing a book which shall contradict one in the market :—the inquisitive gentleman, a bore, and bored in
turn. Then one or two travellers who having long
and hotly advocated some change in our political or
ecclesiastical government, come here at last, to do what
should have been done first—namely, to see how it
works. What can you expect but ex-parte statements
from such people? They are like geological theorists,
who having concocted their system in their library-
chair, come forth and make a tour, in which they would
refer all the phenomena which come in their way to the
test of their own petty conception.

And now I fancy I hear you ask, and to what
order of English travellers in America did you belong?
The Porcine? No. The speculator, theorist, or
demagogue? Neither the one nor the other. The
hasty traveller? Not altogether. The prejudiced and
pompous? I trust not. The sentimental? Decidedly
not.

Then you travelled as a cosmopolitan?—No : I
dislike the word. I love, and prefer, and uphold the
political, social, moral, and religious superiority of my
own native country too sincerely, to claim the title of
‘ a citizen of the world,’ if by that term you mean one
who is equally at home and without preferences where
ever he wanders over its broad surface ; but if by it you
would designate one who reconciles himself easily for
a time to change of place and scene ;—one whose impulse is rather to sing with the native of a foreign land
than to quarrel with him ; to see good everywhere rather than evil ;—one with a facility to form ties with the
natives of every clime, and enter into their usages and
feelings not only with charity but with pleasure, so long
as they are not forbidden by his Bible, and by the sense
of right and wrong which sound education and good
examples may have given him—so far I am a Cosmopolitan, and as such I visited America.

Im TheStory

personalised classic books

"Beautiful gift.. lovely finish.
My Niece loves it, so precious!"

Helen R Brumfieldon

⭐⭐⭐⭐⭐

UNIQUE GIFT

FOR KIDS, PARTNERS
AND FRIENDS

Timeless books such as:

Kids

Alice in Wonderland • The Jungle Book • The Wonderful Wizard of Oz
Peter and Wendy • Robin Hood • The Prince and The Pauper
The Railway Children • Treasure Island • A Christmas Carol

Adults

Romeo and Juliet • Dracula

Highly
Customizable

Change
Books Title

Replace
Character Name
with yours

Upload
Character
inside page

Add
Inscriptions

Visit
Im TheStory.com
and order yours today!